Modernism

Modernism

Second edition

Robin Walz

PEARSON

Harlow, England • London • New York • Boston • San Francisco • Toronto • Sydney
Auckland • Singapore • Hong Kong • Tokyo • Seoul • Taipei • New Delhi
Cape Town • São Paulo • Mexico City • Madrid • Amsterdam • Munich • Paris • Milan

Pearson Education Limited
Edinburgh Gate
Harlow CM20 2JE
United Kingdom
Tel: +44 (0)1279 623623
Fax: +44 (0)1279 431059
Web: www.pearson.com/uk

First published 2008 (print)
Second edition published 2013 (print and electronic)

© Pearson Education Limited 2008 (print)
© Pearson Education Limited (print and electronic)

The right of Robin Walz to be identified as author of this work has been
asserted by him in accordance with the Copyright, Designs and Patents Act 1988.

Pearson Education is not responsible for the content of third-party internet sites.

ISBN: 978-1-4082-6449-2 (print)
        978-1-4082-6618-2 (PDF)
        978-0-273-78888-1 (eText)

British Library Cataloguing-in-Publication Data
A catalogue record for the print edition is available from the British Library

Library of Congress Cataloging-in-Publication Data
A catalog record for the print edition is available from the Library of Congress

10 9 8 7 6 5 4 3 2 1
16 15 14 13 12

Print edition typeset in 10/13.5pt ITC Berkeley by 35
Print edition printed and bound in Malaysia (CTP-PPSB)

NOTE THAT ANY PAGE CROSS REFERENCES REFER TO THE PRINT EDITION

Contents

Acknowledgements   viii
Publisher's acknowledgements   ix
Chronology   xi
Who's who   xv
Glossary   xxiii
Map   xxviii

PART ONE   INTRODUCTION   1

     1   THE PROBLEM   3
          What is modernism?   6
          Further reading   11

PART TWO   THE HISTORICAL ORIGINS OF MODERNISM   13

     2   ART AND MODERNITY IN THE NINETEENTH CENTURY   15
          Further reading   27

     3   THE PERCEPTUAL REVOLUTION   28
          Further reading   38

PART THREE   HIGH MODERNISM   39

     4   EARLY MODERNISM   41
          Further reading   52

5   THE RADICAL AVANT-GARDE   54
     Further reading   65

6   THE NEW SOBRIETY   66
     Further reading   79

PART FOUR   AFTER MODERNISM   81

7   THE NEO-AVANT-GARDE   83
     Further reading   93

8   POSTMODERNISM   94
     Further reading   104

PART FIVE   CONCLUSION   105

9   ASSESSMENT   107
     Further reading   110

PART SIX   DOCUMENTS   111

1   Charles Baudelaire, 'The painter of modern life'   112
2   Virginia Woolf, 'Mr. Bennett and Mrs. Brown'   113
3   Henri Matisse, 'Notes of a painter'   116
4   Wassily Kandinsky, *Concerning the spiritual in art*   118
5   Piet Mondrian, 'Neo-Plasticism: the general principle
     of plastic equivalence'   120
6   Emil Nolde, 'On primitive art'   122
7   F. T. Marinetti, 'The founding and the manifesto
     of Futurism'   123
8   Tristan Tzara, 'Dada manifesto 1918'   125
9   André Breton, 'The manifesto of Surrealism'   127
10   Le Corbusier and Amédée Ozenfant, 'Purism'   129
11   Walter Gropius, 'The theory and organisation of
     the Bauhaus'   132
12   Alfred H. Barr, Jr., *Cubism and abstract art*   134
13   Walter Benjamin, 'The work of art in the age of
     mechanical reproduction'   136
14   Richard Hamilton, 'For the finest art try – POP'   138

15 Peter Bürger, 'The negation of the autonomy of art by
    the avant-garde'   140
16 Jean Baudrillard, *Simulations*   142
17 Fredric Jameson, 'Postmodernism, or the cultural logic of
    late capitalism'   144
18 Lucy R. Lippard, 'Trojan Horses: activist art and power'   146
19 Raymond Williams, 'When was modernism?'   149

    REFERENCES   151

    INDEX   156

Acknowledgements

Among the colleagues and companions who have assisted me in completing this book, foremost mention goes to my first mentors in intellectual history, Donald M. Lowe at San Francisco State University and Eugene Lunn at the University of California, Davis. Their formative influences helped to make this book possible, many years later. I also thank Michael T. Saler, Professor of History at the University of California, Davis, for encouraging me to continually rethink the meaning of modernity. I also owe a great debt to the many students who have taken my courses in Modern European Intellectual History at the University of California at Davis, Pomona College, and the University of Alaska Southeast. Their questions and our discussions have helped me, I hope, write a short cultural history of modernism in a way that is accessible to an undergraduate university audience while still retaining something of its complexity and serving as an inducement for further critical dialogue. The Dean of Arts and Sciences, Marsha Sousa, and my colleagues in the Departments of Social Science and the Humanities at the University of Alaska have provided me with the time and encouragement required to complete this project. I particularly appreciate series editor Gordon Martel for his generous support, and a special thank you goes to Sarah Turpie, Melanie Carter and the staff at Pearson-Longman for their invaluable assistance in ushering this project through from manuscript to book. Finally, a very particular thank you to Carol Prentice, who is neither a cultural nor intellectual historian, but cares deeply for someone who is.

Publisher's acknowledgements

We are grateful to the following for permission to reproduce copyright material:

Plates 1 and 3 courtesy of Giraudon/The Bridgeman Art Library Ltd, © DACS; Plate 2 courtesy of Archives Charmet/ The Bridgeman Art Library Ltd; Plate 4 copyright Barbara Kruger, courtesy: Mary Boone Gallery, New York/ image courtesy of The Broad Art Foundation, Santa Monica.

Document 1 from Baudelaire, C., 'The Painter of Modern Life' in *Selected Writings on Art and Literature* (trans. and intro. P. R. Chavret) (Penguin, 1992); Document 2 from Woolf, V. 'Mr Bennett and Mrs Brown', in *Collected Essays, Vol I* (Harcourt, Brace & World, 1967), reprinted in the US courtesy of Houghton Mifflin, and in the rest of the world courtesy of The Random House Group Limited; Document 3 from Flam, J. (ed.), *Matisse on Art*. Copyright © 1995 by Jack Flam. English translation copyright © 1995 by Jack Flam. Underlying text and illustrations by Matisse. Copyright © 1995, 1973 by Succession Henri Matisse (University of California Press). Reprinted with permission of Georges Borchardt, Inc., for Jack Flam; Document 4 from Kandinsky, W., *Concerning the Spiritual in Art*, trans. Sadler, M. T. (Dover Publications, Inc., 1977); Document 5 from Mondrian, P., *The New Art, The New Life: The Collected Writings of Piet Mondrian* (Thames & Hudson Ltd, 1987), edited and translated by Holtzman, H. and James, M.S.), courtesy of Thames and Hudson Ltd, all of the world except North America, Japan, the Philippines and the Caribbean; Document 7 from Rainey, L. (ed.), *Modernism: An Anthology* (John Wiley & Sons, 2005); Document 8 originally printed in T. Tzara, *Seven Dada Manifestos and Lampisteries* (Calder Publications Ltd, 1981) © Alma Classics Ltd, 2011. Reprinted with permission of Alma Classics; Document 10 from Herbert, R. L., *Modern Artists on Art*, 2nd edn, (Dover Publications, Inc., 2000); Document 13 from Benjamin, W., 'The Work of Art in the Age of Mechanical Reproduction', in *Illuminations* (Pimlico, 1999), reprinted in the UK and Commonwealth (excluding

Canada) courtesy of The Random House Group Limited; Document 14 from Hamilton, R., *Collected Works, 1953–1982* (Thames and Hudson, 1982), reprinted with permission of Hansjorg Mayer, on behalf of Rita McDonough; Document 16 from Baudrillard, J., *Simulations* (trans. Paul Foss, Paul Patton and Philip Beitchman) (Semiotext(e), 1983); Document 17 from Jameson, F., 'Postmodernism, or The Cultural Logic of Late Capitalism', *New Left Review* 142 (1984), 53–65; Document 19 from Williams, R., 'When was Modernism?' in *The Politics of Modernism* (Verso Books, 2007).

In some cases we have been unable to trace the owners of copyright material, and we would appreciate any information that would enable us to do so.

Chronology

Since modernism is not a discrete series of historical events, the following chronology by year provides historical guideposts and cultural touchstones in its development, rather than a comprehensive list of events.

1863 Charles Baudelaire, 'The Painter of Modern Life'

1874 Claude Monet, *Impression, soleil levant* (*Impression, Sunrise*): birth of Impressionism

1890 William James, *Principles of Psychology*

1891 French Expressionist painter Paul Gauguin travels to Tahiti

1893 Edmund Husserl, *On the Phenomenology of the Consciousness of Internal Time*

1896 Henri Bergson, *Matter and Memory*

1900 Paul Cézanne, *Bathers* series of paintings

1901 Death of Queen Victoria
Sigmund Freud, *The Interpretation of Dreams*
Thomas Mann, *Buddenbrooks: The Decline of a Family*

1904 *Die Brüke* group of German Expressionist artists founded

1905 Albert Einstein, 'On the Electrodynamics of Moving Bodies' (special theory of relativity)

1908 Georges Braque, *Maisons à L'estaque* (*Houses in L'estaque*): birth of Cubism

1909 Arnold Schoenberg, *Three Piano Pieces* and *Five Pieces for Orchestra*
F. T. Marinetti, 'The Founding and the Manifesto of Futurism'

1910 Bertrand Russell and Alfred North Whitehead, *Principia Mathematica*

1911 Wassily Kandinsky, *Concerning the Spiritual in Art*

1912 Claude Debussy, *L'Après-midi d'un faune*

1913 29 May: Premiere of *Le Sacre du printemps* (*The Rite of Spring*) by Igor Stravinsky
Virginia Woolf, *The Voyage Out*
Marcel Proust, first volume of *À la recherche du temps perdu* (*In Search of Lost Time*)

Guillaume Apollinaire, *Les Peintres cubistes* (*The Cubist Painters*)

Marcel Duchamp, *Bottlerack* and *Fountain* ('R. Mutt')

1914   August: First World War begins

Wyndham Lewis starts the Vorticist periodical *Blast*

1916   Ferdinand de Saussure, *General Course in Linguistics* (semiotics)

Hugo Ball opens the Cabaret Voltaire in Zurich: birth of Dada

1917   Revolutions in Russia result in the Bolshevik seizure of power

1918   11 November: First World War Armistice

Guillaume Apollinaire, *Calligrammes*

1919   January: Failed Spartacist uprising in Berlin

Bauhaus School of Art and Design in Weimar, Germany founded

Paris Dada begins

1920   First International Dada Fair held in Berlin

1921   *Constructivist Manifesto* issued in Bolshevik Russia

1922   29 October: Mussolini's march on Rome: birth of Italian Fascism

Establishment of the Association of Artists of Revolutionary Russia (AKhRR)

James Joyce, *Ulysses* (previously serialised 1918–20)

Le Corbusier, *Towards a New Architecture*

1923   Union of Soviet Socialist Republics established

First Bauhaus public exhibition held in Weimar, Germany

LEF ('Left Front of the Arts') journal of the Soviet modernist avant-garde founded

1924   'The Manifesto of Surrealism' published in *La Révolution surréaliste*: birth of Surrealism

1925   First *Neue Sachlichkeit* ('The New Objectivity') exhibition held in Mannheim, Germany

1926   Hanah Höche, *Aus einem ethnographischen Museum* ('From an Ethnographic Museum')

Antonio Gramsci begins *The Prison Notebooks*

1927   Julien Benda, *The Treason of the Intellectuals*

Le Tumulte noir lithographs by Paul Colin featuring Josephine Baker

1929   October: Wall Street Stock Market Crashes: Global Economic Depression begins

Thomas Mann receives the Nobel Prize in Literature for *Buddenbrooks*

Bertolt Brecht, *Die Dreigroschenoper* (*The Three-Penny Opera*)

First International Congress of Modern Architecture (CIAM)

1930   José Ortega y Gasset, *The Revolt of the Masses*

1931   May–November: International Colonial Exposition in Paris

Surrealist Counter-Colonial Exposition, 'The Truth about the Colonies'

1932   Paul Nizan, *The Watchdogs*

1933   January: Nazi seizure of power in Germany

Jewish-German artists, writers and intellectuals begin to emigrate from Nazi Germany

Dakar-Djibouti ethnographic mission featured in the Surrealist review, *Minotaure* (no. 2)

1935   21–25 June: International Writers' Congress for the Defense of Culture in Paris

Walter Benjamin drafts, 'The Work of Art in the Age of Mechanical Reproduction'

1936   Left-Center Popular Front governments elected in France and Spain

Fascist-allied General Franco begins civil war against the Second Spanish Republic

Alfred H. Barr, Jr., 'Cubism and Abstract Art' exhibition at the New York Museum of Modern Art (MoMA)

1937   May-November: International Exhibition in Paris

Spanish Pavilion exhibits Joan Miró, *The Reaper* and Pablo Picasso, *Guernica*

July: *Entartete Kunst* ('Degenerate Art') and *Großen Deutschen Kunstausstellung* ('Great German Art') exhibitions in Munich

1939   1 September: Second World War begins in Europe

Clement Greenberg, 'Avant-Garde and Kitsch' published in the *Partisan Review*

Picasso's *Les Demoiselles d'Avignon* (1907) installed at MoMA, New York

1940   Fall of France: beginning of the Nazi Occupation and Vichy France

Pierre Drieu la Rochelle becomes director of *La Nouvelle Revue Française*

Emigration of the modernist avant-garde from Europe to America begins

1942   Peggy Guggenheim opens *The Art of This Century* gallery in New York

1942–3   August–February: Battle of Stalingrad, the war begins to turn against Nazi Germany

1944   Allied invasion of Normandy (6 June) and the Liberation of Paris (19 August)

1945   8 May: End of Second World War in Europe

1948   Robert Motherwell begins the series, *Elegy to the Spanish Republic*

1949   *Life* magazine declares Jackson Pollock the 'greatest living painter' in the United States

Simone de Beauvoir, *Le Dieuxième Sexe* (*The Second Sex*)

1952   *Theater Piece #1*, first neo-avant-garde 'happening' organised by composer John Cage

1955   Kazuo Shiraga, *Challenging Mud*: birth of Gutai ('Concrete Art Group') in Japan

1956   Independent Group, 'This is Tomorrow' exhibition in London

1957   Roland Barthes, *Mythologies*

1960   Yves Klein, *Anthropométries de l'époque bleue* ('Blue Period Anthropometrics'): birth of *Nouveau Réalisme*

Jean Tinguley, *Homage à New York* assemblage catches fire at MoMA

1961   Construction of the Berlin Wall

1962   Andy Warhol, *32 Campbell's Soup Cans* and Roy Lichtenstein, *Blam*: birth of Pop Art

1968   May '68 Student Protests and General Strike in Paris

1974   Peter Bürger, *Theory of the Avant-Garde*

1975   Judy Chicago, *The Dinner Party* exhibition in Chicago
Laura Mulvey, "Visual Pleasure and Narrative Cinema"

1976   Philip Glass and Robert Wilson's opera *Einstein on the Beach* performed at the Metropolitan Opera House in New York

1979   François Lyotard, *The Postmodern Condition: A Report on Knowledge*

1981   Jean Baudrillard, *Simulations*

1984   Frederic Jameson, 'Postmodernism, or the Cultural Logic of Late Capitalism'

1987   First ACT-UP (AIDS Coalition to Unleash Power) action staged in New York

1991   'High & Low: Modern Art, Popular Culture' exhibition at MoMA

1997   Opening of the Guggenheim Museum in Bilbao, Spain, designed by postmodern architect Frank Gehry

Who's who

Apollinaire, Guillaume (pseudo. Whilhelm de Kostrowitzky, 1880–1918): French poet, playwright, critic and impresario of early modernism across the arts, particularly Cubism.

Aragon, Louis (1897–1982): French poet and novelist. A founding member of the Paris Dada and Surrealism movements who shifted his aesthetic and political commitment to communism in the 1930s.

Bacon, Francis (1909–92): Irish-born British figurative painter known for emotionally raw and horrifically garish portraits during the post-Second World War era.

Baker, Josephine (1906–75): African-American entertainer who popularised the fusion of primitivism and modernism in *La Revue Nègre* performances and in Paul Colin's lithographs, *Le Tumulte noir*.

Ball, Hugo (1886–1927): German Expressionist writer and director who founded the Cabaret Voltaire in 1916, the birthplace of Zurich Dada.

Barr, Jr., Alfred H. (1902–81): American art historian and first director of the Museum of Modern Art in New York City. His *Cubism and Abstract Art* exhibition and catalogue (1936) was influential in the canonisation of modernism.

Baudelaire, Charles (1821–67): French poet later recognised by the Symbolists and Surrealists as one of the earliest theorists of the relationship of modernity to art.

Benjamin, Walter (1892–1940): Frankfurt School intellectual who theorised on the rise of modernity and modernist sensibilities. Had a major influence on the development of critical theory and cultural studies.

Braque, Georges (1882–1963): French painter and sculptor whose emphasis upon geometry and multiple perspectives helped to established Cubism. Worked closely with Picasso 1908–1914.

Brecht, Bertolt (1898–1956): German Marxist poet and playwright who provoked audiences to take political action through theatrical techniques of *Verfremdungseffekte* ('alienation effects').

Breton, André (1896–1966): French poet and member of the Paris Dada group, he founded Surrealism and was its chief exponent throughout his life.

Cage, John (1912–92): American musical composer and theorist, he was a leading neo-avant-garde figure, recognised as one of the most influential twentieth-century composers.

Calder, Alexander (1898–1976): American sculptor and visual artist. Influenced by Neo-Plasticism and Surrealism, he is best known for painted steel stabiles and mobiles.

Cendrars, Blaise (pseudo. Frédéric Louis Sauser, 1887–1961): Swiss novelist and poet naturalised in France, his abstract and expressionist early avant-garde writing explored cross influences between art and literature.

Cézanne, Paul (1839–1906): French Post-Impressionist painter who influenced the development of Abstract Expressionism and Cubism.

Christo and Jeanne-Claude (pseudo. Hristo Yavashev, 1935– , and Jeanne-Claude Denat de Guillebon, 1935–2008): Bulgarian and French-Moroccan neo-avant-garde artists best known for their colourful environmental and monumental wrapping projects.

Cocteau, Jean (1889–1963): French poet, dramatist, novelist, critic and cultural impresario who participated in and promoted a wide variety of modernist productions across the arts.

Dalí, Salvador (1904–89): Spanish Surrealist painter whose works enjoyed crossover audience appeal in the art museum and popular culture.

Debussy, Claude (1862–1918): French Impressionist composer. Certain compositions were influenced by Symbolism and primitivism in art and literature.

de Kooning, Willem (1904–97): Dutch-born American Abstract Expressionist painter of the New York School.

Dix, Otto (1891–1969): German *Neue Sachlichkeit* ('New Objectivity') painter and printmaker. Best known for his brutal depictions of the First World War and post-war Weimar society.

Drieu la Rochelle, Pierre (1893–1945): French novelist, essayist and editor who became politically committed to French fascism and was director of the *Nouvelle Revue Française* under the Nazi occupation.

Dubuffet, Jean (1901–85): French painter and sculptor of *art brut* ('raw art'), later known for his colourful and fluid popular art imagery.

Duchamp, Marcel (1887–1968): Provocative French artist whose ready-made sculptures, large glassworks and musical compositions subverted the meaning of art. Was a major influence on Dada and Surrealism.

Eliot, T. S. (Thomas Stearns, 1888–1965): American-born British poet, playwright and literary critic. A prominent figure in English literary modernism, he received the Nobel Prize in Literature in 1948.

Flaubert, Gustave (1821–1880): A leading French Realist novelist, his emphasis upon perfection in literary style anticipated formalist preoccupations in literary modernism.

Freud, Sigmund (1856–1939): Jewish-Austrian founder of psychoanalysis. His ideas about the unconscious and the interpretation of dreams had an inestimable effect upon artistic and literary modernism.

Gaugin, Paul (1848–1903): French Post-Impressionist painter. His colourful and bold paintings set in Brittany and French Polynesia anticipated the use of primitivism in modernist art.

Gautier, Théophile (1811–72): French poetic dramatist and novelist. His art and literary criticism influenced the development of aesthetic theory in Symbolism and modernism.

Gehry, Frank (1929–): Canadian-American architect. His style of 'corporate branding' has made him perhaps the most renowned postmodern architect.

Giacometti, Alberto (1901–66): Swiss sculptor and painter best known for depicting existential alienation in bronze sculptures of elongated human figures.

Glass, Philip (1937–): American minimalist composer whose repetitious musical style has had great crossover appeal in both classical and popular genres.

Gorky, Arshile (Vosdanik Adoian, 1904–48): Armenian-American Abstract Expressionist painter who was strongly influenced by the Surrealists.

Gourmont, Remy de (1858–1915): French Symbolist poet whose literary criticism greatly influenced early modernist poetry in France and England.

Greenberg, Clement (1909–94): Influential American art critic who was the foremost advocate of American Abstract Expressionism in the mid-twentieth century.

Gropius, Walter (1883–1969): German architect and founder of the Bauhaus. Later became an influential figure in American modernist architecture and design.

Grosz, George (1893–1959): German artist who adhered to the Communist Party and was prominent in the Berlin Dada and *Neue Sachlichkeit* ('New Objectivity') movements.

Guggenheim, Peggy (1898–1979): American avid art collector of Cubist, Surrealist and Abstract Expressionist art and the founder of modern art museums in London and New York.

H. D. (Hilda Doolittle, 1886–1961): American poet and writer who, with Ezra Pound and Richard Aldington, was a member of the Imagist group of avant-garde poets.

Hamilton, Richard (1922–2011): A member of the neo-avant-garde Independent Group in London, he was influential in promoting Pop art in the 1950s and 1960s.

Hausmann, Raoul (1886–1971): Austrian artist and writer who was a leading figure in the Berlin Dada movement.

Heartfield, John (pseudo. Helmut Herzfeld, 1891–1968): Member of the Berlin Dada group and the German Communist Party, his photomontages criticised both the Weimar and Nazi regimes.

Höch, Hannah (1889–1978): Berlin Dada artist who pioneered techniques of photomontage, which she continued to develop and refine throughout her life.

Hulme, T. E. (Thomas Ernest, 1883–1917): English critic and poet, he founded Imagism as a form of modern abstract poetry.

James, William (1842–1910): American psychologist and philosopher, his ideas about 'stream of consciousness' in human psychology had a great influence upon literary modernism.

Joyce, James (1882–1941): Irish novelist and poet, he remains one of the most eminent literary modernists of the early twentieth century.

Kandinsky, Wassily (1866–1944): Russian-born painter and avant-garde theorist who pursued Abstract Expressionism and participated in the *Blaue Reiter* ('Blue Rider') group in France and the Bauhaus in Germany.

Klee, Paul (1879–1940): Swiss-German painter who was influenced by multiple modernist art movements including Expressionism, Cubism and Surrealism.

Klein, Yves (1928–62): French painter and performance artist who was a leading member of the *Nouveau Réaliste* neo-avant-garde.

Klimt, Gustave (1862–1918): Austrian Symbolist painter of the Vienna Secession movement who used ancient themes and gold leaf techniques to explore the unconscious and eroticism in modern art.

Kruger, Barbara (1945–): Contemporary American conceptual artist who juxtaposes black and white magazine images with invented captions to deliver feminist and anti-consumerist messages.

Le Corbusier (pseudo. Charles-Édouard Jeanneret, 1887–1956): Swiss-French architect and urban planner whose ideas about rational design had tremendous theoretical influence on the development of modernist architecture.

Léger, Fernand (1881–1955): Prolific French painter, sculptor and filmmaker whose early Cubism later developed into more figurative and popular styles of art.

Lévy-Bruhl, Lucien (1857–1939): French anthropologist whose writings on the 'primitive mind' influenced notions about primitivism in modernism, particularly among the Surrealists.

Lewis, Wyndham (1882–1957): Canadian artist and writer who, together with Ezra Pound, founded Vorticism in art and literature.

Lichtenstein, Roy (1923–97): American Pop artist whose large-scale paintings were often parodies of advertisements and comic book panels.

Mallarmé, Stéphane (1842–98): French Symbolist poet and literary critic. His literary, art and music criticism influenced the later development of modernist aesthetics.

Manet, Édouard (1832–83): French Impressionist painter who used contemporary themes in art and promoted the display of modern art in independent exhibitions.

Mann, Thomas (1875–1955): German novelist and essayist known for exploring the inner psychology in his works. Received the 1929 Nobel Prize in Literature for *Buddenbrooks*.

Marinetti, F. T. (Filippo Tommaso, 1876–1944): Italian poet and avant-garde provocateur. Founder of the Futurist movement, he became a staunch supporter of Fascist Italy.

Matisse, Henri (1869–1954): French painter, sculptor and printmaker. One of the *Fauves* ('wild beasts') painters, he experimented with the expressive use of colour and the qualities of the paint medium.

Mayakovsky, Vladimir (1893–1930): Russian Cubo-Futurist poet who collaborated with the artists and writers of *LEF* ('Left Front of the Arts') and produced agitprop for the early Soviet Union.

Mies van der Rohe, Ludwig (1886–1969): German modernist architect who, with Walter Gropius and Le Corbusier, is considered a pioneer of modern architectural style.

Miró, Joan (1893–1983): Experimental Spanish-Catalan painter and sculptor who was strongly influenced by Surrealism as a path to the unconscious.

Modersohn-Becker, Paula (1876–1907): German painter from the Worpswede group who combined primitive folk and maternal themes with modern Expressionist painting techniques.

Mondrian, Piet (Pieter Cornelis Mondriaan, 1872–1944): Dutch painter who established Neo-Plasticism as a further abstraction of Cubism across the arts.

Morisot, Berthe (1841–95): One of the founders of the Impressionist movement in painting, she used domestic interiors and scenes from private life as subject matter.

Moreau, Gustave (1826–98): French Symbolist painter whose ideas about a painting's integral unity and harmony influenced other Symbolist and modernist artists and writers.

Motherwell, Robert (1915–91): American painter of the New York School whose approach to Abstract Expressionism was heavily influenced by exiled Surrealist artists in New York.

Nolde, Emil (1967–56): German Expressionist painter and member of *Die Brücke* group of artists that sought a fusion of primitivism and modernism in art.

Ozenfant, Amédée (1866–1966): French Cubist painter who collaborated with Le Corbusier to develop the Purist movement in art and architecture.

Picasso, Pablo (1881–1973): Spanish painter, sculptor, ceramicist and set designer. The pre-eminent figure of twentieth-century modernist art, he worked in a variety of styles including Cubism and Surrealism.

Pollock, Jackson (1912–56): American Abstract Expressionist painter best known for his 'action painting' technique of dripping or pouring paint on horizontal surfaces.

Pound, Ezra (1885–1972): American poet and critic who became a major figure in English literary modernism for his leading position in the movements of Imagism and Vorticism.

Proust, Marcel (1871–1922): French novelist who explored the wanderings of memory and inner psychological time over the multi-volume *À la recherché du temps perdu* (*In Search of Lost Time*).

Riley, Terry (1935–). American composer of minimal music pieces that combine musical 'modules' with improvisation choices made by the individual performers within an ensemble.

Reich, Steve (1936–). American composer of minimal music who creates 'phase' effects through the gradual shifting of melodic and rhythmic patterns over time.

Rodchenko, Alexander (1891–1956): Russian Constructivist artist, sculptor and graphic designer in the early Soviet period.

Rosenquist, James (1933–). American Pop artist who drew upon his experiences as a billboard painter to develop techniques of large-scale painting.

Rothko, Mark (1903–70): Russian-American Abstract Expressionist painter whose 'multiform' technique arranged rectangular blocks of contrasting or complementary colours horizontally upon a canvas.

Rousseau, Henri (1844–1910): Self-taught French painter and inspirational figure for the French early avant-garde poets and painters whose 'naïve' style displayed the fusion of modern art with primitive technique.

Saussure, Ferdinand de (1857–1913): Pioneering linguist in the field of semiotics, or the study of signs, which later became the theoretical foundation of structuralism, post-structuralism and postmodernism.

Schoenberg, Arnold (1874–1951): Jewish Austro-Hungarian composer who experimented with musical techniques of atonality, chromatic saturation, dissonance and seriality. Influenced the Second Viennese School of composers.

Schwitters, Kurt (1887–1948): German Dada painter who developed the highly idiosyncratic technique of collage and assemblages he called *Merz*.

Segalen, Victor (1878–1919): French physician, ethnographer and writer who developed the notion of the *exot*, or the psychological alienation of being a foreigner, during his travels in French Polynesia.

Stravinsky, Igor (1882–1971): Russian composer, pianist and conductor who achieved fame in France and the United States. Pursued multi-tonality in music by using overlapping harmonies, rhythms and compositional styles in the same piece.

Stein, Gertrude (1874–1946): American modernist writer who applied theories of abstract painting to literature. An expatriate in Paris, she leant support to the efforts of many modernist artists and authors.

Tinguely, Jean (1925–1991): Swiss painter and sculptor. A member of the *Nouveau Réaliste* neo-avant-garde, he is best known for his fanciful kinetic sculptures and makeshift 'junk' machines.

Tzara, Tristan (1896–1963): Romanian writer who was instrumental in founding the Dada anti-art movement. Participated in the subsequent developments of Berlin Dada, Paris Dada and Surrealism.

Vertov, Dziga (pseudo. David Abelevich Kaufman, 1896–1954). Early Soviet documentary film director who developed sophisticated montage techniques and theories about *Kino-Pravda* ('film truth') and *Kino-Glaz* (the film camera's 'mechanical eye').

Warhol, Andy (1928–87): Controversial American Pop artist, printmaker and filmmaker. Elevated mass consumer culture as art through factory production techniques and sought celebrity fame by association with iconic entertainment and society figures.

Woolf, Virginia (1882–1941): English modernist writer and essayist best known for developing 'stream of consciousness' narrative and language techniques in her novels.

Glossary

Abstract Expressionism: An approach to visual art that combines emotional intensity with abstract or non-figurative painting techniques. A dominant style in modernist art in post-Second World War America.

Art Nouveau: French for 'new art', a late-nineteenth-century style of commercial and decorative art and architecture that featured curved lines and flowing movement inspired by natural forms.

l'art pour l'art: French phrase meaning 'art for art's sake'. Refers to the notion that art has intrinsic value and meaning in itself, independent of any didactic, moral or utilitarian function.

AKhRR (Association of Artists of Revolutionary Russia): An association of Soviet figurative painters that favoured 'heroic realism' over modernist abstraction in ideological support of the proletariat.

avant-garde: Originally a French military term meaning the 'forward guard', in modernism it refers to the vanguard that creates and introduces new forms of art, literature and aesthetic criticism.

Bauhaus: An art and architectural school in Weimar Germany that combined practical training in craft materials with the study of aesthetic theory in a workshop setting towards solving 'form problems' in architecture and design.

Blaue Reiter ('Blue Riders'): A group of Expressionist artists in Germany during the 1910s that sought to express 'spiritual truths' in painting through symbolic associations of colour and the formal qualities of the image.

concrete: An adjective used to modify art, poetry or performance to emphasise direct engagement with the tangible contact elements of media over aesthetic or linguistic meaning.

Constructivism: A radical avant-garde movement in the early Soviet Russia that rejected the idea of autonomy in art in favour of applied modernist art, particularly in the areas of architecture, graphic design, film, fashion and commercial goods.

Cubism: An early form of abstract art in which objects are analysed from multiple viewpoints, broken down into discrete units, and then reassembled as a complex two-dimensional image.

Dada: An anti-art movement originating in Zurich, Switzerland during the First World War that reduced art, language, music and performance to blather or 'da-da'. Berlin Dada and Paris Dada developed in the immediate post-war period.

De Stijl: Dutch term meaning 'the style', title of a journal that promoted Neo-Plastic aesthetics and abstraction in architecture, product design and the visual arts.

Entartete Kunst: German phrase meaning 'Degenerate Art' used by the Nazis in a 1937 exhibition to characterise modernist art as 'Jewish' and 'Bolshevist'.

existentialism: A philosophical attitude popular in the immediate post-Second World War era to create one's individual 'essence' despite living in a disorienting, meaningless and absurd world.

Expressionism: Early modernist movement in visual art, literature and music that gave outward form to subjective experiences, feelings and moods, which expressed the inner life of the individual rather than the representation of external reality.

Fauves: French for 'wild beasts', refers to a group of early-twentieth-century painters who used strong colours and bold brush strokes for purposes of expression over representation.

Fluxus: Latin for 'Flow', refers to neo-avant-garde mixed-media 'happenings' in New York during the 1960s performed by an international network of artists across a variety of disciplines.

Futurism: An early-twentieth-century Italian avant-garde movement that celebrated technology, industrialisation, movement and violence as the basis for future art.

Gutai: Japanese term for 'concrete' or tangible, an association of neo-avant-garde Japanese artists during the 1950s who, in opposition to modernist abstraction, staged performances where artists interacted with physical materials.

Imagism: An early-twentieth-century modernist movement in Anglo-American poetry that promoted an economy of direct, clear and precise language in poetic images over lyrical verse.

Impressionism: A nineteenth-century movement in painting that sought to capture shifting human perceptions of light and movement through the qualities of the paint medium and brushstrokes. Influenced the later styles of Impressionism in music and literature.

Independent Group: An association of painters, sculptors and critics at the Institute of Contemporary Arts in London during the early 1950s who opposed the 'high' status of modernism through the inclusion of 'low' sources of mass culture in artistic productions.

japonisme: Refers to the incorporation of styles and motifs from Japanese wood-block prints, lacquers and porcelains into late-nineteenth-century French art.

jugendstil: German term meaning 'youth style', it was the Art Nouveau form favoured by the Secession artists in Austria and Hungary in the late nineteenth and early twentieth centuries.

Kitsch: German word for cheap and mass-produced art that is popularly regarded as iconic, but is actually imitative, inferior, pretentious, overly sentimental or nostalgic.

minimalism: Movement in art and music after the mid-twentieth century that reveals the essence of a work by eliminating all non-essential features of the medium.

modern: From the Latin *modo* ('just now') meaning 'in the current manner' or up-to-date. Since the Renaissance, history is divided into 'ancient', 'medieval' and 'modern' epochs, and from the nineteenth century forward 'modern' has been opposed to 'traditional'.

modernism: A cultural movement across the arts in the late nineteenth and early twentieth centuries that departed from classical or inherited ideas about art and strove to replace them with new aesthetics that expressed the contemporary moment.

modernity: The experience of living in a contemporary world that is being continually transformed by the processes of modernisation. An attitude, philosophy or worldview that aligns with the conditions of the modern world.

neo-avant-garde: Term given to avant-garde movements after the mid-twentieth century that challenged the status and presumed aesthetic superiority of modernism by staging 'happenings' and by the inclusion of mass-culture sources in contemporary art.

neo-classical: Refers to the impulse to 'return to classical order' in themes and styles of modern art, architecture and literature.

Neo-Plasticism: Meaning the 'new plastic', indicates an abstract aesthetic of asymmetrical balance of harmony and tension achieved through the use of vertical and horizontal lines, rectangular forms, and the primary colours and values.

Neue Sachlichkeit: German phrase meaning 'New Objectivity', a highly politicised modernist style of pictorial painting and collage construction that criticised the collusion between government and big business, and portrayed class conflict in post-war Weimar society.

Nouveau Réalisme: French phrase meaning 'New Realism', refers to a Parisian neo-avant-garde reaction against abstract modernism by staging concrete performances and creating 'junk art' from recycled advertising images, and industrial and consumer goods.

Pop Art: A mid-twentieth-century art movement in the United States and Britain that deployed advertisement images, comics and other popular forms of mass culture in novel ways either to celebrate or ironically comment upon the banality of contemporary life.

postmodernism: Art 'after modernism'. May refer to either a 'crisis of representation' in modernism or a mode of pastiche art that recombines old and new styles in novel ways.

post-structuralism: An approach to art, literature and philosophy that questions the specific meaning of a work in relation to shifts in underlying structures of language and aesthetics.

primitivism: The use of folk and non-Western sources or impulses in modernist art. Also applies to the production of 'naïve' art by untrained artists or the use of 'primitive techniques' such as photomontage.

Prolekult: Russian contraction of *proletarskaya kultura* or 'proletarian culture', refers to the use of avant-garde visual art, literature, drama and film to create a revolutionary working class in the early Soviet Union.

Purism: An early-twentieth-century movement in art and architecture that extended principles of Cubism towards greater rationality and order through the use of geometric form, ratio, and primary colours.

Realism: Nineteenth-century literary and artistic movement that emphasised accuracy in style. Anticipated the modernist emphasis upon form.

Romanticism: A nineteenth-century artistic and literary movement that rejected the supremacy of rationalism and science to emphasise the creative power of the imagination and the emotions. Promoted the status of the 'work of art' and the role of the 'artistic genius'.

Socialist Realism: Modern style of realistic art in the Soviet Union that idealised the heroic role of the Soviet leadership, working class and agricultural workers as the vanguard of future communism.

Surrealism: An early-twentieth-century avant-garde movement in art and literature that sought a 'higher fusion of reality' through explorations of the unconscious and dream imagery, and by making juxtapositions between 'found objects' (*la trouvaille*) in novel ways.

structuralism: An approach to 'semiotics' or the study of linguistic signs that establishes the meaning of a particular work of literature or art by relating it to underlying rules of language or aesthetic principles.

Symbolism: A late-nineteenth-century movement in literature, art and criticism whose response to modernity was a 'retreat to the interior' that gave poetic and imagistic form to the realms of spirituality, the imagination and dreams.

Vorticism: An early-twentieth-century British movement in poetry and art inspired by Cubism and Futurism that strove to capture movement in dynamic images.

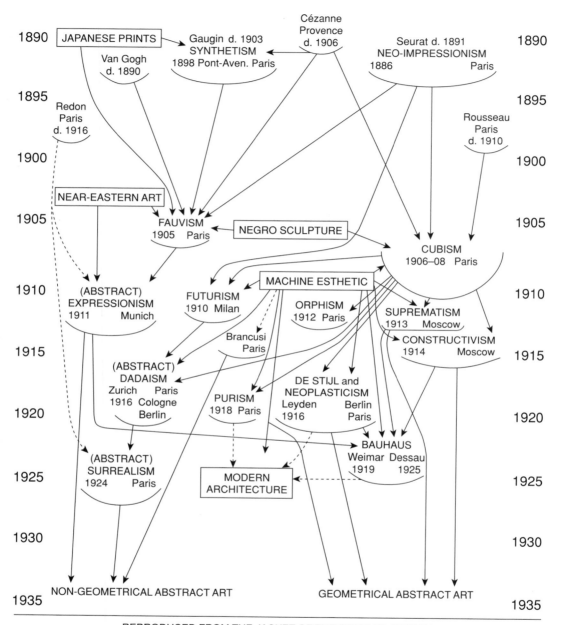

1890

JAPANESE PRINTS → Gaugin d. 1903
Van Gogh   **SYNTHETISM**
d. 1890   1898 Pont-Aven. Paris

Cézanne
Provence
d. 1906

Seurat d. 1891
NEO-IMPRESSIONISM
1886   Paris

1890

1895

Redon
Paris
d. 1916

Rousseau
Paris
d. 1910

1895

1900

NEAR-EASTERN ART

1900

1905

FAUVISM
1905   Paris

NEGRO SCULPTURE

CUBISM
1906–08 Paris

1905

1910

**(ABSTRACT)
EXPRESSIONISM**
1911   Munich

FUTURISM
1910 Milan

MACHINE ESTHETIC

ORPHISM
1912 Paris

SUPREMATISM
1913   Moscow

1910

Brancusi
Paris

CONSTRUCTIVISM
1914   Moscow

1915

**(ABSTRACT)
DADAISM**
Zurich   Paris
1916 Cologne
Berlin

PURISM
1918 Paris

**DE STIJL and
NEOPLASTICISM**
Leyden   Berlin
1916   Paris

1915

1920

BAUHAUS
Weimar Dessau
1919   1925

1920

1925

**(ABSTRACT)
SURREALISM**
1924   Paris

**MODERN
ARCHITECTURE**

1925

1930

1930

1935

NON-GEOMETRICAL ABSTRACT ART

GEOMETRICAL ABSTRACT ART

1935

REPRODUCED FROM THE JACKET OF THE ORIGINAL EDITION

Map: The Development of Abstract Art. In Alfred H. Barr, Jr. *Cubism and Abstract Art.* Reprint edition. New York: Arno Press, 1966. © The Museum of Modern Art, New York, 1936.

Part 1

INTRODUCTION

1

The Problem

During the fall of 1907, the Spanish painter Pablo Picasso invited several friends to his studio in Paris to show them a new painting he had completed earlier that summer. Having recently taken up residence in Paris, the 'capital of **modernity**', Picasso's star was quickly rising on the Parisian arts scene and his works were on display in various galleries. This new painting, which he called his 'brothel', was of a new sort (*see* Plate 1). The canvas was large, two and a half metres tall and nearly as wide. Angular and two-dimensional images of five naked women, looking more like cut-outs than naturalistic figures, seemed to be pasted against a background of massive, irregular geometric shapes of blue and reddish-brown. Two women on the right wore primitive and abstract masks, concealing their faces. Two other women in the centre of the canvas seemed to be staring directly at the viewer. How was the viewer supposed to respond?

The new painting was a calculated provocation, the result of a methodical and intentional process. Over the course of the past year, Picasso had filled sixteen sketchbooks with designs for this particular painting, and he had made a number of preliminary studies of it. Although he was working out of an established nineteenth-century genre, the brothel painting, this particular work had been accomplished in a new style, completely outside the bounds of inherited traditions. Judgements about it were split. Painters Henri Matisse and André Derain did not like it. The American modernist writer Gertrude Stein, a personal friend of Picasso, found 'all of it rather frightening'. The **avant-garde** poet Guillaume Apollinaire dubbed the painting the 'philosophical brothel,' intrigued by its combination of visual provocation and opaque meaning. For the time being, however, it remained in Picasso's studio, known only to a small circle of intimates.

The painting was first placed on public display a decade later, in July 1916, at the 'Modern Art in France' exhibition organised by the poet André

modernity: The experience of living in a contemporary world that is being continually transformed by the processes of modernisation. An attitude, philosophy or worldview that aligns with the conditions of the modern world.

avant-garde: Originally a French military term meaning the 'forward guard', in modernism it refers to the vanguard that creates and introduces new forms of art, literature and aesthetic criticism.

modernism: A cultural movement across the arts in the late nineteenth and early twentieth centuries that departed from classical or inherited ideas about art and strove to replace them with new aesthetics that expressed the contemporary moment.

Expressionism: Early modernist movement in visual art, literature and music that gave outward form to subjective experiences, feelings and moods, which expressed the inner life of the individual rather than the representation of external reality.

Cubism: An early form of abstract art in which objects are analysed from multiple viewpoints, broken down into discrete units, and then reassembled as a complex two-dimensional image.

Futurism: An early-twentieth-century Italian avant-garde movement that celebrated technology, industrialisation, movement and violence as the basis for future art.

Constructivism: A radical avant-garde movement in the early Soviet Russia that rejected the idea of autonomy in art in favour of applied modernist art, particularly in the areas of architecture, graphic design, film, fashions and commercial goods.

Salmon. Titled *Les Demoiselles d'Avignon*, it was Picasso's sole contribution to the exhibition, and it received very little critical attention. In 1924, at the urging of Surrealist André Breton, art collector Jacques Doucet purchased the painting, after the Louvre Museum had declined Picasso's offer to donate it. So the painting remained in Doucet's private collection until his death, when it was sold to an art dealer in 1937. By this time, however, Picasso had become one of the most renowned modernist painters in Europe. Soon, the painting was sold to the Museum of Modern Art (MoMA) in New York City where it was installed in 1939. *Les Demoiselles d'Avignon* has remained there since and today it is viewed by over two and one-half million visitors annually.

This span of time, between the obscure birth of *Les Demoiselles d'Avignon* to its installation in MoMA, coincides with the period of 'high **modernism**' in European history. During these crucial decades, a constellation of avant-garde artists, writers, playwrights, architects, musical composers, film-makers and intellectuals across Europe engaged in a revolutionary project to set Western civilisation upon a new foundation: modernism. Rejecting classical and traditional ideas of aesthetics, modernists insisted that the arts should be founded upon new forms, practices and values derived entirely from the contemporary moment and oriented towards the future. Many of these modernists also believed that they constituted an avant-garde, an artistic elite who were leading a cultural revolution that would transform not only European culture, but human consciousness, social relations and mass politics as well. While the artistic impulses during the period of 'high modernism', from the end of the nineteenth century to the advent of World War II, moved in multiple directions – ranging from **Expressionism**, **Cubism** and **Futurism** to **Constructivism**, **Surrealism** and **Purism** – the goal was the realisation of an entirely new civilisation of modernism.

Today, the notion of modernism has passed into general parlance. Modernist art is a mainstay of contemporary art museums, students learn about literary modernism in university classrooms, scholars critically reinterpret canonical modernist works. Modernist aesthetics have been thoroughly integrated into our contemporary world, part of the cultural air we breathe. When some new work of art or literature debuts, or more common to our daily experience when we are dazzled by newly designed consumer products or digitally generated visual images, such things usually do not shock us. On the contrary, continual innovation in design and creative technique is something we have come to expect. In this sense, culturally we are all **moderns**, whether or not we understand some particular work of modernist art or literature. Yet the aspirations of the early twentieth-century modernist avant-garde were greater than simply to gain general recognition. These modernists were not seeking popularity or looking to win art competitions, they were utopians who wanted to change the world by making new art. We call that collective project 'modernism'. The historical results of that effort have been mixed, and the contemporary status of modernism is uncertain.

This book provides a brief cultural history of modernism, supplemented by a selection of short companion readings and illustration plates for further discussion of critical issues raised by key modernist writers, artists, and critics. The first section focuses upon the historical origins of modernism. Throughout the nineteenth century, as industrialisation and the politics of nationalism and imperialism were rapidly transforming European society, many artists and writers grappled with the issue of what constituted a uniquely modern art and sensibility. The rise of Romantic bohemianism, literary **Realism**, 'art for art's sake,' **Impressionism**, **Symbolism**, and the *Gesamtkunstwerk* 'fusion of the arts' provided some of the aesthetic foundations of modernism for the following century. At the dawn of the twentieth century, a 'perceptual revolution' across academic disciplines – in physics, mathematics, philosophy, psychology, and literature – marked a significant break in the experience of modernity. In a conceptual shift from the experience of linearity to multi-perspectivity, these fields of knowledge were reconfigured upon new conceptual foundations, an intellectual transformation that was seized upon and further developed by the modernist avant-garde.

The second section concerns the era of 'high modernism' in Europe during the first four decades of the twentieth century. At the turn of the century, an early modernist avant-garde began to re-examine and innovate the fundamental modes of expression in such realms as the visual arts, musical composition, and poetry. In the aftermath of World War I and the Russian Revolution, and inspired by the early modernist movements of Futurism and **Dada**, the avant-garde was radicalised. Modernist movements such as Constructivism, Surrealism, and various schools of modernist architecture, had revolutionary goals beyond merely artistic ones to transform mass society and consciousness. With the rise of Fascist Italy, Nazi Germany, the Soviet Union, and global economic depression, however, some modernist avant-garde movements moved towards a "return to sobriety" in which political considerations took precedence over aesthetic experimentation. Under such conditions, modernist art was sometimes placed in the service of the state, while under fascism and communism modernism was censured. In response, an even more radicalised political avant-garde intensified its critique of the status quo.

The third section concerns later developments in modernism in the post-World War II era. During the war and in the following decade, the international centre of modernism shifted from Paris to New York, and a modernist '**neo-avant-garde**' began to emerge beyond the confines of Europe and America. In the last quarter of the twentieth century, the role of the avant-garde was eclipsed by the institutionalisation of modernism in the art

Surrealism: An early-twentieth-century avant-garde movement in art and literature that sought a 'higher fusion of reality' through explorations of the unconscious and dream imagery, and by making juxtapositions between 'found objects' (*la trouvaille*) in novel ways.

Purism: An early-twentieth-century movement in art and architecture that extended principles of Cubism towards greater rationality and order through the use of geometric form, ratio, and primary colours.

modern: From the Latin *modo* ('just now') meaning 'in the current manner' or up-to-date. Since the Renaissance, history is divided into 'ancient', 'medieval' and 'modern' epochs, and from the nineteenth century forward 'modern' has been opposed to 'traditional'.

Realism: Nineteenth-century literary and artistic movement that emphasised accuracy in style. Anticipated the modernist emphasis upon form.

Impressionism: A nineteenth-century movement in painting that sought to capture shifting human perceptions of light and movement through the qualities of the paint medium and brushstrokes. Influenced the later styles of Impressionism in music and literature.

Symbolism: A late-nineteenth-century movement in literature, art and criticism whose response to modernity was a 'retreat to the interior' that gave poetic and imagistic form to the realms of spirituality, the imagination and dreams.

Dada: An anti-art movement originating in Zurich, Switzerland during the First World War that reduced art, language, music and performance to blather or 'da-da'. Berlin Dada and Paris Dada developed in the immediate post-war period.

neo-avant-garde: Term given to avant-garde movements after the mid-twentieth century that challenged the status and presumed aesthetic superiority of modernism by staging 'happenings' and by the inclusion of mass-culture sources in contemporary art.

Pop Art: A mid-twentieth-century art movement in the United States and Britain that deployed advertisement images, comics and other popular forms of mass culture in novel ways either to celebrate or ironically comment upon the banality of contemporary life.

postmodernism: Art 'after modernism'. May refer to either a 'crisis of representation' in modernism or a mode of pastiche art that recombines old and new styles in novel ways.

museum, the rise of the 'culture industry' of mass consumer culture, the attendant '**pop art**' movement, and the advent of '**postmodernism**.' The reading excerpts in the documents section of the book and the plate reproductions of art works not only illustrate and provide texture to these chapters, but also provide the reader with materials for further discussion of the complexities and implications of critical issues raised by this history. As a historical caveat, it is important to bear in mind that the treatment provided here is not comprehensive, as modernism is the subject of a vast scholarship. The modernist movements and the avant-garde figures presented in this book, while important and influential, are neither exclusive nor authoritative, and they do not necessarily deserve some heroic status over their artistic, literary, musical and architectural contemporaries. Still, they constitute a representative and synoptic cultural history of modernism.

Today, the historical implications of modernism are not altogether clear. On the one hand, modernist art has been absorbed into the cultural fabric of the contemporary world, which indicates some measure of success at achieving a fundamental shift in Western civilisation. On the other hand, social and political inequities intensely experienced around the globe today suggest relevance for artistic avant-gardes in the twenty-first century. As a historical process, modernism remains an unfinished project.

WHAT IS MODERNISM?

The term modernism is derived from the root stem 'modern', and it is related to the concepts of modernisation and modernity. Yet while sharing affinities with these terms, modernism should not be equated with or subsumed by them. Modernism does not describe a historical period, large-scale transformations in political economy and society, or even a mentality that favours contemporary values over traditional ones. Rather, modernism marks a radical break in European culture to produce what art critic Harold Rosenberg has called 'the tradition of the new'. In strict usage, modernism is a term of aesthetics, the principles by which a work of art is judged as valid or beautiful. Simply put, modernist aesthetics are different from traditional ones. As both creative innovators and intellectual critics, artists, writers, musicians, designers and architects constituted the vanguard, or avant-garde, of modernism. Rejecting the aesthetic values of their nineteenth-century forebears, the twentieth-century modernist avant-garde sought to set European civilisation upon a new path.

While today we may commonly think of 'modern' and 'new' as nearly synonymous, this has not always been the case. As a historical term, 'modern' refers to European history since the Renaissance and Reformation, so modernism is not synonymous with modern art, which covers the past five centuries. Even the meaning of 'modern' has changed over the centuries. For medieval scholars, to be modern was to be 'current' (from the Latin *modo*) meaning one thought contemporary Christian civilisation was superior to late-Roman antiquity. For the writers and philosophers of the Renaissance 'Republic of Letters', to be current included being knowledgeable about the *prisca sapientia*, or the original 'ancient wisdom' of the Greeks, Hebrews, Egyptians and other civilisations of antiquity. During the Scientific Revolution of the seventeenth century, the breakdown of traditional science (Aristotle, Ptolemy, Galen) was superseded by entirely new knowledge being gained by mathematics, observation, experimentation and global exploration, which was proving to be technologically powerful and commercially profitable. This led to an attitude among the bourgeoisie, a mixture of urban aristocrats, merchants, professionals, and wealthy artisans, that its modern lifestyle and cultural tastes were superior to that of the landed aristocracy and peasantry.

The notion that the modern moment is superior to whatever has occurred in the past began to take root during the Enlightenment of the eighteenth century. When asked, 'What is Enlightenment?' the German philosopher Immanuel Kant responded, *Sapere aude!* – 'Dare to know!' For Kant, the modern, enlightened person thought autonomously for oneself, beyond the limitations of inherited knowledge, authority, custom and superstition. Embracing this new attitude, the writers, artists and intellectuals of the Enlightenment believed that they could help usher in the 'next stage' of knowledge and history with their new philosophies. The crowning achievement of the Enlightenment was the 28-volume *Encyclopédie* edited by Denis Diderot and Jean le Rond d'Alembert (1751–72). A comprehensive dictionary of all known sciences, arts, and crafts, this encyclopaedia was intended as a comprehensive guide to all the world's knowledge for the benefit of humankind. This conceit, that a self-constituted elite discovers the truth, and then compiles and uses that knowledge to guide humanity towards realising a better future, would later be characteristic of the modernist avant-garde as well.

In the nineteenth century, the multiple processes we call 'modernisation' – the expansion of commercial capitalism through industrialisation in tandem with the rise of the modern nation state and imperialism – completely transformed European society and culture. For most of the nineteenth century, many artists and writers largely defined themselves *against* the forces of modernisation. Considering their creative spirit superior to industrial production, many nineteenth-century artists and writers railed against the intellectual pettiness of the bourgeoisie and shopkeepers. Instead, they elevated the 'work of art' above commercially produced mass culture and regarded the superior artist a 'genius'. At the same time, modernisation had produced the very marketplace where their art and literature was sold and thereby had the potential to reach a wide audience. Modernisation thus created an intellectual and practical bind for the artistic elite: is creation of contemporary art an elite enterprise elevated above mass culture, or is the challenge for artists to transform mass culture through a more enlightened modern civilisation? The modernist avant-garde of the twentieth century would come to experience this bind intensely.

Still, whether one was a promoter or critic of modernisation, its transformative effects upon social life and the cultural landscape were self-evident. 'All that is solid melts into air,' Karl Marx proclaimed in the mid-nineteenth century. The critical challenge was not really one of taking a stance for or against modernisation, but how to define art in relation to this modernising condition or 'modernity'. Cultural modernists responded to modernity in two ways. One was the creative goal of trying to capture the experience of modernity, to apprehend what was new about living within rapidly modernising society and culture and to give it expression through art. As the American Abstract Expressionist painter Jackson Pollock put it, 'Modern art is to me nothing more than the expression of contemporary aims of the age that we're living in' (Harrison and Wood, 2003: 583–4). Since the experience of modernity was one of perpetual change, this meant that modernist art had to be continually novel and innovative. In addition to giving expression to modernity, a second goal was to effect a corresponding change in human consciousness. Not only did modernists create new art and literature, they also took on a self-critical role by reflecting upon what they had accomplished by doing so. In turn, they wanted modernist art to transform the minds of their viewers and readers. Modernists, therefore, tried to capture the experience of modernity through new art, and then directed that art towards refashioning consciousness to be more in synch with that modernity. Both of these goals are encapsulated in Ezra Pound's pithy injunction, 'make it new!'

Modernism can be understood, then, as an early twentieth-century cultural movement that strove to achieve a new consciousness about the experiences of modernity through new forms of artistic expression. Yet unlike many nineteenth-century artistic and literary movements, such as **Romanticism**, Realism, Naturalism, Impressionism or Symbolism, modernism cannot be defined in terms of a distinctive style or genre. Modernist movements such as Expressionism, Cubism, **Imagism**, Futurism, Dada, Surrealism, Constructivism, **Neo-Plasticism** and **Abstract Expressionism** were extremely diverse. Their aims were manifold as well, at times even antithetical to one another. Neither did the avant-garde mission of modernism tend towards any particular ideology or politics. Modernist artists and writers can be found across the ideological spectrum, among communists

Romanticism: A nineteenth-century artistic and literary movement that rejected the supremacy of rationalism and science to emphasise the creative power of the imagination and the emotions. Promoted the status of the 'work of art' and the role of the 'artistic genius'.

Imagism: An early-twentieth-century modernist movement in Anglo-American poetry that promoted an economy of direct, clear and precise language in poetic images over lyrical verse.

Neo-Plasticism: Meaning the 'new plastic', indicates an abstract aesthetic of asymmetrical balance of harmony and tension achieved through the use of vertical and horizontal lines, rectangular forms, and the primary colours and values.

Abstract Expressionism: An approach to visual art that combines emotional intensity with abstract or non-figurative painting techniques. A dominant style in modernist art in post-Second World War America.

and fascists, anarchists and corporate managers, mystics and dialectical materialists.

Yet whatever the orientation of a particular modernist artist or movement, all share a strong impulse towards experimentation, that is, to examine, alter and transform the forms and meaning of art, literature, music, architecture or design. As a result, a high value is placed upon innovation and novelty, to make new art that transcends contemporary life and elevates the viewer, reader or audience above the mundane. In all cases, the materials and creative impulses inspiring such new art arise from the contemporary moment; modernist art emerges from within modernity, rather than on the basis of some established rules of aesthetics. Rooted in the experiences of modern life, modernists produced works of art that express modernity in all of its contradictions, while at the same time striving to establish critical perspectives upon the contemporary condition. 'Dauntingly, then,' writes the literary critic James McFarlane, 'the modernist formula becomes "both/and and/or either/or"' (Bradbury and McFarlane, 1991: 88).

Despite the diversity of aims of modernist artists and movements, when considered from a comparative perspective of a total constellation some general contours of modernism may be discerned. Beyond the general impulses towards experimentation and innovation, the intellectual historian Eugene Lunn has articulated four broad dimensions to the modernist aesthetic: self-reflexivity, simultaneity, uncertainty of meaning, and dehumanisation. Through *self-reflexivity*, modernist art simultaneously draws attention to both the work itself – its media materials, as well as the rules and form of its construction – and to the artist who created it. By doing so, artists self-consciously emphasise the direct relationship between the work of art and its creator. One can instantly recognise, for example, a painting as 'a Picasso' or an Apollinaire '*calligramme*'. In this regard, modernist art and literature provide the material expression of the artist's subjective experience of the world, more than an objective description of external reality. Reciprocally, modernists tended to believe that this process is reproduced within the consumer of the work of art as well. The viewer, reader or audience is encouraged to find meaning through a direct, subjective response to the work of art, rather than by judging whether the piece conforms to some set of external aesthetic standards.

The second dimension of modernist aesthetics concerns *simultaneity* in the construction of the work of art. Rather than being a naturalistic representation, the work of art becomes a kind of montage in which form is achieved through the juxtaposition of images, words, media elements and objects set within the same space. Three-dimensional perspective and linear development in time give way to a sense of saturated space and synchronic time; either multiple things occur at the same time, or an abundance of images or words pass through time rapidly. While the work of art may produce a sense or feeling of unity, in fact the elements have merely been placed together (the way, for example, an overwhelming number of still images are imprinted upon celluloid film, juxtaposed through montage editing, and threaded through a projector to produce the unifying illusion of 'moving pictures'). Dreams are perhaps the best lived-experience of this, and many modernist artists and writers were inspired by Freud's *The Interpretation of Dreams*. 'Stream of consciousness' in literature, montage and collage in visual art, and atonality and multitonality in music are common examples of modernist simultaneity.

The third dimension of modernist aesthetics emphasises the *uncertainty of meaning*. In reaction against nineteenth-century positivism, the optimistic belief that scientific knowledge and social progress would nearly automatically produce a more enlightened humanity, modernists were attuned to the paradoxes, ambiguities and uncertainties of contemporary life. Such a 'revolt against positivism' had already been started by such prominent intellectuals as Darwin, Nietzsche and Freud, and was fuelled by more widespread fears about 'the masses', biological regression and moral decadence at the end of the nineteenth century. Modernists also tended to be 'against nature'. One of the goals of modernism became to 'defamiliarise' the world, to draw attention to the realisation that modern life is not natural, but is historically constructed and continually undergoing transformations. Rather than systematically building up knowledge in methodical fashion, the modernist project became to reassemble the fundamental elements of art, literature and the performing arts in ways that demanded the active participation of viewers, readers and audiences. Through the participation of the general population in works of art, the modernist avant-garde hoped this would cause society to re-examine the contemporary world and to perceive it differently.

The final dimension in modernist aesthetics proposed by Lunn is *dehumanisation*. Humans are no longer the measure of all things; instead, human identity is the composite effect of a tremendous number of external forces upon a fragile human psyche. For modernists, personality is not integrated and human nature is not fixed or natural. Rather, humans experience the world subjectively through a 'psychic field' of sensations, perceptions, images and objects. The depiction of humans in modernist visual art is often expressed through distortions of the human body, or simply by treating disembodied body parts as montage elements in some larger image. In modernism, humans have characteristics, but they no longer possess an organic core. It was precisely this belief in the constructed and composite view of human identity that led modernists to believe that they had a mission as an elite avant-garde. A modernist civilisation of their creation, they held, could transform human nature itself. Under the guidance of the avant-garde, modernist art was not only about aesthetics: it offered a path towards social engineering.

These kinds of themes and issues wind their way through this brief cultural history of modernism. While the broad goal of modernism was to set Western civilisation on new foundations, the history of modernism did not constitute a step-by-step development. As the historical contexts changed over time, the aims and activities of various modernist movements shifted as well. That said, by the end of the twentieth century there is little doubt that modernism had transformed contemporary culture in Europe and the world. The modernist imperative towards continual innovation and techniques of abstraction and montage has become the stock-in-trade of advertising, feature films and commercial multimedia that have permeated global contemporary culture at large. What remains to be considered at the dawn of the twenty-first century is to further assess the continuing significance of modernism's historical legacy.

Further reading

Brooker, Peter, Andreij Gasiorek, Deborah Longworth and Andrew Thacker (eds), *The Oxford Handbook of Modernisms*, Oxford: Oxford University Press, 2011.

Bürger, Peter, *Theory of the Avant-Garde* (trans. Michael Shaw; Foreword Jochen Schulte-Sasse), Minneapolis: University of Minnesota Press, 1984.

Calinescu, Matei, *Five Faces of Modernity: Modernism, Avant-Garde, Decadence, Kitsch, Postmodernism*, Durham: Duke University Press, 1987.

Childs, Peter, *Modernism* (Series 'The New Critical Idiom'), London and New York: Routledge, 2000.

Eysteinsson, Astradur, *The Concept of Modernism*, Ithaca: Cornell University Press, 1990.

Foster, Hal, Rosalind Krauss, Yves-Alain Bois and Benjamin H.D. Buchloh, *Art since 1900: Modernism, Antimodernism, Postmodernism*, New York: Thames & Hudson, 2004.

Frascina, Francis and Jonathan Harris (eds), *Art in Modern Culture: An Anthology of Critical Texts*, London: Phaidon Press, 1992.

Gaiger, Jason (ed.), *Frameworks for Modern Art*, New Haven and London: Yale University Press/The Open University Press, 2003.

Harrison, Charles and Paul Wood (eds), *Art in Theory 1900–2000: An Anthology of Changing Ideas* (new edn), Oxford: Blackwell, 2003.

Hughes, Robert, *The Shock of the New: Art and the Century of Change* (revd edn), London: Thames & Hudson, 2004.

Jervis, John, *Exploring the Modern*, Oxford: Blackwell, 1998.

Lunn, Eugene, *Marxism and Modernism: An Historical Study of Lukács, Brecht, Benjamin, and Adorno*, Berkeley: University of California Press, 1984.

Poggioli, Renato, *The Theory of the Avant-Garde* (trans. Gerald Fitzgerald), New York: Harper and Row, 1968.

Rainey, Lawrence (ed.), *Modernism: An Anthology*, Oxford: Blackwell, 2005.

Ross, Alex, *The Rest is Noise: Listening to the Twentieth Century*, New York: Picador, 2007.

Wood, Paul (ed.) *Varieties of Modernism* (Series: 'Art of the 20th Century'), New Haven and London: Yale University Press/The Open University, 2004.

Part 2

THE HISTORICAL ORIGINS
OF MODERNISM

2

Art and Modernity in the Nineteenth Century

In 1863, the French poet Charles Baudelaire wrote an essay on the relationship between art and modernity entitled 'The Painter of Modern Life' (**Doc. 1, pp. 112–13**). The piece was a series of reflections on the artwork of 'Monsieur C. G.', an abbreviated reference to Constantin Guys, a French illustrator for *The London Illustrated News* and other popular magazines. For Baudelaire, Guys was a discriminating observer of the contemporary landscape, someone who objectively observed the modern world, but as an artist who subjectively infused it with an active and poetic imagination. The subjects of his illustrations were exotic in a commercialised and banal sort of way: scenes from the Crimean War, Oriental harems, military parades, portraits of dandies and courtesans, displays of women's fashion and cosmetics. As a panoramic surveyor of modern life, Baudelaire asserted, Guys displayed a superior sensibility that his fellow artists lacked, not content merely to reproduce reality, but to apprehend and distil from it the transient experience of modernity.

Baudelaire's panegyric to the unrecognised genius of Monsieur C. G. may have been somewhat self-serving. At the time he was snubbed by the French literary establishment, and his first collection of poems, *Les fleurs du mal* (*The Flowers of Evil*, 1857), received judicial censure as an 'offence to public and religious morality and to good morals.' Yet whatever his motivations, modernists like the Symbolists and Surrealists later recognised that Baudelaire was one of the earliest critics to articulate what would constitute an entirely new art within the context of a rapidly modernising Europe. The success of future art, Baudelaire predicted, would no longer be judged by its adherence to aesthetic standards, but by whether it gave expression to and reflected back upon the continually transforming modern world. In Baudelaire's conception, modern art would capture, distil, and transcend the experience of modernity. A truly modern art would be both within its historical moment and timeless.

To connect Baudelaire's ideas about art and modernity to the development of modernism in the early twentieth century, it is useful to survey various nineteenth century artistic movements, with their attendant aesthetic and critical impulses, upon the historical terrain of rapidly modernising Europe. Above all, it is imperative to recapture a sense of the multiple and fundamental ways in which economic, social, political and cultural life in Western Europe was completely transformed during the 'long nineteenth century' from the French Revolution of 1789 to the eve of the First World War in 1914. While it may be commonplace today for people to accept that the world in which one's grandparents die is completely different from the one into which they were born, Europeans experienced this for the first time in the nineteenth century.

A few demographic markers make this historical transformation of Europe over the nineteenth century dramatically clear. Over the course of the century, the population of Europe more than doubled to reach 400 million (which is particularly remarkable when considering that tens of millions also migrated to the Americas). Not only were there more Europeans, but more of them were living in cities. At the beginning of the nineteenth century, nine out of ten Europeans still lived on the land, but by the century's end one of three lived in cities. Capital cities became metropolises as well. In 1800, London was the only capital with a population over one million, but by the dawn of the twentieth century thirteen European cities boasted populations over a million (six of them in Great Britain alone), and nearly one hundred cities across Europe had populations over 200,000. The European metropolises also became the centres of vast international empires. By the eve of the First World War, 85 per cent of the world's geography was under European control, directly as imperial colonies (in Africa, south and east Asia, Indonesia and Oceania), as commonwealths (Australia and Canada), or under economic neo-colonialism (Latin America).

The effects of the demographic doubling of Europe's population, the trend towards urbanisation and the pursuit of imperial empires, were fuelled by the combination of the Industrial Revolution and the rise of a mass-consumer economy. Among European nations, only Great Britain had entered the nineteenth century with rapid industrialisation already under way in the areas of textiles, coal mining and iron production. By the end of the century, all of north-western Europe was industrialising, with the addition of steel, petroleum, chemical and pharmaceutical enterprises. Innovations in mass transportation, such as transoceanic steamships and continental railways, reduced international travel to a matter of days and traversing distances within many European countries to a matter of hours. On the local level, the development of commuter rail, tramways and subways reduced daily commutes from suburban neighbourhoods to the city or factory to minutes. The telegraph and telephone made regional, national and even international communication instantaneous. Urban planning and renovations made cities more desirable places to live. By widening boulevards for pedestrian traffic, illuminating city streets with gaslight (later by electricity), and developing underground systems of gas lines, fresh water supply and sewage removal, once dangerous city neighbourhoods were transformed into fashionable ones. Such innovations not only benefited the wealthy, but were also incorporated into the daily lives of ordinary working people.

The grandeur of industrial and commercial progress was put on display in international world's fairs, beginning with Crystal Palace in London in 1851. At the level of everyday life, the dream world of mass-produced commercial goods became a common reality for urban dwellers. Abundant arrays of consumer goods adorned the window displays of store boutiques, the passageways of shopping arcades and the aisles of department stores, which the novelist Émile Zola called the 'Ladies' Paradise'. In the final decades of the nineteenth century, the mass-circulation newspaper turned modern life into an everyday spectacle. Newspapers and magazines, sold by newspaper hawkers or from ubiquitous kiosks along the city boulevards, habituated a highly literate population (over 90 per cent in industrialised north-western Europe) to a taste for daily news and serialised fiction. With the dramatic rise of cheap consumer goods and print mass culture, the experience of modernity affected the quotidian imaginations of Belle Époque Europeans.

In the nineteenth century, Paris was the unsurpassed 'capital of modernity'. The most populated capital on the European continent at the beginning of the nineteenth century, Paris was also a dreadful city of poverty, crime and revolution. In terms of human geography, the tightly packed city of medieval origins was a bewildering configuration of dark streets, labyrinthine alleyways and dead ends, with open sewage and polluted water sources that twice produced cholera outbreaks in the poorer quarters of the city during the early decades of the nineteenth century. Socially, the sophisticates of opera, theatre and café society lived in close proximity with, and in fear of, the vices of the 'dangerous classes' of prostitutes, blackmailers and petty criminals, a terrain of social anxiety depicted in the novels of Honoré de Balzac and in the caricatures of Honoré Daumier. Politically, the frustrated bourgeoisie and downtrodden labouring classes challenged the authority of the Old Regime in periodic revolutionary uprisings, heroically portrayed on the barricades in Eugène Delacroix's painting *Liberty Leading the People* (1830) and in Victor Hugo's novel *Les Misérables* (1862). During the first half of the nineteenth century, nascent modernity in Paris was an admixture of discontent and uncertain future promise. As melodramatically and romantically depicted by Eugène Sue in *Les Mystères de Paris*, such miseries could be transformed into moral redemption. Alternatively, as the former police chief of the Sûreté Eugène-François Vidocq wrote in his *Memoirs*, Paris was a sinister topography of crime.

After mid-century, however, the urban and social landscape was transformed by the 'Haussmannisation' of Paris. Beginning in the 1850s, prefect Baron Georges-Eugène Haussmann undertook a massive project for the renovation of Paris. Poorer and dilapidated neighbourhoods were razed to construct new *grands boulevards* and apartment blocks that traversed and crisscrossed the city. These boulevards opened up new, panoramic perspectives on the city landscape, gloriously captured in the Impressionist paintings of Camille Pissarro, or on a more mundane level circulated as commercial mass culture through photographic images printed in magazines and on postcards. Trees were planted along the expanded boulevards, spacious parks opened up the city centre, and extensive wooded parks were established on the periphery. The construction of new apartment blocks, roads and underground water, sewage and gas lines provided an employment boom for the city's labouring population. The advent of gas street lighting and urban transportation systems of buses, trolleys, and finally subway, also meant that Paris became a round-the-clock entertainment centre. The previously antagonistic social classes of aristocracy, bourgeoisie, small shopkeepers and labourers now mingled more openly, not only on the boulevards and in the parks, but also in the music hall and cabaret, the shopping arcade and the department store. Although real social and political conflicts persisted (most dramatically expressed in the Paris Commune of 1870), the commercial spectacle of life had transformed Paris into the internationally renowned 'City of Lights', celebrated most spectacularly in the *Exposition Universelle* of 1889 with its emblematic symbol of nineteenth-century modernity, the Eiffel Tower.

It is little wonder, then, that new forms of artistic expression arose in nineteenth-century Paris. One of the earliest and most persistent figures to emerge from the milieu of Parisian modernity was the 'bohemian', or the quintessential starving artist. For every successful writer, artist or composer in Paris, there were dozens of aspiring bohemians who lived in poverty on the social margins of bourgeois society. Turning their misfortunes into virtues by claiming that theirs was the truer and nobler pursuit of art, these bohemians were eccentric in manners and costume, longhaired in appearance and rebellious in attitude. Contemptuous of bourgeois values, bohemians garnered an enduring reputation perhaps more for their flamboyant lifestyles than for their artistic accomplishments. The image of the Paris bohemian had a long afterlife, as romantically and nostalgically portrayed in Henry Murger's novel *Scenes from Bohemian Life* (1851) and Giacomo Puccini's opera *La Bohème* (1897). Yet bohemianism was more than just an anti-establishment youth movement. It also contributed to some of the earliest nineteenth-century re-evaluations of the meaning of art in relation to modern society. The early bohemians championed Victor Hugo, the Romantic literary giant who defined the modern genius in art as a fusion of the grotesque and the sublime. In the popularity of new forms of mass culture, such as theatrical melodrama and the *roman feuilleton* (serialised novels published in newspaper or magazine instalments), Hugo found modern corollaries to the Italian *commedia dell'arte* and the plays of Shakespeare.

It was the writer and critic Théopile Gautier, however, who perhaps best envisioned what would constitute a modern art oriented towards the future. Gautier reworked an idea current in his age, **l'art pour l'art** or 'art for art's sake', into the notion of 'the uselessness of literature'. By this Gautier did not mean that art and literature had no purpose, but rather that their truest meaning would not be found in formal aesthetics, elite or popular taste, or the promotion of moral values. Instead, he championed the idea that modern art should achieve the complete liberation of the imagination. Freed from inherited traditions of tragedy, comedy or other classical genres, art would assume new and completely modern forms of expression. Gautier saw theatrical melodrama in the early nineteenth century as exemplary in this regard in the way that it was both superficial and universal. Its formulaic staging of passions, conflicts and fates was entirely artificial; one would never mistake melodrama for 'real life' or consider it 'serious art'. At the same time, melodrama achieved a universal appeal; it reached a socially inclusive audience that ranged from high society to the general population, thereby constituting a truly 'universal' art form that could be enjoyed both by connoisseurs and the unsophisticated.

In addition to the bohemian, another important figure of nineteenth-century modernity was the *flâneur*. The Parisian city idler, the *flâneur* made an avocation of strolling city streets, arcades and department stores. Perusing window display cases, the *flâneur* was not so much interested in making purchases as in visually seeking out those objects or images that would transport him into some reverie of the imagination. Beyond window displays, the *flâneur* took in the spectacle of Paris itself – the hubbub of the boulevard, the glamour of women's and men's fashions, the entertainments of the music hall and cabaret, and their visual mass-culture corollaries in dioramas, wax museums, illustrated magazines and newspapers. Like Baudelaire's Monsieur C. G., the *flâneur* was an observer of modern life. At the same time, he was also a part of the spectacle, either as a 'man of the crowd' who blends in or as a dandy who draws attention to himself. The *flâneur* represents an oscillation in the experience of modernity between objects and the imagination, between identity and cultural absorption. But as Baudelaire critically observed, only the 'painter of modern life' conveyed such an experience of *flânerie* through art.

l'art pour l'art: French phrase meaning 'art for art's sake'. Refers to the notion that art has intrinsic value and meaning in itself, independent of any didactic, moral or utilitarian function.

Yet throughout most of the nineteenth century, the artistic and literary elite largely defined itself against modernisation and modernity. The literary critic Charles Augustin Sainte-Beuve was dismissive of the whole of commercial culture as 'industrial literature', beneath the status of art. Realist novelist Gustave Flaubert concurred, although his ideas about the relationship of literature to the modern world were more nuanced. Having been raised in a bourgeois home, Flaubert came to view the world as vulgar, but he considered it the duty of the Realist artist or writer to accurately depict it in detail, as he had done in *Madame Bovary* (1857) and *L'Éducation sentimentale* (*Sentimental Education*, 1869). The purpose in doing so, however, was not to represent the modern world, but to move from a basis in material reality to a higher contemplation of meaning. For Flaubert, the details of the literary text itself are what bind the author, and subsequently the reader, to the work of art: 'For me, the mental image of things is as true as their objective reality, and what has been supplied by reality very soon ceases, for me, to be distinguishable from the embellishments and modifications I have given it' (Flaubert, 1982: 96). Flaubert's artist is not a Romantic, hoping to restore the world to some kind of material and spiritual wholeness, but a dispassionate creator who produces works of art, and then contemplates what he has created in order to discover meaning in it. The Realist artist or writer is inescapably part of the modern world, but his literary prowess provides him with the ability to establish a perspective above the crowd.

By extension, as intellectual historian Mary Gluck has argued, such literary and artistic figures as Balzac, Daumier, and Baudelaire can be thought of as 'avant-garde *flâneurs*' in the sense that they surveyed the social landscape of Paris, deciphered it, and then transformed it into artistic visions. Pushing beyond Flaubert's Realism, the goal was not simply a higher contemplation of reality as reworked by the artist or writer, but to use art and literature to give new form to the experience of the contemporary world. The work of art thereby gains a kind of autonomy from within, creating a *sui generis* aesthetic from within modernity, rather than by comparing art to formal conventions or to what it is supposed to represent. Such modern art is not a reflection of external reality. Rather, it becomes the outward expression of the artist's or writer's subjective experience of modernity.

One of the early and notable examples of this reworking of modern reality in the visual arts was the Impressionist movement in painting. Beginning around the mid-nineteenth century, painters such as Édouard Manet began to challenge the official art establishment of the Académie des Beaux-Arts. After struggling for recognition as a painter by successfully gaining entry into the Salon of 1861, Manet went on to scandalise art critics and the public by submitting to subsequent exhibitions such works as *Déjeuner sur l'herbe* (1863), of a nude woman picnicking in the woods with two fully dressed men, and *Olympia* (1863), of a naked courtesan being delivered flowers from an anonymous admirer by a black handmaid. For his part, Manet claimed that he was simply using modern settings and individuals to update perennial themes in art, along the lines of Titian's reclining nudes. But what made the strongest impression on his contemporaries was his boldness in the use of modern themes and settings as the subject matter of his paintings, not only portraits of intimate friends and acquaintances, but modern scenes such as the city boulevards, new parks, railway stations and the cafés of Haussmann's Paris.

In 1874, dissident Parisian artists launched their own exhibition, the *Salon des refusés*, which included a painting by Claude Monet entitled *Impression, soleil levant* (*Impression, Sunrise*). The salon was ridiculed in the satirical magazine *Charivari* as the 'Exposition of the Impressionists'. The label Impressionism stuck, and over the next several years a number of painters working in various styles, such as Edgar Degas, Berthe Morisot, Pierre-August Renoir, Camille Pissarro and Paul Cézanne, came to be associated with the term. Although the styles of particular artists varied enormously, broadly these Impressionists shared a general preference for the use of bold colours (enhanced by the chemical innovation of artificial pigments) and the framing of images with careful attention to contrasts of light and shadow (aesthetic concerns established by the new visual technology of photography). The Impressionist style swept across the diverse experiences of the contemporary world as well, from the landscape exteriors of bustling Paris boulevards, apartment building exteriors, monumental cathedral porches, and tranquil water lily ponds painted by Pissarro, Manet and Monet, to the intimate interior spaces of the ballet, cabarets, cafes, family and private life by Degas, Morisot and Renoir. By the following decade, the stress upon the qualities of paint and brushstroke on the canvas, over and above the subject matter of the painting, emerged as the primary aesthetic of Impressionist art. This emphasis on the effects of media and technique over representational content was even more pronounced in the works of Post-Impressionist painters such as Georges Seurat, Pierre Bonnard, Paul Gauguin and Vincent Van Gogh.

Among the earliest champions of Impressionist art were the Symbolist poets, led by Stéphane Mallarmé. Symbolism emerged at the end of the nineteenth century in the train of the Romantic, Parnassian and Naturalist movements in French literature. As the name suggests, the emphasis in Symbolist poetry was not upon the denotative or connotative meaning of words, but upon what the design and delivery of the words in a poem evoked, traits that were particularly pronounced in the experimental poetry of Arthur Rimbaud. This emphasis upon evocation through form was characteristic of other Symbolist arts as well. As the French Symbolist painter Gustave Moreau explained, in terms of visual art:

> . . . a painting should never be explained, that the visual image is integral, complete in itself, and that any attempt to explicate its meaning can only lessen its artistic appeal, diffuse its emotive impact and debase its internal harmony.
>
> (Genova, 2002: 182)

Whatever the artistic mode, Symbolists believed that ideas were expressed directly through literary, artistic and musical forms themselves. Meaning did not come from what the work of art depicted or represented, but was synonymous with its mode of expression and active interpretation.

An elite literary movement, Symbolism strove to create a pure art based upon the complete liberation of the imagination. As defined by Remy de Gourmont in 1896, Symbolism expressed 'individualism in literature, freedom in art, rejection of set formulae, a tendency towards the new, the strange, and even the bizarre' (Genova, 2002: 13). In turn, it became the task of the reader, viewer or audience to synthesise the various elements of a poem, painting or musical performance into comprehension according to one's subjective powers of perception. The power of the individual imagination determined the emotional impact and depth of understanding in Symbolist art. It was an aesthetic that valued the exceptional above the rule, discovered within oneself rather than in the world. This 'voyage to the interior' in Symbolism was especially evident in the poetry of Paul Verlaine, and was pushed even further by Decadent writers such as J.-K. Huysmans, Villiers de l'Isle-Adam, Jean Moréas, Rachilde, and Catulle Mendès.

The Symbolist movement thrived in *cenacles*, or small coteries of writers, artists and musicians, one of the earliest being the Hydropathe group begun by Émile Goudeau. These Symbolist groups also published their own avant-garde literary journals, such as *Le Mercure de France*, *La Plume* and *La Revue Blanche*, which featured essays on literary, art and music criticism, in addition to poetry. Several things are noteworthy about these Symbolist groups and their journals. First was their impulse to become critics, to assume a self-proclaimed role as the purveyors of formal aesthetics and artistic taste. Not only were they the creators of modern art, but they also became the avant-garde authorities on how to interpret it. Further, while the Symbolists shared an elite disdain for mass commercial culture, they also sought to bridge the distance between high and popular culture, particularly in their celebration of decorative arts, such as the **Art Nouveau** style in architecture, furniture, and illustrated magazines and advertising posters.

In addition, both Impressionists and Symbolists were drawn to 'oriental' and 'primitive' motifs in art collected from colonised populations in Asia, Africa, the Americas and Oceania. One of the most enduring reformulations of the primitive in modern European art has been the pursuit of the 'exotic

Art Nouveau: French for 'new art', a late-nineteenth-century style of commercial and decorative art and architecture that featured curved lines and flowing movement inspired by natural forms.

other' in art and literature. This was certainly true of Orientalist art and literature by nineteenth-century Europeans set in the Near East and North Africa. One of the recurring motifs in Orientalist painting was the odalisque, the portrayal of fair-skinned female nudes reclining within harem interiors. The odalisque was a particularly popular figure among such French painters as Jean-Auguste-Dominque Ingres, Eugène Delacroix and Pierre-Auguste Renoir in the nineteenth century and Henri Matisse in the early twentieth century. A measure of anxiety and danger supplemented the erotic oriental female nude through the popularisation of the figures of Salomé and Judith in Symbolist and Decadent art, evident in the works of Gustave Moreau, Aubrey Beardsley and Oscar Wilde, and in the paintings of Gustave Klimt. Orientalism was a major theme in the nineteenth-century literature as well, in exotic historical novels such as Flaubert's *Salammbô* (1862), set in the North African empire of Carthage during the third century, and in the popular novels of Pierre Loti such as *Rarahu* (*Loti's Marriage*, 1880) and *Phantom of the Orient* (1890), supposedly based on his own travels in the South Pacific.

As global colonisation by Europeans during the age of imperialism at the end of the nineteenth century was vigorously and extensively renewed, 'primitive' artefacts forcibly extracted from Africa, the Americas and Oceania poured into Europe and the United States. Such objects were indiscriminately collected, ranging from hunting weapons and canoe paddles to dress garments and decorative accessories, with statuette fetishes and ceremonial masks being particularly coveted. Belle Époque Europeans also developed a fashion craze for furniture, collectibles and prints from Japan, China and Southeast Asia. *Le japonisme*, as it was known in France, directly influenced such Impressionist painters as Édouard Manet, Claude Monet, Vincent van Gogh and Henri de Toulouse-Lautrec, particularly the wood-block prints of Katsushika Hokusai and Ando Hiroshige. On a broader cultural scale, themes of adventure and romance in the orient and colonies received wide circulation through exhibitions at world fairs and colonial expositions, the creation of ethnographic museums, and in such sources of mass culture as dioramas, postcards, popular novels, magazines and illustrated weekly supplements to newspapers. Most Orientalist artists and writers, as well as the European collectors of primitive artefacts, had little contact with non-Western cultures, however. Instead they infused indigenous peoples and cultures with exotic and erotic illusions about a return to natural and instinctive ways of living that existed 'before civilisation', fantasies that were especially projected upon racial and ethnic groups in Africa, the Americas and Oceania.

In the early twentieth century, however, the presumed separation between modern Europeans and the non-Western world of primitive and oriental others began to blur. The sociologist Émile Durkheim and his anthropologist pupil Marcel Mauss saw the distinction between primitive

japonisme: Refers to the incorporation of styles and motifs from Japanese wood-block prints, lacquers and porcelains into late-nineteenth-century French art.

and modern not in terms of differences in human populations, but as cultural differences brought about by the transition from traditional to modern societies. In the *Mental Functions in Primitive Societies* (1910), the ethnographer Lucien Lévy-Bruhl asserted that the difference between primitive and modern mentalities lay in the difference between interpreting the world in terms of magical forces or through scientific rationality. In Lévy-Bruhl's view, even European peasants possessed such a primitive mentality during the medieval age. But magical ways of thinking remained an active psychological function among modern individuals, he asserted, when they encountered experiences that lay outside scientific explanation. In other words, the exotic other was not something modern Europeans discovered in non-Western peoples, but was an expression of their own psychological interior. The exotic was not an independent quality, but something derived from putting the modern and the primitive together.

One of the first modernist artists to grapple with this dynamic was the French Expressionist painter Paul Gauguin, who spent the final quarter of his life living and working in French Polynesia. A native Parisian, Gauguin sought to escape European civilisation by 'going away' to more primitive and exotic settings. For Gauguin, natural and savage locales included rural Brittany in north-western France, as well as the South Pacific colonies. Like most European artists and writers, for most of his life Gauguin's knowledge of the colonies was limited to the artefacts and fetishes displayed in ethnographic collections, visiting world fairs and reading popular fiction such as Loti's novels. In 1891, he set sail for Tahiti, which had become a French colony a decade earlier. Only returning to France briefly once in 1893, Gauguin lived the rest of his life in the islands of French Polynesia until his death in 1903, and thus his work expresses a more prolonged exposure to and a deeper understanding of his native subjects than many other nineteenth-century exotic artists and writers.

By most accounts, Gauguin was quickly disillusioned by what he saw as the degradation of Polynesian life and culture under French colonialism. Rather than simply viewing Polynesia as some kind of contemporary corollary of the Garden of Eden, Gauguin chose instead to rework his experiences with the Tahitians through his Expressionist art. While some of his paintings might be appreciated for their 'natural simplicity', others, such as *Ia Orana Maria* (*We Hail Thee Mary*, 1891) of a Tahitian Madonna and Child with nimbuses, *Manao tupapau* (*Spirit of the Dead Watching*, 1892) of a sleeping, naked Tahitian woman being watched over by a masked and hooded figure, or *Market Day* (1892) of contemporary Tahitian women in colourful embroidered dresses sitting on a park bench, are difficult to divide up into exclusive categories of modern or primitive, Western or non-Western. Instead, his Tahiti paintings are a hybrid that combines the modern and the primitive, a tendency that had already been present in Gauguin's earlier Breton paintings, particularly *The Yellow Christ* (1889). While something of the exotic clearly remains in his Polynesian works, Gauguin realised that the mixture of the primitive and the modern yields uncertain and ambivalent meanings, a subject he further explored in his illustrated autobiography, *Noa Noa* (1901).

The French writer Victor Segalen arrived in the Polynesian Marquesas Islands a few months after the death of Gauguin. A friend of the Decadent writer Joris Huysmans, Segalen acutely understood the experience of the exotic as the uncertain co-mingling of the primitive and the modern. In his uncompleted 'Essay on Exoticism' (1908), Segalen wrote that contact with indigenous colonial populations was more likely to produce intense psychological anxiety than confidence in Europeans. Segalen called Europeans who lived among colonial populations '*exots*'. He referred to colonial administrators and tourists as false *exots* in that they imposed primitive character types upon colonials in an attempt to maintain a sense of European distinction from and superiority over indigenous populations. By contrast the true *exot* tried to embrace native perspectives, Segalen emphasised, but found that by doing so the fusion of identities tended to heighten, rather than diminish, the European's sense of feeling alien within the colonial setting. Instead of developing assurance about inhabiting the colonies, the *exot* experienced increased anxieties and uncertainties because of this new hybrid identity, an insight Segalen later developed in his novels *Stèles* (1915), *Le Fils du Ciel* (*The Son of Heaven*, 1917), and *René Leys* (1922). In this way, the subjective experience of fusing the European modern and the colonial 'primitive' foreshadowed a later modernist impulse to emphasise uncertainties of meaning and destabilise identity.

Within Europe, some of the Symbolists were committed to the high-culture fusion of literary, visual and musical arts into the 'Great Work'. This pursuit was perhaps most clearly expressed through an explosion of essays and journals devoted to Wagnerian studies. Devoted to the critical exploration of the theories of German composer Richard Wagner, particularly his idea of the *Gesamtkunstwerk* or the unification of all the arts in modern opera, Wagnerian journals were established across Europe. Rather than pursue such a grand synthesis of the arts, Impressionist composer Claude Debussy experimented with the crossing of artistic forms as a mode of musical composition. Such hybrid musical works by Debussy include the ballet *Prélude à 'L'Après-midi d'un faune'* (1894) based on a poem by Mallarmé, the opera *Pelléas et Mélisande* (1893–1902) adapted from a theatrical work by the Belgian playwright Maurice Maeterlinck, and three 'symphonic sketches,' *La Mer* (1903–1905), inspired by the Japanese print illustration *The Wave* by Hokusai. International musical styles as diverse as Javanese music and American ragtime jazz, which Debussy heard at world fairs, were incorporated into his compositions as well.

Such developments highlight the cosmopolitan nature of emergent modernism, again particularly notable among the Symbolists. Some leading figures travelled internationally, such as Mallarmé, who had spent years as a young man in London where he made the acquaintance of several English writers and poets. Upon his return to Paris, Mallarmé became a cultural correspondent for the London *Athenaeum*. Parisian Symbolists welcomed non-French writers into the fold as well, most notably the Irish writer Oscar Wilde and the Norwegian playwright Henrik Ibsen. Symbolism became an important avant-garde influence outside France as well, in central Europe, Russia and Scandinavia. Rejecting the conception of national literature that had become the official pedagogy of the newly emerging European nation states in the late-nineteenth century, the Symbolist conception of modern art and literature strove for universal status across international lines.

This nascent modernism of the Belle Époque was a quintessentially 'metropolitan art' in its impulses and contradictions, first taking root in the capital cities of Europe. While Paris was the unparalleled capital of modernity in the nineteenth century, the glory of Vienna rivalled it by the dawn of the twentieth century. The modernisation of Vienna occurred around the *Ringstrasse*, a former military parade field converted into a marvellous circular boulevard at the city centre. New government and municipal buildings, the Opera House and Art History Museum, rows of multi-storeyed apartment buildings and corporate businesses along the *Ringstrasse* attested to both Vienna's imperial and modern status. It was also home to one of Europe's most innovative artists, Gustav Klimt, a Symbolist painter who worked in the Art Nouveau style (known in Austria as the Secession). Drawing upon ancient Egyptian, Greek and Hebrew motifs, particularly the figures of Athena and Judith, Klimt painted undulant nudes in bold and patchwork colours, and he employed Byzantine techniques of gold illumination to frame, decorate or conceal those images. Yet Klimt employed these ancient motifs not to invoke some Golden Age of past humanity, but to depict a particularly modern conflict between material passions and spiritual aspirations. Klimt's artistic expression of such ambivalent tensions had corollaries in the ideas of his philosophical contemporaries Arthur Schopenauer and Friedrich Nietzsche, as well as in Freud's psychology of the unconscious.

Other European capitals provided dynamic cultural terrains for the cultivation of modernism as well. In the pre-war years of the early twentieth century, London was the gathering spot for modern English writers, whether British, Irish or American, among them Henry James, Oscar Wilde, W. B. Yeats, Joseph Conrad, George Bernard Shaw, E. M. Forster, James Joyce, Ezra Pound, H. D. (Hilda Doolittle), T. S. Eliot, and D. H. Lawrence. Berlin was the third largest capital in Europe, behind London and Paris, and was rapidly gaining continental renown for its support of modern theatre, promoting the works of the Scandinavian dramatists Henrik Ibsen and Arthur Strindberg. In Saint Petersburg, the modern metropolis of the economically underdeveloped Russian empire, literary circles formed around the Symbolist poets Andrei Biely (Bugayev) and Alexandr Blok, and the Acmeist poets Osip Mandelstam and Anna Akhmatova.

That such arts flourished in European metropolises that were imperial centres of culture and power was not particularly new; Western civilisation since antiquity had arisen from urban-based empires. Further, the vast majority of the art being produced in these rapidly modernising metropolises was not perceived as avant-garde. The cultural elite continued to uphold salon art, while the general population consumed commercial entertainments as mass culture. What would be required to achieve modernism, as Baudelaire had presciently articulated in the mid-nineteenth century, was the emergence of a new kind of art that, from within the maelstrom of change, could provide a new foundation to modern life. Modernist art would have to be simultaneously ephemeral and eternal. To realise that paradox required not only grappling with material and cultural changes wrought by the modernisation of Europe, but also by making an intellectual shift, a 'perceptual revolution'.

Further reading

Berman, Marshall, *All That Is Solid Melts Into Air: The Experience of Modernity*, New York: Penguin, 1988.

Clark, T. J., *The Painting of Modern Life: Paris in the Art of Manet and his Followers*, Princeton: Princeton University Press, 1984.

Frascina, Francis (et al.), *Modernity and Modernism: French Painting in the Nineteenth Century*, New Haven: Yale University Press, 1993.

Genova, Pamela A., *Symbolist Journals: A Culture of Correspondence*, Aldershot, Hampshire: Ashgate Publishing, 2002.

Gluck, Mary, *Popular Bohemia: Modernism and Urban Culture in Nineteenth-Century Paris*, Cambridge, MA: Harvard University Press, 2005.

Graña, César, *Bohemian versus Bourgeois: French Society and the French Man of Letters in the Nineteenth Century*, New York: Basic Books, 1964.

Harvey, David, *Paris, Capital of Modernity*, New York: Routledge, 2006.

Schorske, Carl E., *Fin-de-Siècle Vienna: Politics and Culture*, New York: Vintage Books, 1981.

Schwartz, Vanessa, *Spectacular Realities: Early Mass Culture in Fin-de-Siècle France*, Berkeley: University of California Press, 1998.

Siegel, Jerrold, *Bohemian Paris: Culture, Politics, and the Boundaries of Bourgeois Life*, New York: Penguin, 1986.

3

The Perceptual Revolution

On 18 May 1924, the modernist novelist Virginia Woolf delivered a paper at the Cambridge Heretics Society entitled 'Mr. Bennet and Mrs. Brown' (**Doc. 2, pp. 113–15**). Co-founded by the writer and editor Charles Kay Ogden and the philosopher John McTaggart Ellis in 1909, the society sponsored public lectures to promote new trends in modern philosophy, science, literature and the arts. Early on in the talk, Woolf proposed 'that in or about December, 1910, human character changed.' Her choice of 1910 as a watershed decade was not arbitrary. The current experience of modernity, she emphasised, was not simply the accumulation of effects inherited from the nineteenth century. Rather, in the opening decade of the twentieth century all aspects of material and intellectual life had been radically altered. What this reconfiguration portended, no one really knew. But Woolf saw it as the task of modern authors to capture, express and reveal the inner workings of this new condition, which included immersing oneself in an uncertain era of subjective perceptions and multiple perspectives.

The historical condition that Woolf sought to express through literature is what the intellectual historian Donald M. Lowe has called the 'perceptual revolution', a fundamental shift from linearity to multi-perspectivity that occurred around the first decade of the twentieth century. Widespread changes in knowledge across the fields of physics, mathematics, philosophy, psychology and linguistics, as well as the early rise of modernism in literature and the arts, expressed a shift in the collective mentality of how Europeans perceived and experienced time, space and the body. The intellectual historian Stephen Kern has pursued a similar line of thought by characterising modernism as the 'culture of time and space'. In addition to the new intellectual trends, innovations in new communications and transportation technologies at the turn of the century were also creating new experiences of multiplicities of time and space. As a result of these changes, the linear and progressive modernity bequeathed by the nineteenth century exploded into simultaneities of time and space in the early decades of the twentieth century.

To understand the radical nature of the break in this reorientation of knowledge through the perceptual revolution, it is useful first to briefly recall the emergence of progressive and evolutionary systems of thought in the nineteenth century. Well into the eighteenth century, most European philosophers conceived of progress in rather static terms, as the accumulation of knowledge across all fields, most notably expressed in Diderot's multivolume *Encyclopédie* (1751–77). In the early nineteenth century, this Enlightenment concept of progress as the synthesis of all knowledge was called 'positivism' or scientism, as articulated by the French philosopher Auguste Comte. In Comte's system, knowledge was progressively staged in a hierarchy of understanding from the religious, to the metaphysical and finally to the scientific, that is, as knowledge that can be empirically verified. As an intellectual endeavour, the endgame of positivism was the compilation of all knowledge as empirically verifiable in both the natural and the human (or social) sciences. The notion that economic liberalism, social utility, individual liberty and education had universally positive benefits for society became increasingly accepted by those with positivist sentiments over the course of the century.

As the transformative effects of modernisation became increasingly apparent over the nineteenth century, some intellectuals adopted the perspective that knowledge was not merely accumulating, but was also actually changing due to realignments in the basic structures of the economy, politics and society. One of the first philosophers to come to grips with this realisation was Georg Wilhlem Friedrich Hegel in the early nineteenth century. With the political restructuring of traditional kingdoms and smaller principalities into larger nation-states, which subsumed ethnically and linguistically diverse populations into 'national' identities and languages, and through the further European colonisation of the globe, which forced diverse civilisations to submit to the home country's political rule and economic policies, it became self-evident that no single existing philosophical system encompassed the totality of what was actually occurring in the world at present. So, the Idealist philosopher Hegel postulated an Absolute Mind in a continual process of 'becoming' was the guiding force of history. For Hegel, knowledge was not merely cumulative, but was continually evolving on a hierarchy that extended from the local and particular to the universal, with the dialectical formulation of new and higher truths continually superseding the previous ones.

It was Karl Marx, though, who brought Hegel's system down to earth and directly applied it at mid-century to the material conditions of modernising Europe. For Marx, the socio-economic transformations resulting from industrial capitalism were transforming political systems, social relations, material and intellectual culture, and ideology as well. As famously expressed in *The Communist Manifesto*, 'All fixed, fast-frozen relationships, with their train of venerable ideas and opinions, are swept away, all new-formed ones become obsolete before they can ossify. All that is solid melts into air . . .' The material conditions of a rapidly changing reality in Europe were transforming human experiences and knowledge. From within the conditions of modernisation, actual social conflicts and political struggles destroyed old laws and worldviews, rendering the past culture obsolete as it created a new and different modern reality. While Marx agreed with Hegel that new stages of history superseded previous ones, he had less confidence in the ability of philosophy to predict the future outcomes. The resolution of actual conflicts in the changing realities of material, social, political, cultural and intellectual life – with transformations, not mere accumulations, of knowledge and ways of knowing – would configure the 'next stage' of human history, whatever that might be.

The notion that the future emerged from changes in material reality was reinforced with the introduction of the notion of biological evolution, which yielded social and political consequences as well. In the mid-nineteenth century, Charles Darwin synthesised what was known about the taxonomy and diversity of existing life forms with the discovery of geological time and the fossil record, and brought them together in the general theory of biological evolution. Arising during the age of Victorianism, it is unsurprising that the key mechanism Darwin invoked in the never-ending 'struggle for existence' – cutthroat competition among individuals within and between species for scarce food resources in order to increase the chances for successful reproduction – was a notion lifted directly from classical political economy, laden with class prejudices. It is equally unremarkable that, in the age of European Imperialism, 'scientific racism' favoured 'superior' Europeans over 'savage' indigenous peoples and the 'arrested development' of Asian civilisations.

But the critical implications of Darwinism as an intellectual system, derived from empirically verifiable scientific inquiry, ran deeper than social prejudices. The intellectual optimism of scientific positivism, inherited from the age of Enlightenment, was based upon the belief that humans were responsible for discovering, accumulating and applying knowledge towards the universal and progressive improvement of the human condition. Darwinism suggested that the fate of species, individually and collectively, was the product of blind material forces, not that of the systematic accumulation and application of scientific knowledge. History was no longer a linear and progressive inevitability, but a multifaceted evolutionary process of random variation branching into diversification, with the multiplication of species requiring the vast extinction of most life forms. Evolutionary 'progress', now

defined as the survival of the 'most well fitted', was due to a random inheritance encountering contingent exigencies which, as the geological record demonstrated for biological evolution, could be radically reconfigured according to
the ecology of the present. Progress defined as the diachronic achievement of
rational designs and empirically verifiable knowledge, keys to positivism,
had been swept aside by an alternative scientific viewpoint that an uncertain
future emerges from the success or failure of individuals, whose inheritance
stems from what may now be an irrelevant past, confronting the synchronic
configuration of the present. Within a continually changing modernity, historical progress was in no way guaranteed.

By the end of the nineteenth century, the presumption of cumulative and
linear historical progress was being challenged from numerous quarters. The
philosophers Arthur Schopenhauer and Friedrich Nietzsche led this 'revolt
against positivism' by casting modern Western civilisation in terms of
nihilism, that is, a state of cultural exhaustion and enervated human vitality.
While individual 'supermen' (*Übermenschen*) with strong wills to power
might achieve greatness, rationality and science had extinguished heroic
civilisation. More widespread than the threat of cultural nihilism was the fear
of social 'degeneration'. Darwinian evolution accounted not only for the
development of species, but also for their regression. As a social corollary,
fears of degeneration led to the proliferation of legal and medical discourses
about the presumed negative effects that criminals, the indigent, alcoholics,
'hysterical' women, and other 'undesirable' groups exerted upon society. In
the debates over degeneration, the Symbolist and Decadent poets and artists
were exceptional in their embracing of the supposed degraded human condition as an invitation to turn to the psychological interior to find meaning.

Beyond these irrational fears, concerns that modernisation was a source
of social and individual discontent were gaining credence from the newly
emerging social sciences. The foundational French sociologist Émile
Durkheim attributed the cause of rising suicide rates over the course of the
nineteenth century not to degeneration or biological causes, but to *anomie* or
the 'social anxiety' produced in the transition from traditional and simple
societies to modern and complex ones. The German economic historian Max
Weber argued that the rationalisation of social life effected by the efficiency
of the capitalist marketplace and the bureaucratic organisation of corporations and governments constituted an 'iron cage of reality'. In order to function efficiently within modern society, Weber emphasised the imperative to
train individuals for technical and professional careers, which replaced the
traditional notion of realising a personal vocation. The German sociologist
Georg Simmel concluded that life in the modern metropolis increased both
a sense of social isolation and individual alienation. In the emerging field of
psychoanalysis, Sigmund Freud pitted an individual's fragile ego against a

powerful unconscious comprised of a frustrated biological libido, repressed traumas and internalised moral prohibitions. Under such pressures, the rational individual hardly stood a chance; humans could never be happy, only less miserable. As Europeans entered the twentieth century, the notion of linear progress was in crisis: did the accumulation of scientific knowledge and its application through modernisation pave the way towards a brighter future, or did it portend the degradation of humanity?

Against this impasse of doubts about progress, the perceptual revolution of the early twentieth century emerged as an alternative way of perceiving and interpreting modernity. In place of time's arrow, the modern moment splayed into a synchronic field of multiple events that are experienced simultaneously. Knowledge was not simply discovered through the objective study of cause and effect relationships, but was something subjectively established by positioning oneself in relation to the phenomena being registered. Put more succinctly: the participation of the investigator and the apparatuses being utilised to undertake investigations would determine both the content and form of the knowledge gained. Through such a perceptual revolution in time, space and the body, the convergence of multiple, relativistic and subjective fields of knowledge superseded the quest for scientific positivism.

In historical terms, one of the earliest acknowledgements of this intellectual shift came from the 'hardest' of the sciences, physics. While everyone knows that Einstein came up with the theory of relativity, rarely do we apply his ideas in everyday life for the simple reason that we do not experience life at or near the speed of light. In the paper 'On the electrodynamics of moving bodies' (1905), Einstein demonstrated that at the speed of light, time and space become a continuum, no longer capable of being perceived as separate phenomena. Einstein postulated that the speed of light remains constant at 300,000 kilometres per second, irrespective of whether an observer was moving towards or away from its source. However, time itself would vary if the observer were moving at or near the speed of light. What an observer would then experience as 'time', he concluded, is actually a fourth dimension in space. Under such conditions, the notion that time provides an independent measure of distance no longer applies.

While Einstein was reworking classical physics on a cosmic scale, Newtonian physics was being challenged at the atomic level. The most familiar image used to model the atom is the one developed by Ernest Rutherford, which resembles a miniature solar system of a relatively massive and positively charged nucleus being orbited by a 'cloud' of negatively charged electrons. This atom presented problems for Newtonian physics. First, Newtonian laws suggested that these electrons should lose energy and spiral into the proportionally massive nucleus; in fact, they maintained their orbits. This meant that gravitational forces were negligible at the atomic level; subatomic forces, not gravity, governed the behaviour of atoms. Towards resolving this problem, physicist Neils Bohr postulated that an electron in orbit is not a mass in the ordinary sense, but a quantum of energy. Further, physicists came to understand that electrons behave both as particles and waves at the same time, a paradox for Newtonian physics. These kinds of discoveries would be later worked out mathematically as quantum mechanics.

Beyond these particular examples, the broader implication of these developments in early twentieth-century physics is that the entire physical universe does not conform to a single and uniform set of laws and principles, but to multiple sets: Newtonian physics for the everyday world, Einstein's relational time–space continuum at the speed of light, quantum mechanics at the level of atoms. All are verifiable, yet the physics involved in demonstrating each is different, at times even mutually exclusive. Which physics applies is dictated by the level of physical reality being explored. While some physicists were troubled by the implications of opening up the Newtonian universe to a plurality of physics, others were more sanguine about accepting the emerging multiplicities of knowledge about physical reality, notably the physicist Werner Heisenberg who later articulated the 'uncertainty principle'. Statistical probability is all we can count on, Heisenberg asserted, and for practical purposes it is a sufficient threshold. But on a more critical level, the uncertainty principle asserts that known pluralities of knowledge take precedence over certainty or 'absolute' knowledge. These pluralities of established knowledge must be accepted as true, Heisenberg asserted, even when – especially when – the logic of non-contradiction tells us such things cannot be possible. The totality of reality cannot be embraced by 'either/or' ways of understanding, only by inclusive 'either/and' paradoxes.

Such insights might have remained of limited consequence had they been restricted to the discipline of physics. However, developments across multiple intellectual pursuits in early twentieth-century Europe reinforced the idea of multiple and synchronous experiences of time and space. In the field of mathematics, the English logicians Bertrand Russell and Alfred North Whitehead demonstrated in the *Principia Mathematica* (1910–13) that mathematical truths are not founded upon external reality, but are established according to formal logic derived from axiomatic principles (proof theory). The German mathematician David Hilbert developed the idea of formalism or finitism, which argues that mathematical symbols have only finite configurations as determined by previously agreed upon rules. Against analytical logic and formalism, the Dutch mathematician L. E. J. Brouwer developed the notion of intuitionism, the idea that the logic of mathematics is derived from the consistent application of self-evident laws rooted in complex mental processes of the human mind. In these ways, mathematics, too, became a relativistic field of knowledge.

The study of human consciousness underwent a perceptual revolution as well. At the end of the nineteenth century, the American psychologist William James introduced the concept of a 'stream of consciousness' in the *Principles of Psychology* (1890). The notion of a 'state' of consciousness, James emphasised, was misleading; thoughts are not the compilation of ideas or discrete experiences, like so many bricks stacked together, but are continually flowing. The European philosophers Edmund Husserl and Henri Bergson pursued related ideas. In *On the Phenomenology of the Consciousness of Internal Time* (1893–1917), the German phenomenologist Husserl asserted that experiences are registered against a flow of consciousness already occurring within a person's mind. It is the conscious awareness of its subjective passage that makes time meaningful for a person. In *Matter and Memory* (1896), the French philosopher Bergson argued that humans do not experience time in discrete units, but as duration, as a flow of sensations and memories that become intelligible upon conscious reflection. For Bergson, images produced from memories deep within the unconscious were particularly important, as they actively participated in the ongoing formation of human consciousness. While none of these philosophers would deny the objectivity of chronological time, the awareness of multiple and overlapping experiences of subjective time had far greater meaning for human psychology.

Dreams provided Sigmund Freud with another way of understanding multiplicities of consciousness. In the multi-levelled ego–id–superego model of human psychology, Freud provided a methodical route to probe the irrational realms of the unconscious through dream work. Freud's basic proposition in *The Interpretation of Dreams* (1901) appears simple enough: 'The dream is a wish fulfillment.' However, what is being wished for, Freud insisted, is not found in the manifest images we dream, but in our latent desires. For Freud, dream images are not symbols that are easily decoded, but function like a rebus that overlays concealed desires and repressed experiences. Some dream images are condensations, the same wish appearing in many guises. Others are displacements, images that appear instead of the wished for image. In all cases, these dream elements possess a power and crazy logic of their own, impervious to the restrictions of cause and effect, and they lie outside everyday experiences of time and space altogether. If humans could admit forbidden desires to themselves through ordinary thoughts and language, particularly those of unrestrained sexuality and violence, they would. But they cannot, and therefore such desires are expressed through the irrational logic of dreams. In Freudian analysis, it takes serious effort to recall and rework dream imagery to achieve a deeper, and sometimes darker, understanding of the human experience.

Such ideas about human consciousness had a particularly strong resonance in literary modernism in the 1910s and following. Modernist literature contributed directly to the perceptual revolution, as Woolf had suggested in 'Mr. Bennett and Mrs. Brown', by experimenting with a variety of literary techniques to reveal multiplicities of time, memory and psychology. A new emphasis upon the literary text to produce a flow of consciousness within readers, to help them experience and be aware of multiple and overlapping realities, emerged as one of the major features of modernist literature. Woolf grappled with this dynamic in her literary production. As literary critic Susan Rubinow Gorsky has noted in relation to Woolf's first published novel, *The Voyage Out* (1913), 'Woolf suggests that two worlds exist simultaneously: an everyday world of facts where one can plan to marry, take sea voyages, live, and die, and an inner world where those events have a different significance and even a different meaning.' As importantly, these multiple worlds exist within the same person: 'These two kinds of life have their own realities; they can coexist for most people, and they can coexist in a single work of art' (Gorsky, 1989: 6). Woolf went on to become perhaps the foremost author of 'stream of consciousness' novels in *Jacob's Room* (1922), *Mrs. Dalloway* (1925), *To the Lighthouse* (1927) and *The Waves* (1931). As an approach to experimental literature, 'stream of consciousness' provided a way to explore a multiplicity of relationships between authors, readers and the novel.

Literary modernism was not limited to stream of consciousness writing, but expressed the intellectual perceptual revolution in a variety of ways. An emphasis upon the use of subjective perceptions to give form to reality emerges in Thomas Mann's early novel *Buddenbrooks: The Decline of a Family* (1901). A *Bildungsroman*, it is the coming-of-age story of Thomas Buddenbrook whose family's rise and decline in commercial fortune as Northern German merchants is expressed through his own physical and psychological exhaustion. What makes this a modernist novel is the way that Buddenbrook's subjective condition transforms common reality. Not only had the Buddenbrook family been driven out of business by larger forces of modernisation, Thomas Buddenbrook's self-consciousness of his own enervated condition constitutes the exhausted *fin de siècle* of the age. Mann was among the first of the modernist writers to collapse this distance between private and public spheres by establishing an ironic perspective on the modern age through the examination of oneself, an approach that he more fully developed in his subsequent works, *Tonio Kröger* (1903), *Death in Venice* (1913) and *The Magic Mountain* (1924).

Beyond the new emphasis upon the subjective interpretation of reality, a preoccupation with time-consciousness predominates in other early works of literary modernism, perhaps most notably in Marcel Proust's *In Search of Lost Time* (*À la recherche du temps perdu*). A seven-volume series that spans more than a decade, from *The Way by Swann's* (1913) to the posthumous *Time Regained* (1927), the meandering series summons up memories and episodes from the life of its narrator. Unlike previous multi-generational novel series from the nineteenth century, such as the 'La Comédie humaine (Human Comedy)' series by Honoré de Balzac or the 'Rougon-Marquart' series by Émile Zola, no linear or evolutionary development is discernable from Proust's multi-thousand paged work. Instead, the narrator's search for 'lost time' becomes fully synchronous, with past, present and future sharing the same textual space. According to the literary critic Christopher Prendergast, 'not only does the novel look back as it thrusts forwards, it also moves sideways, in a complex set of lateral shifts and swerves, deploying a technique of digression so systematic as to empty the notion of "digression" of its normal meanings' (Proust, 2002: 36). Proust's writing digresses not only in the storytelling, but also at the level of syntax through lengthy sentences whose complexity of construction renders such common grammar guideposts as subject, verb or object superfluous. Digression becomes both the method and the meaning. The text is less a description of Proust's world than an expression of his own meandering time consciousness, a modernist fusion that matches style and expression with subjective experience.

In *Ulysses* by the Irish author James Joyce (1918–20), synchronous multiplicities of time and space emerge as the novel's dominant quality. The story revolves around the lives of Leopold Bloom and Stephen Dedalus, and Bloom's wife Molly, in Dublin on 16 June 1904. Joyce explodes that single day into a modernist epic. On one level, the novel broadly parallel's Homer's epic poem, with Bloom, Stephen and Molly loosely cast into the roles of Ulysses, Telemachus and Penelope, and each of the novel's eighteen episodes are named after different characters or events in the *Odyssey*. The story does not occur in mythic time, however, but within a single day oversaturated by time and memory. The broad narrative recounts the parallel lives of Bloom and Stephen that day, their chance meeting and joint visit to a brothel in the evening, and it culminates in a soliloquy on love by an adulterous Molly. Rather than developing in sequential chapters, each episode is done in a different literary style, set in various locations, at different hours of the day, and is governed by a different artistic muse. Any 'grand design' to the novel eludes the reader. The juxtapositions and discontinuities in the novel's construction express the way that the characters' minds work through free associations, not by an overarching narrative.

French avant-garde poet Blaise Cendrars employed yet another set of literary techniques to evoke the perceptual revolution in time and space in the avant-garde poem *La prose du Transsibérien et de la Petite Jehanne de France* (*Prose of the Trans-Siberian and of Little Jeanne of France*, 1913). The poem weds locomotion technologies, subjective travel experiences and experimental verse to a modernist depiction of multiplicities of time and space. Rather than opening up one event to multiplicities of time and space, as Joyce had done, Cendrars reversed the direction by having a multiple of places and times occur simultaneously. Ostensibly a record of a voyage by train that Cendrars took from Paris to Russia in the years just before the Russian Revolution of 1905, the poem is neither a chronological travelogue nor any conventional form of writing. Rather, Cendrars called the poem a 'simultaneous text', one that combined upon the same sheet of paper various locations (Moscow, Montmartre, Novgorod, Prague, Flanders, Patagonia, Fiji, Japan, Mexico), times (Friday morning, St Bartholomew's Day, five days, a few days' respite), geography (as defined by the train-line routes Basel–Timbuktu, Paris–New York, Madrid–Stockholm, Saint-Germain–Montmartre), mythic allusions (the Old Man of the Mountain, the Quiet Ones, the hanging gardens of Babylon, the Land of Cockaigne), magical images of modern objects (a nickel-plated Browning revolver, an enraged locomotive) and, above all, train noises (the opening and closing of compartment doors, the squeal of metallic wheels, steam blasts and whistles) and rail rhythms (4/4, 5/4, and 7/4). The original publication was printed on a single sheet 36 centimetres wide and nearly 2 metres long, and was folded like an accordion so it could be read either sequentially in pages, like a book, or unfold as one continuous space. The multiple lines of the poem were each short in length, printed in several fonts of various lengths, and read from the top to the bottom the length of the page. Resembling an interminable telegram, the words led in serial succession from one to another without punctuation or other standard formatting devices to guide the reader as to where phrases started or stopped. The page was also illustrated along the left-hand side by a full-colour 'synchrome painting' by Sonia Delaunay. The combined effect yielded an illustrated text that took the place of time, space and lived experience. It was engagement with Cendrars's poem, not actual experience in the world, which organised the reader's temporal sense.

In these ways and others, literary modernism was a critical dimension of the perceptual revolution in time and space. Literary modernism in the early twentieth century is, of course, a vast topic that encompasses numerous authors in Great Britain and Ireland, and across continental Europe. And as the twentieth century developed, increasingly modernists would not be content simply to give form to the perceptual revolution through their works of art and literature. In addition to a heightened self-consciousness about the radical reorientation in modernity from the nineteenth to the twentieth century, many artists and writers began to see it as their task to constitute themselves into self-stylised vanguards of an entirely new, modernist aesthetic. The philosophical and political imperatives of the modernist avant-garde would not only be to remake art anew, but to effect a cultural revolution that would set Western civilisation on entirely new foundations.

Further reading

Asendorf, Christoph, *Batteries of Life: On the History of Things and Their Perception in Modernity* (trans. Don Reneau), Berkeley: University of California Press, 1993.

Bradbury, Malcolm and James McFarlane (eds), *Modernism: A Guide to European Literature 1890–1930* (new Preface), New York: Penguin, 1991.

Healey, Kimberly J., *The Modernist Traveler: French Detours, 1900–1930*, Lincoln: University of Nebraska Press, 2003.

Hughes, H. Stuart, *Consciousness and Society: The Reorientation of European Social Thought 1890–1930*, New York: Alfred A. Knopf, 1958.

Gregory, Rosalyn and Benjamin Kohlmann (eds), *Utopian Spaces of Modernism: Literature and Culture, 1885–1945*, New York: Palgrave MacMillan, 2012.

Kern, Stephen, *The Culture of Time and Space 1880–1918*, Cambridge, MA: Harvard University Press, 1983.

Levenson, Michael (ed.), *The Cambridge Companion to Modernism*, Cambridge: Cambridge University Press, 1999.

Lowe, Donald M., *History of Bourgeois Perception*, Chicago: University of Chicago Press, 1982.

Rainey, Lawrence (ed.), *Modernism: An Anthology*, Oxford: Blackwell, 2005.

Rosenbaum, S. P. (ed.), *A Bloomsbury Group Reader*, Oxford: Blackwell, 1993.

Shone, Richard, *The Art of Bloomsbury: Roger Fry, Vanessa Bell, and Duncan Grant*, Princeton: Princeton University Press, 2001.

Werth, Margaret, *The Joy of Life: The Idyllic in French Art, circa 1900*, Berkeley: University of California Press, 2002.

Part 3

HIGH MODERNISM

4

Early Modernism

The premiere of *Le Sacre du printemps* (*The Rite of Spring*), composed and conducted by Igor Stravinsky, choreographed by dancer Vaslav Nijinsky and performed by Serge Diaghilev's Ballets Russes, occurred at the Théâtre des Champs-Élysées in Paris on 29 May 1913. It is one of the most celebrated events in the history of early modernism. Since 1909, the Ballets Russes had performed across Europe and enjoyed great acclaim for its Russian and oriental themes, music and costuming. Over the previous year, however, the ballet company had begun to stage more modern and scandalous performances, such as the debut of Debussy's *L'Après-midi d'un faune* in 1912, which featured Nijinsky as a faun in leotards with horns and a tail, convulsively making love to a young wood nymph. The audience gathered at the Théâtre des Champs-Élysées that evening represented a wide cross-section of the public – fashionable Parisian socialites, latter-day bohemians and members of the newly emerging Parisian literary avant-garde such as Gertrude Stein, Jean Cocteau and Guillaume Apollinaire. The programme libretto written by Stravinsky announced, 'The Rite of Spring is a musical choreographic work. It represents pagan Russia and is unified by a single idea: the mystery and great surge of the creative power of spring. The piece has no plot.' Everyone knew it was chic to be in attendance, but no one knew what to expect.

Protests of whistles and hisses began during the overture, even before the curtain was raised. The dancers appeared on the stage, began jumping up and down, and led by their pelvises ran pigeon-toed across the stage, out of synch with Stravinsky's powerfully rhythmic music. The audience divided into those who shouted in protest at the dancers and others who applauded enthusiastically, urging them on. It was hard to tell where the more remarkable performance was occurring, on the stage or in the auditorium. The artist Valentine Gross (Hugo), whose action sketches of Nijinsky and the dance company were exhibited in the theatre's foyer, celebrated the maelstrom. 'I thought there was something wonderful about the titanic struggle which must have been going on in order to keep these *inaudible* musicians and these *deafened* dancers together in obedience to the laws of their invisible choreographer. *The ballet was astoundingly beautiful*' (Eksteins, 2000: 9). While some commentators have suggested that the scale of the uproar and significance of the event have been over-exaggerated, in the mythology of modernism the premiere of *Le Sacre du printemps* has become legendary.

From self-promotional accounts penned after the event, it is clear that scandalising the public was precisely what Diaghliev, Stravinsky and Nijinsky had in mind. However, equating the avant-garde with outrageous acts only takes our understanding of modernism so far. It is worth remembering that since the mid-nineteenth century, effrontery had already become a regular feature of the modern visual, literary and musical arts; scandalising the public was not particularly new in 1913. Nonetheless, the 'shock of the new' is an important dimension to modernist art. Beyond offence, its purpose was to provoke the public into perceiving modern reality differently through new art. The Spanish philosopher José Ortega y Gasset understood the shock of the new in terms of the role the artistic avant-garde performed in society at large: 'the new art also helps the elite to recognise themselves and one another in the drab mass of society and to learn their mission which consists of being few and holding their own against the many' (Harrison and Wood, 2003: 325). It became the task of an elite, self-conscious and self-constituted artistic avant-garde to awaken a slumbering population from their common aesthetic and intellectual habits, to open their eyes to the effects of the rapidly changing world and to provide a new basis to comprehend modernity. As the literary critic Ástráoður Eysteinsson has observed, it is perhaps best to understand the avant-garde function in modernism 'as an attempt to *interrupt* the modernity that we live and understand as a social, if not "normal", way of life' (Eysteinsson, 1990: 6). As the artistic 'shock troops' ahead of the rest of society, the avant-garde would reinvent modern culture, transform human consciousness, and revitalise society.

However, at the beginning of the twentieth century few early modernists in that avant-garde were the kinds of cultural iconoclasts and political revolutionaries that would be commonly associated with the radical avant-garde that later emerged in the wake of the First World War and the Russian Revolution. Many early avant-garde artists and writers were primarily motivated by a strong desire to innovate art, literature and music. By experimenting with the forms of their artistic crafts, and then critically reflecting upon what was being accomplished by doing so, this early avant-garde began to develop the techniques and language of the modernist idiom. By the eve of the war, the aesthetic innovations of the avant-garde had become highly developed, and some of its artistic production and manifesto declarations quite bold and jarring. The development of this early avant-garde is perhaps best reconstructed by charting the emergence of ideas through some representative and influential early modernists.

In the field of painting, Henri Matisse is emblematic of the kind of avant-garde artist who was an innovator while remaining respectful of the traditions of his craft. A leading member of the **Fauves** ('wild beasts') group of Parisian painters, Matisse had followed in the footsteps of the impressionists and neo-impressionists, and specifically the painting of Paul Cézanne. Working broadly within a representational mode – where human figures, home interiors and exterior landscapes are easily recognisable, even if not 'naturalistic' – Matisse's aesthetic shifted to the abstract elements of the painting medium itself and the expressive impact the work of art made upon a viewer. For Matisse, the elements of the painting medium were foundational to form and meaning: the size and strength of the brushstroke, the boldness and lustre of paint colours, the harmony of elements upon the canvas. The purpose for putting paint to canvas was less to reproduce reality than to evoke a strong response in viewers that would resonate with the inner world of the artist. As Matisse articulated in *Notes of a Painter* (1908),

> The entire arrangement of my picture is expressive: the place occupied by the figures, the empty spaces around them, the proportions, everything has its share. Composition is the art of arranging in a decorative manner the diverse elements at the painter's command to express his feelings. (**Doc. 3, pp. 116–17**)

Such an expression of the external representation of an artist's or writer's inner reality became a fundamental modernist aesthetic, influential among both visual artists and writers, particularly in central and northern Europe, well into the 1920s.

Matisse had a profound impact upon Wassily Kandinsky, the Russian-born painter who, together with Franz Marc and Paul Klee, was one of the founding collaborators of the **Blaue Reiter** ('Blue Rider') group of artists. Trained as a lawyer and economist, Kandinsky was an art enthusiast who moved to Munich in 1896 to study *Jugendstil* (Art Nouveau) painting. During the first decade of the twentieth century, Kandinsky travelled extensively throughout Europe and quickly emerged as one of the continent's foremost avant-garde artists. In 1909, he helped to establish the New Artists' Association (NKV), a group of Expressionist artists in Munich, including Marc. Together, they founded the Blue Rider group, whose journal *Der Blaue Reiter Almanach* (estb. 1912) featured the work of a range of innovative contemporary artists, such as Hans Arp, Georges Braque, André Derain, Paul

Fauves: French for 'wild beasts', refers to a group of early-twentieth-century painters who used strong colours and bold brush strokes for purposes of expression over representation.

Blaue Reiter ('Blue Riders'): A group of Expressionist artists in Germany during the 1910s that sought to express 'spiritual truths' in painting through symbolic associations of colour and the formal qualities of the image.

Jugendstil: German term meaning 'youth style', it was the form of Art Nouveau favoured by the Secession artists in Austria and Hungary in the late nineteenth and early twentieth centuries.

Klee, Ernst Nolde and Pablo Picasso; it also highlighted folk and primitive art from Europe and the overseas colonies.

Kandinsky pushed ideas about abstraction and expressionism further than Matisse, articulating his theory about the language of colour and form in painting in *Concerning the Spiritual in Art* (1911) (**Doc. 4, pp. 118–19**). For Kandinsky, art not only expressed the inner feelings of the artists, it also constituted an actual depiction of the human soul. Colours, lines and shapes, he believed, invoked sympathetic spiritual vibrations: the more abstract the work of art, the more directly it corresponded to the 'inner need' of the viewer, he claimed. Kandinsky cast the artist into an avant-garde role by charging him with no less than the spiritual care of humanity. Drawing upon the form of an ascending triangle, an important compositional element in the history of art that Kandinsky traced from Renaissance art through the *Bathing Women* paintings by Cézanne (1898–1905), he established a correspondence between the soul of the artist and the collective spirit of humanity itself. Only the true artist, Kandinsky claimed, occupied the pinnacle of the triangle, and thus only he had the capacity to lead humanity to a greater spiritual reality. This would be accomplished by degrees, Kandinsky believed, with the artist moving from simpler 'melodic' paintings to more complex 'symphonic' ones. These symphonic paintings, in turn, would resonate in viewers through a series of ascending stages, first as 'impressions', then 'improvisations', and finally as complex 'compositions' (all three terms were used as series titles for paintings by Kandinsky). The avant-garde task of the artist, then, was to give exterior expression of the inner needs of the soul.

The language of music was not accidental in Kandinsky, for in addition to the colour harmony notions of Matisse, he was also influenced by the musical theories of Austrian composer Arnold Schoenberg. A pioneer in the field of atonal music – the infinitesimal division and saturation of dissonant tones between the conventional notes in the tempered scale – for Schoenberg, music amounted to phenomenological philosophy in a different form. Schoenberg's avant-garde project was to realise a new language of music, to turn a composition into a 'text' constructed of musical 'sentences'. The structure of such atonal musical compositions would express a radically different 'logic' than the one provided by standard music theory. The goal was to move beyond the comforts of melody and harmony and to achieve a 'total chromaticism' that would provoke strong, conflicting, deep emotional responses within the listener. Dissonance was the foremost element in such chromatically saturated music, first realised in *Three Piano Pieces* (1909) and *Five Pieces for Orchestra* (1909), and it served the goal of unleashing the 'logic of the unconscious'. For Schoenberg, the audience's capacity to withstand musical dissonance through a nearly unbearable saturation of varied, juxtaposed, non-repetitious sounds equalled the emancipation of consciousness.

It was the obligation of the avant-garde composer, in his view, to construct musical pieces designed to invoke such a self-consciously subjective response within listeners. Although atonality would not become a dominant mode of modernist music, a Schoenberg following developed in the Second Viennese School of composers that included Anton Webern and Alban Berg, and his ideas about dissonant 'noise' and a 'new logic' in music briefly resonated with Italian Futurist and Russian Constructivist music composition as well.

The composition of language was being reworked in modernist poetry as well. In London, the American poet Ezra Pound emerged as the leader of the Imagist poets, begun by T. E. Hulme, which included H. D. (Hilda Doolittle) and Richard Aldington. In Pound's view, words should be self-constituted image-symbols, not symbols of 'something else'. From the Imagist perspective, the Symbolists remained a step removed from this realisation, as their poetry alluded to another reality, typically the psychological interior. For Pound, however, poetry should strive to be less figurative, and instead the words employed in a poem should instantaneously convey an entire complex of intellectual and emotional meanings to the reader as directly and economically as possible. As early as 1912, Pound issued a litany of advice in 'A Few Don'ts by an Imagiste' about how to achieve such poetry saturated with meaning:

> Use no superfluous word, no adjective, which does not reveal something.
>   Don't use such an expression as 'dim lands of peace.' It dulls the image. It mixes an abstraction with the concrete. It comes from the writer's not realizing that the natural object is always the adequate symbol.
>
> (Rainey, 2005: 95)

A modernist poet's training in craft, Pound proclaimed, was no less rigorous than that of a musician or a painter. The imperatives of Imagism would later be refined and extended in Pound's subsequent movement, **Vorticism**, which applied to both poetics and visual aesthetics. Pound emphasised that words and images are not abstractions, but are impulses that are brought together into a **concrete** coalescence: 'The image is not an idea. It is a radiant node or cluster; it is what I can, and perforce, call a VORTEX, from which, and through which, and into which ideas are constantly rushing' (Bradbury and McFarlane, 1991: 237). Pound insisted that poetry should never be static, that it must be energetic, perpetually in motion, continually reformulated, and always carefully crafted. In creative and intellectual rigour, Pound promoted the superior, avant-garde role of an elite of modernist poets, and Anglo-American poets as widespread as William Butler Yeats, T. S. Eliot, D. H. Lawrence, William Carlos Williams, Wallace Stevens and Marianne Moore came under his influence.

Vorticism: An early-twentieth-century British movement in poetry and art inspired by Cubism and Futurism that strove to capture movement in dynamic images.

concrete: An adjective used to modify art, poetry or performance to emphasise direct engagement with the tangible contact elements of media over aesthetic or linguistic meaning.

Across the English Channel, Guillaume Apollinaire was a great innovator of modernist poetry as well. A leading avant-garde figure in early twentieth-century France, Apollinaire became renowned as a lyrical modernist poet with the publication of the collection *Alcools* (1913). During the years that he served in the First World War, Apollinaire developed a new technique of concrete poetry in which the typographical layout of the text reinforced the poem. Posthumously published as the collection *Calligrammes* (1918), the sonorous and visual are drawn together in Apollinaire's typographic poems as the words are assembled into the visual form of the poetic image. For example, one of those poems, '*La colombe poignardée et le jet d'eau*' ('The stabbed dove and the water fountain') is shaped like a dove flying above a water spray. Poetic lines constitute the water jets, each recalling another poet or artist, or the memory of an image or feeling. These lines shower upward from flowering lips at the bottom of the page, whose downward corollaries are the tears and prayers descending from a 'dove in rapture' flying overhead. That dove bears the names of Apollinaire's past women lovers, now 'sweet, stabbed figures' (*see* Plate 2). In such calligrammes, Apollinaire created the 'poem-object', a self-contained symbol whose meaning is generated by the oscillation between the graphic text and the visual image.

In addition to his own literary production, Apollinaire became the champion of other modernist artists, musicians and writers. He wrote art criticism in support of the emerging modernist trends in art, literature, music, and theatre, most notably *Les Peintres cubistes* (*The Cubist Painters*, 1913). The birth of Cubism is often marked by Pablo Picasso's *Les Demoiselles d'Avignon* (1907), a painting recognised at the time as simultaneously primitive (of roughly drawn female nudes, some wearing 'savage' African masks) and multi-perspective (in that multiple views of the figures had been combined and flattened out upon the two-dimensional canvas surface). Art critic John Golding has defined basic aesthetic of Cubism as

> the construction of a painting in terms of a linear grid or framework, the fusion of objects with their surroundings, the combination of several views of an object within a single image, and of abstract and representational elements in the same picture.
>
> (Butler, 1994: 67)

In collaboration with painter Georges Braque, Picasso pioneered this Cubist aesthetic, working from semi-recognisable still-life paintings to entirely abstract and non-representational works. While Braque and Picasso are the most well-known Cubists, the technique was utilised by other painters of the era as well, including Robert Delaunay, Henri Le Fauconnier, Juan Gris and Fernand Léger.

Three different trajectories emerged from Cubism. One lay in the direction of Cubist collage, which juxtaposes diverse images, words and materials in a multimedia montage picture. Newspaper clippings, advertising images, product packaging, strips of wallpaper and pieces of wood or metal were glued upon a painted canvas to create the collage. In this way, Cubist collage infused the materials of popular culture with modernist aesthetics, blurring distinctions between 'high' and 'low' culture. In addition, like photography and the cinema, Cubists self-consciously assembled the collage elements within a 'frame', thus incorporating a stock-in-trade technique from the commercial arts into the aesthetic repertoire of modernism. Yet while these collages were derived from the materials of everyday life and commercial culture, their meaning remained abstract and ambiguous. The concept of collage derives from the French *collé*, meaning 'glued', but colloquially it suggests something sham or fake. Yet even if the meaning of Cubist collage remained dubious, the introduction of commercial multimedia elements broke with the kind of avant-garde snobbery that defined modernist art as distinct, autonomous and above everyday commercial culture. This blending of avant-garde sensibilities with the commercial materials of everyday life later became even more pronounced in the subsequent modernist movements of Dada, Surrealism, and Constructivism, and again in the late twentieth-century movements of Pop Art and postmodernism.

Alternatively, Cubism led in the direction of further abstraction, most notably in the works of the Dutch painter Piet Mondrian. In 1912, Mondrian had come to Paris to study Cubism, but was forced by the outbreak of the First World War to return to the Netherlands. In contrast to Braque and Picasso's attempt to suffuse Cubism with the elements of everyday life, Mondrian sought the further abstraction of the elements of Cubist art towards a more universal aesthetic that he called 'Neo-Plasticism' (**Doc. 5, pp. 120–1**). Through this technique, Mondrian simplified all images to their most elemental components – black horizontal and vertical lines, squares and rectangles, and spaces painted in primary or secondary colours, white, grey, or black – and then assembled them in ways that would suggest visual movement. Through paintings he called 'compositions', Mondrian assembled these simplified elements into asymmetrical patterns designed to resist the viewer's ability to see the work of art as harmonious whole. Upon this 'new plastic method', which combined 'the unconscious and the conscious, the immutable and the mutable', Mondrian sought to produce a sense of tension and dissonance in art that resonated with the perpetually changing experience of modernity. He also believed that the principles of Neo-Plasticism governed not only painting, but all of the arts. Along these lines, his ideas were first incorporated into modernist architecture through the **De Stijl** movement.

De Stijl: Dutch term meaning 'the style', title of a journal that promoted Neo-Plastic aesthetics and abstraction in architecture, product design and the visual arts.

Primitivism: The use of folk and non-Western sources or impulses in modernist art. Also applies to the production of 'naïve' art by untrained artists or the use of 'primitive techniques' such as photomontage.

Primitivism, inherited from the nineteenth-century notion of the exotic but reformulated in the modernist idiom, was a third current in Cubism readily seen in Picasso's *Les Demoiselles d'Avignon*, visible in the African masks painted directly upon the female nude figures. But primitivism influenced a number of other early modernist movements as well. One example of the modernist primitive was 'naïve' or simple art produced by untrained artists, perhaps best illustrated in the art and life of Henri Rousseau. Neither a cosmopolitan nor intellectual, Rousseau was a Paris toll tax collector (called *Le Dounier*, 'the customs agent', by Apollinaire and other Parisian avant-garde poets), who retired early and lived on a small pension in order to paint every day. His paintings were primitive in the sense that Rousseau had absolutely no training in art. His self-taught technique employed bold and primary colours, flattened perspective and disproportionate relationships between objects. In addition to his naïve aesthetic, many of his paintings depicted exotic settings, colonial or jungle scenes, such as *Sleeping Gypsy* (1897), *The Snake Charmer* (1907), and *The Dream* (1910). Yet the imagery in those paintings did not originate in colonial sources, but came from the botanical collections and the zoo at the Jardin des Plantes in Paris. It was the simplicity of the man and his art, not his familiarity with primitive cultures, which was heralded as a modernist achievement.

Another approach to primitivism in modern European art was to treat peasants as though they were original peoples. In the nineteenth century, the Realist painter Jean-François Millet portrayed the nobility of peasants in such works as *The Gleaners* (1857) and *The Angelus* (1857), and Breton villagers were the subjects of the Post-Impressionist painters Émile Bernard, Vincent Van Gogh and Paul Gaugin. In the 1890s, a group of German painters from Düsseldorf and Munich settled in the peasant village of Worpswede north of Bremen. Influenced by Volkish notions about untamed nature and idealising peasant women as both fecund and pious, Worpswede painters such as Fritz Mackensen and Otto Modersohn depicted the peasantry in romantic, quasi-mystical terms. Within this community of artists, Paula Modersohn-Becker became the most renowned Worpswede painter, best known for such works as *Poorhouse Woman in the Garden* (1906) and *Kneeling Mother and Child* (1907). During the first decade of the twentieth century Modersohn-Becker travelled frequently to Paris, where she became familiar with Expressionism in painting, particularly through the works of Cézanne and Gauguin. Her adoption of more bold painting techniques – vivid colours, simplified forms, distorted perspectives – was not a direct expression of her subject matter, labouring peasant women or nursing children, but resulted from her fusion of modernist aesthetics and folk simplicity.

There were also avant-garde movements in painting that drew upon primitive source materials to produce highly modernist art. One of the earliest of these was the Fauves, the 'wild beasts' painters that included Henri Matisse, André Derain and Maurice de Vlaminck. Often selecting pastoral and mythological scenes as the imagery for their Expressionist paintings, the combination of simplified and bold colours predominated in their land-scapes and portraits. German Expressionist artists from the Brücke group, such as Ernst Ludwig Kirchner, Erich Heckel, and Emile Nolde, were even more bold. The sources of primitivism employed by the Brücke artists included techniques such as the revival of woodcut block-print methods, and the graphic depiction of sexualised female nudes as an affront to 'civilised' bourgeois values and aesthetics. For both the Fauves and the Brücke group, primitivism was employed less for exotic or erotic ends, than to exploit such primal sources towards creating an entirely new and modern-ist art. In the case of the Brücke, their particular variety of Expressionism amounted to nothing less than a Nietzschean effort to sweep away Western civilisation, at least as it was embodied in the Wilhelmine German Empire, and to replace it with a modernism infused with primitive and vivid imagery, produced by artisanal techniques (**Doc. 6, pp. 122–3**).

What this relatively small cast of artists, writers and musicians reveals is a dynamic of cross-influences that occurred within and between early modernist movements. Few of these modernists lived in isolation. Most lived and worked in the capital cities of Europe – Paris, London, Vienna, Berlin, St Petersburg, Prague, Budapest – and their immediate circles included net-works of artists, writers and intellectuals. Further, as can be seen from these examples, aesthetic innovations in one artistic field were sometimes trans-ferred to another. Geographic displacement was also a common experience among modernists. As the cosmopolitan metropolis, Paris attracted artists and writers from across Europe – the Spanish Picasso, the Dutch Mondrian, the Irish James Joyce and the Polish Apollinaire, for example. American liter-ary modernists largely ignored at home, such as Gertrude Stein, Ezra Pound and T. S. Eliot, thrived in Europe (as would the subsequent generation, the American 'Lost Generation' and Harlem Renaissance writers, living in post-war Paris). Modernism had quickly become a cross-cultural and interna-tional phenomenon across Europe and the Atlantic.

Yet modernism's broader cultural impact remained limited in these early decades. Public response to modernist art in Paris, the capital of modernity, was largely negative during this era. Mystified by what was being viewed, read or heard, most people considered modernism a 'joke' (*blague*, in French), and modernist works were often parodied and satirised in news-paper reviews, cartoons, in the theatre and the music hall. Neither was the spirit of entertainment lost on the avant-garde. The French artist Marcel Duchamp, for example, deliberately provoked art connoisseurs by displaying ready-made objects such as *Bicycle Wheel* (1912), *Bottlerack* (1913) and

Fountain (a urinal signed 'R. Mutt', 1913) in exhibitions. Only a small cross-section of the public experienced modernist works at this time, and an even smaller percentage felt transformed by the encounters.

In order to achieve the avant-garde goal of transforming Western civilisation, modernism would have to reach the masses. The first murmurs of such an across-the-board transformation began to be heard on the eve of the First World War, in an early radical avant-garde movement called Futurism. The 'Manifesto of Futurism' by Italian poet Filippo Tommaso Marinetti, as much a provocateur as a man of letters, appeared in the Parisian daily newspaper *Le Figaro* on 20 February 1909 (**Doc. 7, pp. 123–5**). Art, Marinetti insisted, should be revolutionary, bold, energetic, fervent, destructive, violently sweeping away the old world with the newest technologies, towards the goal of hurling humanity into a chaotically beautiful future. Artists of the future, he declared, would value action over thought, speed over stasis, aggression over contemplation, ecstasy over repose, and masculinity over femininity. The Futurist, he proclaimed, embraces the entirety of the modern world in a dynamic image:

> *We shall sing of the great masses shaken with work, pleasure or rebellion; we shall sing the multicoloured and polyphonic tidal waves of revolutions in the modern metropolis; shall sing the vibrating nocturnal fervour of factories and shipyards burning under violent electrical moons; bloated railway stations that devour smoking serpents; factories hanging from the sky by their twisting threads of spiralling smoke; bridges like gymnasts who span rivers, flashing at the sun with the gleam of a knife; adventurous steamships that scent the horizon, locomotives with their swollen chest, pawing the tracks like massive steel horses bridled with pipes, and the oscillating flight of airplanes, whose propeller flaps at the wind like a flag and seems to applaud like a delirious crowd.*
>
> (Rainey, 2005: 5)

Marinetti's rant might have simply remained just that, had it not been for the convergence of several historical factors. First, Futurism was not the idea of a solitary individual, but was a multifaceted movement across the arts. While Marinetti was the principal public spokesman for the movement, other Italian writers, such as Mario Carli, Emilio Settimelli, Bruno Cora and Arnaldo Ginna, constituted a constellation of contributors to the literary review, *L'Italia Futurista*. Major Futurist painters and sculptors included Giacomo Balla, Umberto Boccioni and Carlo Carrà. These artists also produced avant-garde theoretical treatises such as *Futurist Painting: Technical Manifesto* (1910) and *The Technical Manifesto of Futurist Sculpture* (1912). With roots in Symbolism, Neo-Impressionism, the Fauves and Cubism, Futurism radically pushed modernist aesthetic sensibilities rapidly forward.

Its aesthetics emphasised synesthesia (the breaking down and blurring of sensory boundaries), kinaesthesia (the breaking down of movement into discrete moments) and the use of new technological media (particularly photography and the cinema) in a wholesale effort to sweep aside all past culture and artistic traditions. Futurism was also the first artistic avant-garde movement to base its aesthetics on industrial modes of production, both in the use of modern materials like metals and in the use of the commercial marketplace to advertise its art, and it applied industrial principles to all artistic realms, including architecture, music and photography, beyond literature and painting. The Futurists fully embraced technology, industrial production, political revolution and warfare as the means of propelling Western civilisation into the future. The Italian Futurist movement was so dynamic that it was one of the few early avant-gardes to re-emerge after the First World War.

Second, Futurism influenced the development of other radical avant-garde movements throughout Europe. Marinetti was not only a publisher of manifestos, he was also an energetic proselytiser who travelled extensively to promulgate Futurism. While Futurism itself was short-lived or modified outside of Italy, its imprint was widespread. German Expressionist art in Berlin and Prague was transformed by Futurism. In Russia, Cubo-Futurism was embraced by the poet and playwright Vladimir Mayakovsky. In England, the Vorticist movement in poetry and visual art promoted by Ezra Pound and Wyndham Lewis was animated by Futurism. In France, Marinetti's speaking tour in Paris influenced the development of late-Cubist works by Léger, Gris and Delaunay. After the war, the Paris Dada and Surrealist movements openly acknowledged their inspirational debts to Marinetti (although they distanced themselves from the Italian Futurist movement itself, which became openly fascist in the post-war era).

Yet for all its success as an early, radical avant-garde movement, Futurism's emphases upon hyper-masculinity, ultra-nationalism, and the glorification of violence constitute a difficult and disturbing legacy. While it may be possible to interpret Futurist imagery metaphorically, Marinetti made it clear that he was literal about his art. In an essay on 'Contempt for Woman' in *Le Futurisme* (1911), Marinetti hurled invective language at women as love-dependent creatures, wholly inferior to men physically, intellectually, emotionally and erotically, and he singled out the politically and sexually liberated modern woman for particular abuse. In *Technical Manifesto of Futurist Literature* (1912), he called for the abolition of the individual ego in human psychology, and he extolled patriotism as the heroic basis for social solidarity in *Destruction of Syntax – Wireless Imagination – Words-in-Freedom* (1913). When Marinetti writes of artistic and literary lyricism, he frequently refers to the movement and sounds of locomotives, airplanes, cars, machine guns and bomb explosions. For Marinetti, the symphony of life had little to do with rebirth and renewal and nearly everything to do with the masses engaging in political revolution and technological warfare. Marinetti's apocalyptic vision of the future was far more convulsive than the fallout from any scandal in Paris over the debut of *Le Sacre du printemps*.

Barely five years after the appearance of Marinetti's Futurist manifesto, the conflagration of total war would engulf Europe and traumatise millions of ordinary people. During the First World War, the terrible beauty of the modern world no longer remained images fashioned by a Futurist avant-garde, but became the subjective reality of the masses. In what intellectual historian Stephen Kern has called the 'Cubist War', millions of soldiers from Europe and the imperial colonies would suffer the physical and psychological afflictions of No Man's Land. A physical space alternating between sun-parched land and mud-flooded ravines, for long stretches of time nothing occurs. Suddenly, time is compressed by a chaotic flurry of bombardments, machine-gun fire, gas and gas masks, a tangle of shovels spades and bayonets, soldiers running and falling. The chaos continues for hours, days, sometimes weeks. Then, inexplicably, everything is quiet again, and the landscape is littered with corpses and body parts. In the aftershock, the soldier's experience of No Man's Land is internalised and becomes part of his personal psychology. Among the members of the artistic and literary avant-garde who survived the war, both as soldiers and civilians, those traumatic experiences of war re-emerged in politically radicalised modernist visions.

Further reading

Apollinaire, Guillaume, *The Cubist Painters* (trans. Peter Read), Berkeley: University of California Press, 2004.

Barron, Stephanie (ed.), *German Expressionism: Art and Society*, New York: Rizzoli, 1997.

Butler, Christopher, *Early Modernism: Literature, Music and Painting in Europe 1900–1916*, Oxford: Oxford University Press, 1994.

Elderfield, John, *The 'Wild Beasts': Fauvism and its Affinities*, New York: Museum of Modern Art, 1976.

Eksteins, Modris, *Rites of Spring: The Great War and the Birth of the Modern Age*, New York: Mariner Books, 2000.

Flamm, Jack, *Matisse on Art* (revd edn), Berkeley: University of California Press, 1995.

Gordon, Donald E., *Expressionism: Art and Idea*, New Haven: Yale University Press, 1987.

Green, Christopher (ed.), *Picasso's Les Demoiselles d'Avignon,* Cambridge: Cambridge University Press, 2001.

Harrison, Charles, Francis Frascina and Gill Perry, *Primitivism, Cubism, Abstraction: The Early Twentieth Century*, (Series: 'Modem Art: Practices and Debates'), New Haven and London: Yale University Press/The Open University, 1993.

Lloyd, Jill, *German Expressionism: Primitivism and Modernity*, New Haven: Yale University Press, 1991.

McCully, Marilyn (ed.), *A Picasso Anthology: Documents, Criticism, Reminiscences*, Princeton: Princeton University Press, 1997.

Mondrian, Piet, *The New Art–The New Life: Collected Writings* (trans. and ed. Harry Holtzman and Martin S. James), New York: Da Capo Press, 1993.

Perloff, Marjorie, *The Futurist Moment: Avant-Garde, Avant Guerre, and the Language of Rupture*, Chicago: University of Chicago Press, 1986.

Rosenblum, Robert, *Cubism and Twentieth-Century Art* (revd edn), New York: Harry N. Abrams, 1977.

Rubin, William (ed.), *'Primitivism' in 20th Century Art: Affinity of the Tribal and the Modern*, 2 vols, New York: The Museum of Modern Art, 1984.

Rubin, William, Helene Seckel and Judith Cousins, *Les Desmoiselles d'Avignon*, New York: The Museum of Modern Art, 1994.

Weiss, Jeffrey, *The Popular Culture of Modern Art: Picasso, Duchamp, and Avant-Gardism*, New Haven: Yale University Press, 1994.

5

The Radical Avant-Garde

The First International Dada Fair was held in Berlin in June 1920 at the gallery of art collector Dr Otto Burchard. The artists who organised the exhibition boasted absurdly grandiose titles: 'Marshal' George Grosz, 'Dadasopher' Raoul Hausmann and 'Dadabserver' John Heartfield. Among the paintings on display were *War Cripples* by Otto Dix, of amputated, blinded and wheelchair-bound veterans on parade, and *Germany, A Winter's Tale* by George Grosz, a satirical cubist montage of a dining bourgeois man flanked by a priest, a general and a politician and set against a fragmented urban landscape of destroyed buildings, cemeteries, criminals and prostitutes. A life-sized mannequin of a German military officer with a pig's head was suspended from the ceiling. Among the numerous photomontages was Hannah Höch's *Cut with the Dada Kitchen Knife through the Last Weimar Beer-Belly Cultural Epoch in Germany*, a chaotic image of cut-out magazine images of portraits, human figures and machine parts, and the printed phrases 'Dada', 'Anti-Dada' and 'Dadaisten' (total doubt about everything). Raoul Hausmann displayed *Mechanical Head (Spirit of the Age)*, a wooden mannequin head with rulers and metal parts glued and nailed on to it. The assemblage-sculpture *Plastic-Dada-Dio-Drama: The Glory and Decadence of Germany*, created by the 'Superdada' messiah and architect Johannes Baader, depicted history as a heap of commercial debris.

A number of signs were posted on the wall: 'Take Dada Seriously', 'Dada is Political', and 'Art is Dead, Long Live Tatlin's New Machine Art'. The combined effect of the images, objects and messages was more that of a demented commercial advertisement than an art salon. In the exhibition catalogue, Hausmann proclaimed, 'Straight away one must emphasise that this Dada exhibition consists of the usual bluff, a cheap speculation preying upon the public's curiosity – it is not worth visiting.' With the newly established Weimar government in the throes of political, social and economic crisis, he decried the Dada exhibition as a bunch of 'pathetic rubbish' mounted by a 'decadent group, so totally void of ability or of serious intention' (Huelsenbeck, 1993: 135). In other words, the Berlin Dada Fair was a faithful, radical and absurd expression of the immediate post-war era.

The traumatic effects of the First World War on European economy, politics, society and culture can hardly be overestimated. With nearly 40 million casualties – 8.5 million soldiers dead, 25 million physically maimed or psychologically impaired, 4 million missing altogether – and with rationing and volunteerism demanded of the home front civilian population, the war had devastating effects on nearly everyone. At the level of political geography, Austria, Germany and Russia each lost their empires and the map of central Europe was entirely redrawn. The successful Bolshevik Revolution in Russia, the brief rise and collapse of the Bavarian Socialist and Hungarian Soviet Republics in 1918–19, and the failed 1919 Spartacist uprising in Berlin, had turned the spectre of communism into a political reality. Everywhere, Europeans suffered from material deprivations in the immediate aftermath of the war, most severely felt in Germany because of the extensive war reparations demanded by France and Britain. Over the next few years, a social and political consensus for a 'return to normalcy' emerged among the former combatants, as European nations across the continent strove to put the catastrophe of the war quickly behind. But the collective psychological trauma of war was not so easily assuaged.

Modernism was galvanised as a result of the war experience, particularly for artists and writers who served as soldiers as part of the 'Generation of 1914'. The general trajectory was one of frustrated heroism, entrenched disillusionment, and outright rejection of the politics and values of their elders. For some modernist artists and writers, this wholesale rejection translated into politically radicalised avant-garde movements. Many of these radical avant-garde groups adhered to the revolutionary communist left or at least displayed political sympathies in that direction. But others moved to the nationalist right, with the most extreme becoming supporters of fascism. And for the first time in history, with the advent of new communications technologies, the avant-garde had the potential means to distribute its messages directly to the masses.

In the early 1920s, wireless radio was transformed from a correspondence communications technology into a mass medium via both governmental and corporate broadcast systems. Daily news reportage, musical performances and dramatic productions, live or recorded, now could be heard by thousands or millions of people simultaneously. Innovations in phonograph recording technology, from cylindrical rolls to high-fidelity records that were easier to produce, permitted the unlimited and uniform sound reproduction for mass audiences for the first time in history. The cinema matured as well.

While movies during the pre-war era in many ways were still a 'primitive' medium – the early films of the Lumière brothers and Thomas Edison were more a sideshow attraction than a main feature – the decade following the First World War constituted the golden age of the silent cinema. During the 1920s, movies became a truly universal medium through the common language of film techniques (shots, lighting, montage), internationally famous screen stars (Charlie Chaplin, Fatty Arbuckle, Theda Bara, Pearl White, Douglas Fairbanks, Rudolph Valentino), renowned directors (Cecil B. DeMille, D. W. Griffith, Abel Gance, Fritz Lang, F. W. Murnau), and the establishment of worldwide film distribution systems. As Surrealist poet Philippe Soupault wrote to a mass newspaper audience, 'Faithful readers, we are not isolated, and we hear the heartbeat of the world itself' (Walz, 2000: 41). The dream of the avant-garde was to direct such media technologies towards the transformation of mass consciousness.

The first murmurs of the radical avant-garde were heard during the war, raised by an assortment of nonconformists and pacifists who refused to participate in patriotic slaughter and took refuge in the Swiss city of Zurich. There, in February 1916, the German Expressionist writer Hugo Ball opened the Cabaret Voltaire, an entertainment venue featuring chanteuse Emmy Hennings, who sang popular songs from Munich and Paris. Within a few months the cabaret had developed into something of an artistic and literary bohemian club, attracting an émigré clientele of artists and the curious from Germany, France, Italy, Hungary and Romania. In short order, the appearance and performances in the Cabaret Voltaire took on bizarre aspects. Abstract and primitivist art by Hans Arp and Augusto Giacometti were displayed on the walls. 'Simultaneous poetry' in multiple broken languages was performed by Tristan Tzara, Marcel Janco and Richard Huelsenbeck. Backed by a 'brutist' musical accompaniment of piano, banjos and drums, dancers in primitive masks designed by Janco hopped around the stage and shouted 'negro' chants. By the time the landlord closed down the club in July 1916, because of its utter commercial failure, the art and performances of the Cabaret Voltaire had a name – Dada.

The birth of Dada marked a crucial turning point for modernism as an anti-art movement. Convinced that European art, literature, philosophy and religion had produced the kind of nationalistic jingoism responsible for fanning the flames of war, the avant-garde project begun in the Cabaret Voltaire amounted to no less than the total rejection of the aesthetics and values of Western civilisation and their replacement by Dada, or baby blather (in French 'dada' is a child's word for hobbyhorse). Preferring Dada over the discontents of civilisation, the Dadaists sought a direct connection between the objective world and the subjective human experience by reducing art, language and music to their most primitive elements and endlessly recombining them in novel images, poetry and performances. The whole of Western civilisation would be swept away by Dada. 'DADA MEANS NOTHING', Tristan Tzara proclaimed in the *Dada Manifesto* of 1918 (**Doc. 8, pp. 125–7**). Provocation and irony were the critical tools of the anarchistic Zurich Dada movement.

To a degree more fully realised than any other modernist movement to that point, Zurich Dada employed primitivism in a modernist assault on contemporary society and values. The primitivism of Dada fed off an anti-art impulse to attack all cultural conventions, and then randomly reassemble the most basic elements of art, music, and language in new and novel ways. The Dadaist *Lautgedicht* (sound poem), for example, separated vowel and consonant sounds from the German language, and then recombined them to recreate a kind of primordial language, as this fragment from 'Karawane' ('Caravan', 1917) by Hugo Ball illustrates:

> jolifanto bambla ô falli bambla / grossigna m'pfa habla horem / égiga gora-men / higo bloiko russula huju / hollaka hollala / anlogo bung / blago bung / blago bung / bosso fataka / ü üü ü . . .
>
> (Huelsenbeck, 1993: 61)

While 'Karawane' was recited, other Dadaist *Lautgedichte* were concrete poems of typographic letters and symbols repeated to fill entire pages, as individual characters in random combination or as the same word printed over and over. Dubious transliterations of 'indigenous languages', presented as Maori work songs or 'negro' chants, and recited in live performance or published in Dada tracts, were experienced by modern Europeans only as an unintelligible cacophony of sounds. The culmination of the primitive *Lautgedichte* would later be realised in Kurt Schwitters's sound poem *Sonate in Urlauten* (*Sonata in Ur-Language*). Composed over a ten-year period, 1922–32, Schwitters continually compiled and revised his primordial language sonata, until the text ran over thirty pages in length and required several hours to perform. Radically democratic in impulse, Schwitters's *Ur-Sonata* reduced musical composition to the zero point, and then used the simplest poetic elements – sounds, rhythm, cadence – as a mode of direct, unmediated communication, and he entirely left it up to the performers to make determinations about tempo, pitch, dynamics, and emotional feelings.

Towards the end of the war, Dada collaborator Richard Huelsenbeck returned to Berlin and linked up with the artists George Grosz, Wieland Herzfelde, and John Heartfield to form Club Dada in January 1918. Continuing with the anti-art agenda from Zurich, the early impulse in Berlin Dada was, as the editor of the English translation of the *Dada Almanach* puts it, one of 'bluff and counter-bluff, bewilderment, and parody'. Club Dada chose writer and artist Raoul Hausmann as the movement's 'Dadasopher' and heralded an apocalyptic Christian prophet named Johannes Baader as their 'Superdada'. Yet with the collapse of Imperial Germany in November 1918, the subsequent communist uprisings in Bavaria and Berlin, and the slaughter of communists by the roving paramilitary *Freikorps*, Berlin Dada quickly moved in a revolutionary political direction. With disdain for the newly established Weimar Republic and admiration for the successful Bolshevik Revolution in Russia, Berlin Dada produced deliberately provocative political art from the ephemeral materials of mass media. Montages from newspaper print and magazine images emphasised dehumanisation within the chaos of post-war life. Photomontage posters, particularly those of John Heartfield, criticised the government and military. The Dada Advertising Company attacked the values of capitalism and the decadent lifestyles of the bourgeoisie. The culmination of the movement was realised in the First International Dada Fair of 1920 and the subsequent publication of the *Dada Almanach*, edited by Huelsenbeck, with contributions from an international Dada cadre that included Tristan Tzara, Francis Picabia, Philippe Soupault, Georges Ribemont-Dessaignes, Hans Arp and Walter Mehring.

As in Zurich, Berlin Dada continued to fuse the modern and the 'primitive' through a variety of techniques. Foremost among these was photomontage, a relatively simple technique of cutting and pasting images and words from the media ephemera – newspapers, magazines, advertising images, photographs, movie stills – and then reassembling them into pastiche collages. In Berlin Dada, the 'primitive sources' were crude photographic reproductions of industrial machinery, mass consumer culture, and portraits of political leaders published in newspapers and magazines, assembled to deliver radical political and social critiques directed against the Weimar Republic (and later Nazi Germany), perhaps most skilfully accomplished by John Heartfield. Even when masks, statuettes, or artefacts from Africa or Oceania were incorporated in Berlin Dada photomontages, such as the *Aus einem ethnographischen Museum* ('From an Ethnographic Museum,' 1926) series by Hannah Höch, the purpose of the hybrid primitive-modern imagery was to create critical images through which moderns perceive themselves as an *exot*, foreign or 'other', within contemporary society and culture. When combined with a keen sense of modernist aesthetics, this relatively simple production technique yielded highly provocative images of uncertain meaning.

In the mid-nineteen twenties, the politically committed **Neue Sachlichkeit** or 'New Objectivity' movement surpassed the radical impulses of Berlin Dada. Leading artists in the movement included George Grosz and Otto Dix, members of the German Communist Party who painted unflinchingly stark depictions of middle-class greed, commodified sexuality, and military and political corruption into their works. In the arts journal *Das Kunstblatt*,

Neue Sachlichkeit: German phrase meaning 'New Objectivity', a highly politicised modernist style of pictorial painting and collage construction that criticised the collusion between government and big business, and portrayed class conflict in post-war Weimar society.

Grosz wrote about the inability of aesthetic techniques alone to be revolutionary, and he admonished avant-garde artists to become more politically engaged:

> Go to a proletarian meeting; look and listen how people there, people just like you, discuss some small improvement of their lot.
> And understand – these masses are the ones who are reorganizing the world. Not you! But you can work with them. You could help them if you wanted to! And that way you could learn to give your art a content which was supported by the revolutionary ideals of the workers.
>
> (Harrison and Wood, 2003: 273)

For Grosz, this meant an objective, practical, political and applied art, not the 'inner psychology' of Expressionist art, which he lambasted as 'stuffed with cabalistic and metaphysical hocus-pocus'. *Neue Sachlichkeit* also gained expression in the theatre, in the politically engaged plays of Bertolt Brecht such as *Mann ist Mann* (*Man Equals Man*, 1927) and *Die Dreigroschenoper* (*Three-Penny Opera*, 1929), and in stage adaptations of controversial films and novels by Edwin Piscator.

It was in the newly established Soviet Union, however, that the radical avant-garde was put directly into the service of communism. During the early and experimental years of the New Economic Policy (NEP) in the 1920s, after the October Revolution of 1917 and following a bitterly fought civil war, Anatoly Lunacharsky was made the Bolshevik Commissar of Enlightenment. Lunacharsky recruited artists, poets, actors and filmmakers into the **Prolekult** ('proletarian culture') movement to proselytise the new Soviet citizenry about the virtues of communism. Some avant-garde artists and writers readily responded to Lunacharsky's call to participate in this utopian political project of building a new communist society from scratch. Foremost among these was Constructivism, the leading radical avant-garde movement in Eastern Europe at that time that had emerged from the earlier Supremacist movement in geometrical abstract painting.

Prolekult: Russian contraction of *proletarskaya kultura* or 'proletarian culture', refers to the use of avant-garde visual art, literature, drama and film to create a revolutionary working class in the early Soviet Union.

The *Constructivist Manifesto* of 1921 proclaimed, 'We consider self-sufficient studio art and our activity as mere painters to be useless . . . We declare industrial art absolute and Constructivism its only form of expression' (Gleason et al., 1985: 204). Constructivists utterly rejected the nineteenth-century notion of 'art for art's sake' and insisted upon an immediate and applied function to art, fusing technology with modern design towards solving practical problems in everyday life. Yet many Constructivists were also committed to the most aesthetically radical aspects of modernism, such as abstract painting and sculpture, experimental theatre and music, and modernist poetry, literature and photography published in the review *LEF* ('Left

Front of the Arts'). Some Constructivist projects were visionary to the point of grandiosity, such as architect Vladimir Tatlin's model for the unrealised *Monument to the Third International* (1919), a proposed iron and glass skyscraper based on the principle of an ascending spiral, designed to house Soviet governmental planning agencies (*see* cover image).

Placed in direct service to the state, Constructivists were employed to apply their art for everyday purposes. For example, Russian Cubo-Futurist poet Vladimir Mayakovsky collaborated with Constructivist painter and photographer Alexander Rodchenko to design posters, advertising copy and product logos for ordinary Soviet consumer goods and clothing fashions. Motion pictures represented perhaps the supreme expression of the Constructivist fusion of technology and art. Whether or not Lenin actually said 'of all the arts, for us the cinema is the most important', there is no doubt that the Soviets seized upon film's propaganda potential. Constructivist techniques in film montage in both feature films and documentaries, pioneered by Sergei Eisenstein in *Battleship Potemkin* (1925), Vsevolod Pudovkin in *Mother* (1926) and Dziga Vertov in *Man with a Movie Camera* (1929), were cutting edge in their era and have had a lasting impact upon the development of cinema. Not limited to the Soviet Union, Constructivism became an international movement with two major conferences held in 1922, the Constructivist Congress of Progressive Artists in Düsseldorf and the Dada-Constructivist meeting in Weimar. Constructivism aspired to close the distance between art and industry towards an internationalist agenda of creating a new, socialist world.

In post-war France, the cultural and political situation was altogether different. Unlike defeated Imperial Germany or Tsarist Russia, the victorious French Third Republic had survived the Great War. But victory had been achieved at the cost of one and a half million French soldiers killed and more than double that number permanently maimed and psychologically traumatised. In homage, war memorials were constructed across northern France, the site of the Western Front. Soon, though, the mood of the country shifted towards a desire to 'return to normalcy'. In this search for wholeness, some members of the pre-war avant-garde retreated from some of their more radical modernist experiments, such as Picasso who returned to a neo-classical period of portraiture and paintings. Others sought to forget the immediate past by losing themselves in the frivolities of *les années folles*, the 'crazy years' of the jazz age. For the fashion set, popular entertainment was preferable to dwelling upon war trauma.

Among some of the young Frenchmen of the 'Generation of 1914', however, the war was not something to be commemorated and then forgotten, but served as the impetus to revolutionise consciousness and society through art. These young war veterans included André Breton, Louis Aragon, Paul

Éluard, Benjamin Péret and Philippe Soupault, who embraced the provocative tactics of Dada as their anti-establishment mode of expression. The zeal
of Paris Dada was reinforced by the subsequent inclusion of the artists Marcel
Duchamp, Max Ernst, Francis Picabia and Zurich Dada founder Tristan
Tzara into the Paris Dada entourage. Within a few years, however, Breton
in particular had become dissatisfied with the anti-art stance of Dada, and
he proposed a new movement – Surrealism. Where Dada dismantled art,
Surrealism would create a new reality, a *sur*-reality, that would embrace the
modern world at a higher level of consciousness.

In the *Manifesto of Surrealism* (1924), Breton declared, 'Surrealism is based
on the belief in the superior reality of certain forms of associations hitherto
neglected, in the omnipotence of dream, in the disinterested play of thought'
(**Doc. 9, pp. 127–9**). The goal was to reconfigure consciousness by breaking old patterns of thought, what Breton called the 'paucity of reality', to
form entirely new, richer and more complex images of modern life based
upon juxtapositions between seemingly dissimilar elements. Surrealist art
was not to be based upon preconceived ideas or aesthetics, but would be
expressed through dream imagery drawn from the Freudian psychological
unconscious, as well as from the vast terrain of found objects (*la trouvaille*)
littering the modern cultural landscape. The Surrealists developed a range of
techniques to invoke the kinds of uncanny, disturbing experiences that
would enhance surreal perceptions, from word-and-image 'exquisite corpse'
games to 'automatic writing' in semi-trance dream states, to create new and
superior forms of literature and art that would be experienced by readers
or viewers as 'convulsive beauty'. While many early surrealists' works were
literary, it was later through painting that Surrealism became more widely
known through the work of such artists as André Masson, Yves Tanguy,
Salvador Dalí and René Magritte.

Like Berlin Dada and Russian Constructivism, Paris Surrealism associated itself politically with the socialist and communist left. But the political
orientation of the radical avant-garde was not necessarily leftist, and in
some instances modernist artists and movements moved in the direction
of fascist right. In 1919, Marinetti and other Futurists participated in the
foundation of the Italian Fascist Party. After spending twenty-one days in
prison with Mussolini at the end of that year, Marinetti became fervently
anti-communist. In *Futurism and Fascism* (1924), he proclaimed his
avant-garde movement to be the forerunner of Mussolini's 'New Italy' and
his support remained unabated in his openly fascist journal *Futurismo* of
the 1930s.

In France, too, some modernists were drawn to fascism. French writer
Pierre Drieu la Rochelle, like many of his Surrealist contemporaries, had
been part of the disillusioned Generation of 1914. But unlike his leftist

colleagues, Drieu had been exhilarated by the experience of war and felt deflated afterwards by the absence of its intensity. In works of fiction, most notably in *Gilles* (1939), as well as in his life, Drieu flirted with fascist fantasies of power. During the collaborationist Vichy era, Drieu became the chief editor at the Gallimard publishing firm and director of its highbrow literary review, the *Nouvelle Revue Française* (NRF).

The American poet Ezra Pound was enticed by fascism as well. Together with the Canadian modernist writer Wyndham Lewis, the two co-founded the Anglo-American literary and visual movement of Vorticism in direct and sympathetic response to Marinetti's Futurism. In 1925, Pound moved to Italy, became an open admirer of Mussolini, and even made pro-fascist radio broadcasts during the Second World War. (After the war, Pound was arrested by Italian partisans as a traitor, and he was subsequently deported to the United States where he was confined to a mental asylum.) Such fascist affiliations suggest that the modernist fantasies of revolutions in consciousness and politics among the avant-garde could drift in various radical directions.

Yet there were other members of the radical avant-garde for whom modernist art itself, more than its explicit political uses, remained the impetus for the transformation of mass consciousness and society. This was the case with Purism in painting, which grew out of Cubism (**Doc. 10, pp. 129–32**). Inspired by Fernand Léger's ideas about analytical Cubism and by the De Stijl movement in design, the modernist painter Amédée Ozenfant and the Swiss draftsman and writer Le Corbusier (the pseudonym of Charles-Édouard Jeanneret) launched the Purist movement in art and architecture as a call to 'return to order' (*rappel à l'ordre*). As articulated in a co-authored article on Purism from 1920, 'The highest delectation of the human mind is the perception of order, and the greatest human satisfaction is the feeling of collaboration or participation in this order' (Harrison and Wood, 2003: 241). In the same way that Taylorism or 'scientific management' was being applied to factory production, Le Corbusier advocated a scientific attitude of 'serious rigour' in art and architectural design, as advocated in his monthly international review *L'Esprit Nouveau* and his essays collected in *Towards a New Architecture* (1922). From the Purist perspective, standardisation should be as universal in art, design and architecture as it was in machine production.

The International Exposition of Decorative Arts held in Paris in 1925 provided Le Corbusier with an opportunity to promote his ideas in a public forum. From Le Corbusier's point of view, Art Deco, the pre-eminent modern style of the era, was not truly modernist in design. Instead of making geometric patterns fundamental to architectural, interior and object design, he criticised Art Deco for relegating geometric designs to decorative elements that masked over the fundamental features of buildings, rooms or household objects. Instead, Le Corbusier sought uniformity between designs, materials and manufacturing methods. After much haggling, Le Corbusier was permitted space to display a model apartment based on his designs in the Exposition (although his exhibition project for a prefabricated apartment and garden complex remained unrealised). From Le Corbusier and Ozenfant's Purist perspective, artist-engineers should plan out all aspects of modern life, from urban planning to the level of daily life of homes, furniture and commodities, to bring humans into greater harmony with rational design. Whether humans would want to be transformed by Le Corbusier's world, however, was a separate issue. With the later exceptions of some housing projects in the United States and the urban planning of Brazilia, few of Le Corbusier's architectural plans were fully realised. His influence upon modernist architectural theory, however, was tremendous.

The **Bauhaus** school of modernist art and design by contrast, founded in Weimar in 1919, had widespread international resonance on both the theoretical and practical levels. First directed by the German architect Walter Gropius, the Bauhaus synthesised the aesthetic concerns of the arts academy with the practical activities of the arts and crafts school across the trades: sculpture, carpentry, metalwork, pottery, stained glass, painting, textiles, and finally architectural design. In sharp contrast to Le Corbusier's narrowly analytical and hierarchical model, where elite artist-engineers dictate which designs are implemented for public benefit, the Bauhaus developed a workshop model of innovation and application (**Doc. 11, pp. 132–4**). Under the guidance of workshop masters, at the first level of instruction students were introduced to craft materials. At the second level, they grappled with form problems that examined how theoretical problems of space, colour and composition are addressed with specific tools, construction methods and representational values. This workshop model attracted renowned artists from throughout Europe to the Bauhaus, including the Dutch Neo-Plasticist Theo van Doesburg, the Russian Constructivist El Lissitzky, the German-American Cubist Lyonel Feiniger, the Swiss Expressionist and Cubist Paul Klee, and the Russian Abstract-Expressionist Wassily Kandinsky.

While the nomenclature of workshops might seem to suggest a return to artisanal modes of production, the Bauhaus developed in the direction of modern industrial design and production methods, particularly after the addition of the Hungarian Constructivist László Moholy-Nagy to the faculty. This orientation was made explicit in a position paper, 'Art and Technology: A New Unity', delivered by Gropius at the first Bauhaus exhibition of 1923. The exhibition provided the first major opportunity for the Bauhaus to showcase its products: an experimental house with angular design and a flat roof, a model for a thirty-storey glass skyscraper, painted wall murals, crafted items from book typography to electric lamps, and a 'Bauhaus Week'

Bauhaus: An art and architectural school in Weimar Germany that combined practical training in craft materials with the study of aesthetic theory in a workshop setting towards solving 'form problems' in architecture and design.

of musical and dramatic performances. Through this public event, Gropius tried to steer a neutral political course through the turbulent political waters of the early Weimar Republic, although the Bauhaus's affiliations with Constructivism caused friction with the more conservative political elements within the local city government.

In April 1925, the Bauhaus was forced to close down in Weimar, reopening later that year in the industrial city of Dessau. After the relocation, the school set up its own company, Bauhaus GmbH (Ltd), to begin to produce and distribute commercial products in addition to being architectural and design laboratories. The principles of Bauhaus, Gropius declared, encompassed the total fusion of modern aesthetic, human and industrial needs:

> A decided positive attitude toward the living environment of vehicles and machines.
> The organic shaping of things in accordance with their own current laws, avoiding all romantic embellishment and whimsy.
> Restriction of basic forms and colours to what is typical and universally intelligible.
> Simplicity in complexity, economy in the use of space, materials, time and money.

> (Willet, 1978: 119)

Through the exploration of modernist aesthetics, the Bauhaus avant-garde became deeply committed to social change. That is, innovations in technique and theory alone were insufficient to bring about a cultural revolution: the implementation of large-scale and collective projects based upon modernist aesthetics would be required in order to achieve social transformations. Over the next few years, Gropius designed and supervised the construction of the Törten housing estate and municipal buildings for the city of Dessau. While starting from different foundations, Gropius came to share with Le Corbusier the goal of engineering better modern living through industrial design, which influenced an entire generation of modernist architects.

By the mid-1920s, the radical avant-garde had reached a crisis point. Arising from the ashes of the First World War, Zurich Dada had constituted a frontal assault on the aesthetics and values of Western civilisation, but within a few short years its anti-art impulse had been reshaped and diversified into a variety of modernist movements. In Russia, the Constructivist avant-garde assisted in building the Soviet Union, while in Berlin the highly politicised *Neue Sachlichkeit* operated in opposition to the Weimar Republic. In Italy, Futurism had committed itself to the fascist state. In France, Surrealism strove to expand human consciousness through dismantling reality and reassembling it all into new and more powerful images. In Germany, the Bauhaus attempted to unify modernist aesthetics with industrial methods to address real social and commercial needs. In all of its varieties, modernism was no longer simply an aesthetic and theoretical enterprise, but had become a concerted effort to effect widespread transformations in European society and culture.

Further reading

Andrews, Richard and Milena Kalinovska (eds), *Art into Life: Russian Constructivism 1914–1932*, New York: Rizzoli, 1990.

Batchelor, David, Paul Wood and Briony Fer, *Realism, Rationalism, Surrealism: Art Between the Wars*, New Haven: Yale University Press, 1993.

Bayer, Herbert, Walter Gropius and Ise Gropius, *Bauhaus 1919–1928*, New York: The Museum of Modern Art, 1938.

Caws, Mary Ann, *Surrealism*, London: Phaidon Press, 2010.

Gleason, Abbot, Peter Kenez and Richard Stites (eds), *Bolshevik Culture: Experiment and Order in the Russian Revolution*, Bloomington: Indiana University Press, 1985.

Kaes, Anton, Martin Jay and Edward Dimendberg, *The Weimar Sourcebook, 1918–1933*, Berkeley: University of California Press, 1995.

Le Cobusier (Charles-Edouard Jeanneret), *Towards a New Architecture* (1922), Thousand Oaks, CA: BN Publishing, 2008.

Motherwell, Robert (ed.), *The Dada Painters and Poets: An Anthology* (2nd edn, trans. Ralph Manheim), Cambridge, MA: Belknap Press of Harvard University Press, 1988.

Nadeau, Maurice, *The History of Surrealism* (trans. Richard Howard), Cambridge, MA: The Belknap Press of Harvard University Press, 1989.

Polizzotti, Mark, *Revolution of the Mind: The Life of Andre Breton*, New York: Farrar, Straus and Giroux, 1995.

Witkovsky, Matthew S. (ed.), *Avant-Garde Art in Everyday Life: Early Twentieth-Century European Modernism*, Chicago: Art Institute of Chicago, 2011.

6

The New Sobriety

I n the 1930s, Europe was in the throes of severe political crises. The Nazi seizure of power occurred in Germany in 1933, and the regime quickly allied with the Italian Fascist state that had already been in existence for over a decade. In June 1935, the International Writers Congress for the Defence of Culture convened in Paris to deliver speeches before an assembled international audience of nearly 3,000 people that called for a 'Popular Front' against fascism. In 1936, a broad coalition of centrist and leftist political parties successfully formed Popular Front governments in France and Spain. In June of the same year, the Spanish nationalist General Francisco Franco, with military backing from Fascist Italy and Nazi Germany, launched a civil war to overthrow the legitimately elected Second Spanish Republic. The only nation to give direct military assistance to Spain was the Soviet Union, which at the time was in the process of conducting purges of the old Bolshevik leaders, as well as against massive numbers of the rank and file Communist Party membership. With the Spanish Civil War in full flame, French Socialist Prime Minister Léon Blum called for an International Exhibition in Paris the following year to symbolise the united power of parliamentary democracies to combat fascist oppression.

However, when the World's Fair opened in May 1937, the intended centrepiece, the Peace Pavilion, was dwarfed by the massive presence of Europe's two most powerful anti-democratic regimes, Nazi Germany and the Soviet Union, whose pavilions symbolically faced off across the Champs de Mars. The tallest was the German Pavilion, designed by the Nazi architect Albert Speer in a **neo-classical** style with an enormous eagle perched upon the precipice to command the view below. Opposite, the Soviet pavilion was a colossal cement block building designed by the architect Boris Iofan, crowned by the heroic and multi-storeyed statues, *Industrial Worker and Collective Farm Woman* designed by the sculptor Vera Mukhina, raising hammer

neo-classical: Refers to the impulse to 'return to classical order' in themes and styles of modern art, architecture and literature.

and sickle to the heavens. The hope that the Popular Front could use the world's fair to realise a brighter future through the collective strength of a united humanity was overshadowed by these monumental twin spectres of power and might.

Among the nations participating in the International Exhibition, the beleaguered Second Spanish Republic had assembled a pavilion. Spain's Popular Front government was being torn asunder by severe political and social discord, Franco's civil war from the ultra-nationalist right and by political agitation for greater regional autonomy in Catalonia from the anarchist left. Amidst this crisis, the Surrealist painter Joan Miró suppressed his strong Catalan sympathies and agreed to support the Republic. His major contribution to the Spanish Pavilion was a wall mural, five and a half metres high and three and a half metres wide, called *The Reaper*. Although done in an abstract style with bold colours, primarily red, blue, yellow, white and black, the painting was recognisably a portrait of a peasant holding a sickle in one hand, raising his other arm in a salute to the Republic, and wearing the traditional red Catalonian cap – a didactic Popular Front message calling for the union of socialism, republicanism and regional autonomy against the fascist enemy. Even more explicit was Miró's poster, mass-produced for sale to tourists at the low price of one franc apiece, of a man with a massive forearm raised in a fist and bearing the slogan *Aidez l'Espagne* (*Help Spain*) (*see* Plate 3). While Miró's images were unquestionably modernist, the messages were unambiguous.

The Spanish Republican government had also commissioned Picasso, by then the most renowned modernist artist in all of Europe, to make a monumental work for the pavilion. For several months Picasso had prepared a series of sketches for a multi-panelled mural called the *Dream and Lie of Franco*. But he abruptly changed course after learning about the massacre in the Basque capital of Guernica on 26 April. At the request of General Franco, an attack squadron of Nazi bombers and fighter planes had levelled the entire town within three short hours, killing one-third of its inhabitants. On May Day, the previously apolitical Picasso made the radical decision to scrap the mural project, and he began a series of sketches that became the colossal oil painting, *Guernica*. The horizontal counterpart to Miró's mural, Picasso's enormous Cubist montage was three and one-half metres tall, nearly eight metres wide, and painted entirely in grey tones. The painting's stark images depict a fallen soldier in agony, terrified women crying and screaming, a frightened horse braying, an impassive bull staring at the viewer, and an electrical light that resembled a mechanical eye illuminating the entire scene. The emotionally provocative modernist painting was difficult for some tourists to assimilate. Purportedly when a Nazi officer visiting the exhibition asked Picasso, 'Did you do that?' the painter replied, 'No, you did' (Foster et al., 2004: 285).

The story of the Paris International Exhibition, with its contrasts between Miró's and Picasso's contributions to the Spanish Pavilion, provide a historical point of departure for re-evaluating a variety of challenges faced by the modernist avant-garde as the self-stylised harbingers of a cultural revolution during the 1930s. Not only were Nazi Germany and Soviet Russia powerful political antagonists, each totalitarian regime put an end to the modernist artistic experimentation that had flourished in their respective countries during the previous decades. Now, Hitler and Stalin each promoted his particular version of heroic art. For Nazi Germany, state-sanctioned art was rendered in a grandiose neo-classical style that promoted the 'Aryan' ideals of the *Volksgemeinschaft* ('German national community'). In the Soviet Union, the official policy in art became **Socialist Realism**, an idealised version of reality that portrayed a brighter communist future as a continuation of the present. Along related lines, Fascist Italy, which had originally been receptive to Futurism, cooled to avant-garde modernism in favour of more heroic and government-sponsored art and architectural projects. In all these cases, the modernist avant-garde had either submitted to official policy, or it had been eliminated.

Socialist Realism: Modern style of realistic art in the Soviet Union that idealised the heroic role of the Soviet leadership, working class and agricultural workers as the vanguard of future communism.

In the case of the Popular Front, the differences between the contributions by Miró and Picasso to the Spanish Pavilion highlight tensions in the relationship of modernist art to politics that troubled parliamentary and socialist democracies during the 1930s. Of the two artists, Miró was more rigorous in his theoretical understanding of modernist aesthetics, and he was already politically dedicated to the cause of Catalonian political autonomy. Yet given the political exigencies, for the Spanish pavilion Miró proved willing to tone down his radical ideas and commitments to produce a kind of modernist art that would be accessible to a wide audience. The clarity of the message for the public trumped modernist impulses towards experimentation and innovation, with their attendant ambivalences and uncertainties of meaning. Equally uncharacteristic for Picasso, at a time when he had finally secured international recognition as one of the greatest artists of the age, his art became radicalised. For the Spanish Pavilion he had produced a modernist painting so politically charged and viscerally shocking that some visitors to the exhibition avoided it. For a brief moment, *Guernica* expressed the complete fusion of avant-garde cultural and political revolutionary agendas. Yet this accomplishment would prove to be the exception, both within the broader spectrum of modernist art during this era and in Picasso's career.

The art critic and historian John Willett refers to this period in modernism, extending from the late 1920s to the eve of the Second World War, as 'the new sobriety'. For some modernists, sobriety entailed the trade-off of giving up some of their more radical avant-garde ideas and projects in order to secure corporate and government contracts or to gain commercial success in galleries and publications. That is, success in modernist art was redefined to mean that it should reach a broad public, and that this goal should be placed above ideological or avant-garde aspirations. By contrast, for politically engaged artists and writers sobriety meant that modernist art needed to be less ambiguous, esoteric and frivolous, and instead more explicit and direct in its political messages. In both cases, the earlier avant-garde assumption that the transformation of modernist aesthetics alone would create a cultural revolution now seemed insufficient.

One of the fields where modernism first began to have visible effects on a wide scale was in architecture. When the Bauhaus moved to Dessau, Walter Gropius contracted with the city to build housing estates and municipal buildings for the Törten industrial region south of the city in the late 1920s. Under the guidance of similarly minded modernist architects, such as Adolf Meyer and Ludwig Mies van der Rohe, additional housing estates followed in Berlin, Frankfurt-am-Main, Stuttgart, Breslau and several other major cities in Weimar Germany. Not limited to Germany, architecture became the first modernist field to benefit from international organisation and a common aesthetic, known as the International Style. By 1929 the International Congress of Modern Architecture (CIAM) had been established, with representatives from England, France, Finland, Hungary, Poland, Sweden, Switzerland, the Soviet Union and the United States, with Gropius and Le Corbusier as the movement's guiding figures.

In Fascist Italy, modernist architecture achieved indirect success through Mussolini's 'New Towns' project that included housing construction in more than 13 towns and 60 rural settlements between 1928 and 1940. In contrast to the high architectural modernism of Bauhaus and *L'Esprit Nouveau*, these fascist New Towns were supposed to blend ancient imperial Roman and traditional medieval forms with modern housing design. Since Mussolini wanted these housing projects to be completed quickly, within a year if possible, centralised planning was required. This had the effect of drawing many of Italy's leading Rationalist architects, such as Giuseppe Terragni and Pietro Lingeri, into the New Town projects. The towns themselves were supposed to be modelled after Roman villas, with the town's buildings organised into a fascist hierarchy, placing the town hall and the Casa del Fascio (Fascist Party headquarters) at the city centre. Generally, the larger the urban centre, the more modernist the architecture, as was the case with the Casa del Fascio designed by Terragni in the northern Italian city of Como. In small town and rural settings, housing tended to blend modern, ancient and medieval design, although even here in low-income apartment projects, such as those in the provincial capital of Littoria, modernist style sometimes predominated. Thus, while the New Town movement was driven by fascist politics, the participation of Rationalist architects and urban planners to accomplish the vast housing projects meant that modernism was becoming a daily reality for average Italians.

In England, the expansion and renovation of the London Underground brought modernism to the masses not only through architectural design, but also through the display of modernist art, sculpture and advertising posters within the subway system. Frank Pick, the de facto director of the Underground Group and the managing director of the London Passenger Transport Board after 1933, led the effort to renovate and expand the Underground. Pick was committed to the idea that everything about the subway system, from the architecture of the stations to interior design, benches and trash bins, should be thoroughly modern and of high quality. The designers charged with carrying out this task were members of the Design and Industries Association (DIA), an arts and crafts movement whose conception of modernism was moderated by the utopian ideas of the late-Victorian art critic John Ruskin and the romantic socialist William Morris.

The modernist architect Charles Holden designed the new Underground stations, concurring with Pick's notion that everything about the system should be modern, rational and edifying for passengers. Therefore, in addition to architectural design, the exteriors and interiors of the stations were decorated with modernist art. Modernist sculptures by Jacob Epstein, Eric Hill and Henry Moore were commissioned for the new Underground corporate headquarters. Most Underground passengers encountered modernist posters done in Post-Impressionist, Fauvist, Cubist and Surrealist styles by such renowned artists as E. McKnight Kauffer, Paul Nash, Graham Sutherland, Edward Wadsworth and Man Ray. The objective was to turn the Underground into 'the people's picture-gallery'. Bloomsbury artist and critic Roger Fry resoundingly approved of the Underground poster-art project, commenting upon 'the alacrity and intelligence people can show in front of a poster which if it had been a picture in a gallery would have been roundly declared unintelligible' (Saler, 1999: 101). While tightly knit communities of artists, writers and critics such as the Bloomsbury Group constituted modernist avant-garde elites, the London Underground brought modernism to the masses.

In the Soviet Union, by contrast, avant-garde modernism was swept aside with Stalin's rise to power. In the wake of the Bolshevik Revolution, modernist artists and writers had benefited from the support of the state and exercised partial autonomy in the nascent Soviet Union as organised under the New Economic Policy (NEP). In an effort to rapidly modernise the economy and create the new communist society, NEP mixed state projects with commercial initiatives. With the ascension of Stalin to power in 1927, and the implementation of the first industrial Five Year Plan and the collectivisation of agriculture the following year, the favour previously enjoyed by avant-garde artists, writers and intellectuals came to an end. Initially, members of the modernist avant-garde who had benefited under NEP, such as those writers and artists who constituted the LEF ('Left Front of the Arts'), rallied behind Stalin as their new patron. Within short order, however, all independent movements and groups were banned and were replaced by official Communist Party organisations, such as the Union of Soviet Writers established in 1932.

Aesthetics became official under the Stalinist state, a development welcomed by those Soviet artists and writers who had little patience with elitist avant-garde movements such as Constructivism. The Association of Artists of Revolutionary Russia (**AKhRR**), founded in 1922, insisted that art should be made for, and readily understood by, the working class. The AKhRR judged that the modernist experiments in abstraction and montage, evident in the poetry of Vladimir Mayakovsky, the visual art of Alexander Rodchenko and the *Kino-glaz* ('camera's eye') techniques of filmmaker Dziga Vertov, were incomprehensible and unpopular. Instead, the AKhRR advocated a 'heroic realism' in art and literature, a position favoured by such traditional portraiture painters as Alexander Deineka, Isaak Brodsky and Alexander Gerasimov. The truth of art, the AKhRR argued, was not derived purely from aesthetics, but was established through ideological support for the proletariat as displayed through art. Or, as Stalin put it in more blunt terms, proper Soviet art should be 'pictures that were comprehensible to the masses, and portraits that did not require you to guess who was portrayed' (Foster et al., 2004: 263). In place of confusing modernist aesthetics, Soviet art moved towards a near photo-realism in portraits of famous leaders, such as Lenin and Stalin, and heroic imagery of proletarian men and women in the factories and the fields.

This kind of heroic realism was made official state art policy by Cultural Commissar Andrei Zhdanov in the First All Union Congress of Writers in 1934. Known as Socialist Realism, official Soviet art adhered to five principles. The first was *narodnost* (art 'of the people'), an imperative to portray common Soviet workers with dignity as understood by popular sentiment. The second was *klassovost* ('class consciousness'), which conveyed the historic role of the working class in leading the Communist revolution worldwide. Third, *partiynost* ('party adherence') required that art conform to officially established Soviet standards. The fourth principle, *ideynost* ('ideologically correct'), meant that any new forms or attitudes in art had to be approved by the Party. Finally, *tipichnost* ('typicality') stipulated that iconic socialist figures such as industrial workers and farm labourers should be portrayed heroically and in familiar settings.

In a complete reversal of modernist aesthetics, and in sharp contrast to the Constructivist avant-garde which had pursued artistic experimentation and innovation as a means of transforming human consciousness, the political

AKhRR (Association of Artists of Revolutionary Russia): An association of Soviet figurative painters that favoured 'heroic realism' over modernist abstraction in ideological support of the proletariat.

and ideological demands of Socialist Realism restricted the possible meanings of art. Some eminent NEP artists, such as the writer Maxim Gorky, the
film director Sergei Eisenstein and the architect and designer El Lissitsky,
successfully made the transition to Stalinism and in some instances even
continued to flourish. Others, such as the artist Alexander Rodchenko and
the writer Boris Pasternak, strove to adapt but became disillusioned with
Stalinism over time. Still others became victims of the regime, such as the
poets Vladimir Mayakovsky, who took his own life in 1930, and Osip
Mandelstam, who was exiled to the Siberian gulag (where he subsequently
died). For the next half-century, modernist art was driven underground in
the Soviet Union.

In Germany, by contrast, the new sobriety entailed redoubled efforts
toward political radicalisation. Although the Weimar Republic had achieved
some measure of political stability by the mid-1920s, from the perspective of
leftist artists and writers severe social and economic inequities continued to
plague the country. Class conflicts were caricatured in oppositions of a decadent bourgeoisie versus an impoverished proletariat, often embodied in the
figure of the female prostitute. Portrait painting emerged as one of the preferred genres among *Neue Sachlichkeit* artists. However, the 'new objectivity'
did not seek photo-realism in portraiture, but combined Abstract Expressionist
and Cubist techniques with figurative painting, producing jarring effects
that were characteristic of the works of Max Beckmann, George Grosz and
Otto Dix. Through their disorienting and provocative paintings, these *Neue
Sachlichkeit* artists were strident in their anti-bourgeois ire and explicit in
their sympathy with the working class. Such harsh depictions of economic
hardship, class conflict and political corruption were not limited to the
highly politicised art of the *Neue Sachlichkeit*, but were also becoming common in the mass media, as seen for example in the long-established satirical
weekly magazine *Simplicissimus* and in movies like G. W. Pabst's *Pandora's
Box* (1929) and *The Blue Angel* (1930).

With the onset of global economic depression in 1930, however, the
fragile political consensus of the Weimar Republic collapsed. As the Social
Democrats lost the centre coalition, both the radical right and left quickly
picked up seats in parliament, the Nazis at twice the rate of the Communists.
In this changed political context, the German radical avant-garde turned its
activities against Nazism, perhaps best seen in the 1930s' photomontages
of John Heartfield for the covers of the *Arbeiter-Illustrierte-Zeitung* (*A.-I.-Z.*,
'Workers' Illustrated Paper'). In one photomontage entitled 'The Meaning
of the Hitler Salute', a diminutive Führer with arm raised behind his head
received a big wad of money from a fat capitalist who stood behind him, with
the caption, 'Millions stand behind me!' Another called 'German Natural
History' depicted the evolution of a caterpillar with the head of Friedrich

Ebert, the First President of the Weimar Republic, crawling along an oak branch twig, followed by a hanging pupa with the head of the successive President, Paul von Hindenburg, and finally to Hitler as a death-skull moth liberated in flight above. All wore the same top hat to remind *A.-I.-Z.* readers that this was indeed the metamorphosis of the same political creature. In 'Hurray, the butter is all gone!' a poor working-class family gathered around the dinner table eat bicycle parts, metal weights and gardening tools, while the baby in a carriage takes a bite out of a hatchet with a swastika on it. The photomontage displayed a quote by Nazi leader Hermann Goering about how iron makes the nation strong, while butter and lard make people fat. Through these kinds of interplay between photographic images and captions, standard techniques used in commercial advertising, Heartfield assembled his photomontages in support of the working-class struggle against Nazism.

With the burning of the Reichstag parliament building and Hitler's ascension to power in 1933, however, the radical avant-garde was eliminated in Germany altogether. In short order, the Nazi Party purged over 20,000 works of modernist art from museums, and then put hundreds of the pillaged pieces on display in the **Entartete Kunst** ('Degenerate Art') exhibit in Munich in 1937. Works by Kandinsky, Klee, Picasso and other renowned modernist artists, as well as a reconstruction of the Berlin Dada Fair, were presented to the public as negative examples of 'Jewish' and 'Bolshevistic' art. Concurrently, the *Großen Deutschen Kunstausstellung* ('Great German Art Exhibition') opened in Munich to showcase heroic and 'Aryan' works produced by over 1,600 approved German artists. Ironically, five times as many people visited the degenerate art exhibit, which the Nazis toured throughout Germany and Austria over a three-year period.

Entartete Kunst: German phrase meaning 'Degenerate Art' used by the Nazis in a 1937 exhibition to characterise modernist art as 'Jewish' and 'Bolshevist'.

While the true power of Hitler's state derived from the industrial production of warfare, Nazi art generated fantasies about the glory of the German nation through monumental, heroic and neo-classical imagery. Typical Nazi art included larger than life statues of muscular and nude 'Aryan' men or women, or portraits of Nazi leaders heroically ennobled in ancient or medieval garb. While such officially sanctioned Nazi art is generally regarded as **Kitsch** (a German word invented at the time to denote excessively garish, overly sentimental or nostalgic images and objects), nonetheless the regime recognised the propaganda value of innovative design through its patronage of such accomplished individuals as architect Albert Speer and filmmaker Leni Riefenstahl. As for members of the radical avant-garde, a very few like Emil Nolde tried unsuccessfully to accommodate themselves to the Nazi regime, while others like Hannah Höch managed to survive the war years within Germany by lying low. However, a great number of modernist artists, writers and intellectuals chose or were forced to emigrate.

Kitsch: German word for cheap and mass-produced art that is popularly regarded as iconic, but is actually imitative, inferior, pretentious, overly sentimental or nostalgic.

In France, the Surrealists strengthened their commitment to Marxist social and political revolution with the founding of a new journal, *Le Surréalisme au service de la revolution* (1930–33). But it was in their critique of French colonialism that the Surrealists had their most profound political impact. Influenced by the writings of Freud on the unconscious, by Lévy-Bruhl on the primitive mentality, and as avid collectors of indigenous art, the Surrealists regarded primitive art as one of the primary sources of the 'marvellous', that is, the experience of the unconscious as mediated by simple stories, images and objects. The Surrealists understood, perhaps more than many other modernist movements of the era, the tremendous accomplishments of indigenous art, both within its own cultural and historical context and in relation to modern art. Articles devoted to primitive art and photographic reproductions of indigenous artefacts frequently appeared in Surrealist journals, and a special issue of the Surrealist arts review *Minotaure* (no. 2, 1933) was entirely devoted to the Dakar–Djibouti ethnographic mission across Africa. Surrealist Michel Leiris participated in the mission, which became the basis for *L'Afrique fantôme* (*Phantom Africa*, 1934), the autobiographical journal that marked the beginning of his lifelong career as a research ethnographer. While traditional and indigenous cultures had direct access to sacred realms, Surrealism sought to expand modern human consciousness by re-enchanting the contemporary world with marvellous primitive art.

Given these multiple connections, it is unsurprising that the Surrealists railed against the Paris International Colonial Exposition of 1931. A world's fair sponsored by France to showcase the successes of European imperialism, the International Colonial Exposition promised visitors a 'Tour of the World in One Day'. Fairgoers either walked or took a small railway through the park to see a mélange of exhibition halls, recreated village scenes, and amusements from French colonies in West and Equatorial Africa, North Africa, Madagascar, Indo-China, Tahiti, Oceania and Guyana, as well as exhibitions from the Belgian and Dutch colonies. The European centre of the fair featured the Metropolitan Section, the City of Information and the Colonial Museum, all constructed in a high modernist architectural style. The various colonial exhibition halls were based upon modern architectural designs, but the building exteriors were decorated to emphasise the cultural regionalism of the various colonies with towers, roofs, pillars, portals and windows that imitated their geographic origins. The interiors were entirely modern, with colonial artefact collections rationally organised in dioramas and display cases. In the imperial vision of the International Colonial Exposition, modernism had reorganised and improved upon the primitive civilisations of the world.

Against this kind of modernism, which worked in tandem with imperialism to justify the remaking of 'primitive' colonial culture into a 'superior'

European image, the Surrealists organised a Counter-Colonial Exposition called 'The truth about the colonies'. Co-sponsored by the Communist Anti-Imperialist League and displayed in a Constructivist pavilion built by the Soviets in 1925 for the Decorative Arts Exposition, the Surrealist exposition was a direct attack upon European imperialism for its brutality, exploitation and violence in the pursuit of political domination and world capitalism. The tone of the counter-exposition was vehemently anti-imperialist, supplemented by two vitriolic manifestos, *Don't Visit the Colonial Exposition!* and *Preliminary Balance Sheet of the Colonial Exposition* (written after the loss of thousands of irreplaceable artefacts in a fire at the Dutch South-east Asian pavilion). One of the Surrealist displays, for example, featured a statuette of a 'Hottentot Venus', an African child with a collection plate that read *'merci'* ('Thank You'), and a black Madonna and Child under the collective title 'European fetishes'. For the Surrealists, the notion that superior Europeans had a civilising mission to improve primitive cultures was patently false. Further, the Surrealists denied that there was any genuine distinction between primitive and modern mentalities. That part of human psychology that interprets the world in metaphoric, mythic and sacred terms was no less active in moderns, the Surrealists insisted, than among so-called primitives. The Counter-Colonial Exposition was not above and beyond primitivism but drank from the same wellspring.

But the imperialist cultural challenge facing the Surrealists was greater than protesting against official events such as the International Colonial Exposition. At the level of commercial popular culture, the intersection of primitivism and modernism in Paris was becoming commonplace. With the influx of African-Americans in Paris in the post-First World War era, black culture became chic in Paris. In some ways, the post-war Parisian passion for 'primitive' African culture, particularly black jazz from America, was simply the latest incarnation of a popular urban fascination with social marginalisation as a source of exoticism, previously filled by nostalgia for bohemian Paris, popular stories about the Parisian underworld of *apaches* (not Apache Indians, but criminal thugs), and *tzigane* or 'gypsy' music. With the entry of African-Americans into Paris, their collective experience was one of relative openness and toleration, if not acceptance, by the French. While the Harlem Renaissance was flourishing in New York City, blacks throughout America at the time experienced intense social discrimination and suffered under legal segregation. By contrast, the many African-American jazz performers who performed in Paris during the 1920s, including blues singers Ada Louise 'Bricktop' Smith, jazz saxophonist Sidney Bechet and band leader Noble Sissle, found the social atmosphere in the French metropolis more relaxed in terms of race relations.

In the jazz craze for primitive African music and rhythms, Parisians tended to prefer African-American performers to actual Africans from the colonies, revealing a tendency towards exotic fantasies. Perhaps no one embodied this fantasy better than Josephine Baker, an obscure performer from East St Louis who became the most celebrated African-American in Paris during the jazz age. Proclaiming at the end of her signature song *J'ai deux amours* that she adored both 'my native country' and Paris ('*mon pays et Paris*'), Baker willingly played whatever exotic role was summoned by her French audience – an American negro minstrel show performer, a tribal African dancer in a banana skirt, an Algerian street urchin with aspirations of becoming a high society lady, a Haitian or Hawaiian plaintively singing about her island home, or a young Vietnamese woman in love with her Legionnaire. Baker did not so much embody the primitive, as, through popular entertainment, she reflected back to Parisian audiences their own narcissistic, exotic and erotic fantasies.

In addition, Baker is an important figure for understanding how the fusion of primitivism with modernism had started to gain popular appeal at this time. Paul Colin, a frustrated Parisian painter who had settled into a career as a publications illustrator, designed the poster used to advertise Baker's 1925 premiere in *La Revue Nègre*. After seeing Baker perform, Colin coaxed the entertainer into posing for a series of sketches that was published two years later under the title *Le Tumulte noir*, an oversize folio book of forty-five hand-coloured lithographs. Colin's lithographs of Baker were at the centre of the collection. But the volume included an even greater abundance of images of popular French entertainers such as entertainers Maurice Chevalier, Damia and Mistinguett, who were all depicted as dark skinned even though in fact they were light skinned. There were also portraits of black jazz musicians in tuxedos and of mixed black and white couples dancing, sometimes completely poised in full costume or elegant evening dress, at other times rendered partially or fully naked and deliriously gesticulating. The message seemed to be that even the formal and overly civilised modern French can 'go native' by performing jazz or dancing the Charleston.

On a more formal level, some of Colin's lithographs also suggest that the fusion of primitive and modernist art now had widespread exposure, if not acceptance. His representation of ballet dancer Jean Borlin is a parody of Cubist portraiture and the film actress Marcelle Parysis is depicted as an African statuette fetish. Two illustrations were done in the style of Apollinaire's *calligrammes*, one as a portrait of a blackface performer in a bowler hat and the other of a palm tree. The penultimate image in the collection was a quasi-Cubist landscape with a big band playing jazz in the foreground and symbols of modernity – a factory, skyscraper apartments, an ocean liner, Paris and the Eiffel Tower – in the background. Taken together, these elements in Colin's *Le Tumulte noir* suggest that by the late 1920s, seeing connections between primitivism and modernism had ceased to be an avant-garde insight. Yet even as the association of primitivism with modernism became more familiar, the meaning of that fusion remained unclear. As seen in the different ways primitive art and culture were fused together at the International Colonial Exposition and in the Surrealist Counter-Exposition of 1931, it remained an open question whether the union of modernism and primitivism would produce a cultural revolution or would yield to exotic and erotic fantasies that could be exploited by powerful commercial and political forces.

This tension between the aspirations of the modernist avant-garde and mass culture was becoming a critical issue for many writers and intellectuals in Western Europe, who began to call for greater social and political engagement in literature and the arts. In *The Treason of the Intellectuals* (1927), French philosopher Julian Benda criticised intellectuals who were mere careerists or state functionaries, and he urged them to re-engage their historic role as a scholarly elite charged with the ennoblement of humanity. The Spanish philosopher José Ortega y Gasset referred to the fusion of popular culture and politics as *The Revolt of the Masses* (1930), and he charged the avant-garde elite with the task of creating 'living fictions' through new art, literature and music, believing that this would reanimate a modern world that had been spiritually impoverished by mass culture. Imprisoned in Fascist Italy, the socialist philosopher Antonio Gramsci wrote in *Prison Notebooks* (1926–37) of the need of 'organic intellectuals' with roots in the working-class and agricultural cooperatives to create a 'counter hegemony' in art, literature and philosophy to combat the domination of the Italian population by fascist politics and culture. In *The Watchdogs* (1932), the French writer Paul Nizan urged intellectuals to quit the university and instead to publish in newspapers and magazines that ordinary people read. Literature, Nizan insisted, should be about the routine of daily life, its problems and frustrations, but most of all its successes, so that common people with full knowledge of their own social difficulties might translate those experiences into political action. In various ways, all of these intellectuals exhorted artists and writers to perform their avant-garde mission in concrete ways that could address pressing political, social and cultural issues, rather than pursue abstract experiments in aesthetics.

It was in this spirit of engagement and sobriety that the International Writers Congress for the Defence of Culture convened in Paris during 21–25 June 1935. Organised by the literary paragons André Gide and André Malraux, an international array of eminent writers including Aldous Huxley, E. M. Forster, Louis Aragon, Henri Barbusse, Bertold Brecht, Robert Musil, Maxim Gorky, Boris Pasternak, Malcolm Crowley, John Dos Passos, Langston Hughes and others delivered speeches against fascism for five consecutive days to audiences of 2,500 to 3,000 persons. The participants generally regarded the congress as a success, and the proceedings concluded with the audience singing the *Internationale*. As an outgrowth of the conference, the International Writers Association for the Defence of Culture was established, headquartered in Paris but with an international board that would meet in a different country every year to assure that each participating nation would 'struggle on its own terrain, which is culture, against war, Fascism, and in a general manner, against all threats to civilization' (Lottman, 1982: 97).

As it turned out, the cultural unity of the Popular Front was only apparent. During the congress, the machinations of the Soviet representative Ilya Ehrenberg proved that party discipline would become a greater force than democratic consensus. On the eve of the proceedings, André Breton was banned from participation after having slapped Ehrenberg on the face for insulting remarks the Communist author had made about Surrealism amounting to little more than 'pederasty and dreams'. When representatives from various countries pressed to bring the case of Victor Serge, an émigré anarchist who had returned to Russia during the Bolshevik Revolution and subsequently had been imprisoned by Stalin for being a 'Trotskyite', to the conference floor, Ehrenberg objected and most conference participants either justified the Soviet Union's actions or remained silent. The crowning blow was delivered on the closing night of the conference, when the French poet and novelist Louis Aragon publicly renounced Surrealism and embraced Socialist Realism as the only method of revolutionary art and literature.

Such ideological rifts between the Communists and other political groups within the Popular Front became even wider once the Spanish Civil War began the following year. While various artists and writers made individual choices about whether to volunteer to fight in defence of the beleaguered Second Spanish Republic, Blum's Socialist government in France adopted a policy of non-intervention, leaving the Soviet Union the only country to officially provide the Spanish Republic with material assistance during the civil war. On the ground, however, the Communists proved to be more interested in political manoeuvring to eliminate rival leftist factions than in winning the civil war, a tragic history detailed in George Orwell's *Homage to Catalonia* (1938). Caught between fascist and communist systems of repression, the Popular Front of engaged artists and writers in the defence of culture proved ineffectual. By 1939, the Spanish Civil War had ended in Franco's victory, the Popular Front government in France had collapsed, and Nazi Germany had unleashed a second war upon the European continent. As the Second World War deepened, modernist artists and writers who had not been driven underground, imprisoned or killed, became refugees. And the international centre of modernism shifted across the Atlantic Ocean to New York.

Further reading

Blake, Jody, *Le Tumulte noir: Modernist Art and Popular Entertainment in Jazz-Age Paris, 1900–1930*, University Park, PA: The Pennsylvania State University Press, 1999.

Brown, Matthew Cullerne, *Art under Stalin*, New York: Holmes and Meier, 1991.

Brown, Matthew Cullerne, *Socialist Realist Painting*, New Haven: Yale University Press, 1998.

Ghirardo, Diane, *Building New Communities: New Deal America and Fascist Italy*, Princeton: Princeton University Press, 1989.

Greeley, Robin Adele, *Surrealism and the Spanish Civil War*, New Haven: Yale University Press, 2006.

Hughes, H. Stuart, *Between Commitment and Disillusion*, Middletown: Wesleyan University Press, 1986.

Kaplan, Alice Yeager, *Reproductions of Banality: Fascism, Literature, and French Intellectual Life*, Minneapolis: University of Minnesota Press, 1986.

Lottman, Herbert R., *The Left Bank: Writers, Artists, and Politics from the Popular Front to the Cold War*, New York: Houghton Mifflin, 1982.

Morton, Patricia A., *Hybrid Modernities: Architecture and Representation at the 1931 Colonial Exposition, Paris*, Cambridge, MA: MIT Press, 2000.

Saler, Michael T., *The Avant-Garde in Interwar England: Medieval Modernism and the London Underground*, Oxford: Oxford University Press, 1999.

Stovall, Tyler, *Paris Noir: African Americans in the City of Light*, New York: Houghton Mifflin, 1996.

Willet, John, *Art and Politics in the Weimar Period: The New Sobriety 1917–1933*, New York: Pantheon Books, 1978.

Part 4

AFTER MODERNISM

7

The Neo-Avant-Garde

In October 1942, the American art collector Peggy Guggenheim opened a gallery called 'Art of this Century' in New York. Heiress to a small fortune from her family's copper mining company, Guggenheim had moved to Paris in the 1920s where she made the acquaintance of various avant-garde artists and writers, including Man Ray and Marcel Duchamp. In 1938 she moved to London and opened the Guggenheim Jeune gallery, where she exhibited the drawings of French writer and impresario Jean Cocteau, the paintings of the Surrealist Yves Tanguy, the Abstract Expressionist Wassily Kandinsky, the former Dadaist now Abstract-Creationist Jean (Hans) Arp, and the abstract sculptures of Constantin Brânșusi. Guggenheim also made it her goal to 'buy a picture a day', and she quickly built up an extensive collection of modernist art. After the bombing of London began and England was drawn further into the Second World War, Guggenheim moved her collection into safe storage at a chateau in Vichy France. Continuing south to Marseilles, she gathered up an entourage of refugee artists and raised the funds to bring them back with her to New York.

To create the space for her Art of this Century gallery in New York, Guggenheim commissioned De Stijl architect Frederick Kiesler to renovate two former tailor shops on West 57th Street. Three rooms were for Guggenheim's permanent collection, the Abstract, Kinetic and Surrealist galleries, while one room was set aside for temporary shows. In addition to the European artists she had featured in London, the Art of this Century gallery also displayed works by Georges Braque, Giorgio de Chirico, Salvador Dalí, Max Ernst, Alberto Giacometti, Paul Klee, Fernand Léger, Piet Mondrian, Joan Miró, Pablo Picasso and other prominent European artists. The works of several American modernists were showcased as well, including Alexander Calder, Willem de Kooning, Robert Motherwell, Jackson Pollock, Mark Rothko and Clyfford Still. Assessing the importance of Guggenheim's gallery, the American Abstract Expressionist painter Lee Krasner later declared, '"Art of this Century" was of the utmost importance as the first place where the New York School could be seen . . . Her Gallery was the foundation, it's where it all started to happen' (Foster et al., 2004: 301).

A more balanced judgement is that Guggenheim was intensifying the attention focused on modernist art in America, which had already been happening for some decades. As early as the 1910s, works like Maurice Prendergast's *The Promenade* (1913) showed the direct influence of Post-Impressionist style upon American painting. In 1913 the photographer Alfred Stieglitz organised the Armory Show in New York to showcase the Expressionist paintings of Cézanne, Gauguin, Van Gogh and works by various Cubist and Fauve artists. During the First World War, Marcel Duchamp came to the United States, where he gained the admiration and patronage of Walter and Louise Arensberg who collected and displayed his works. During this same period, the American painters Joseph Stella, John Marin, Arthur Dove and Marsden Hartley began to produce works influenced by European Cubist, Cubo-Futurist and Dadaist styles. After the war, the 'Lost Generation' of modern American authors, such as Sherwood Anderson, Djuna Barnes, Kay Boyle, John Dos Passos, F. Scott Fitzgerald, Janet Flanner and Ernest Hemingway, became expatriates in Paris and London. Within New York, the Harlem Renaissance in African-American literature thrived, bringing such writers as Nora Neale Hurston, Claude McKay and Langston Hughes into public prominence. By the late 1920s and early 1930s, American figurative painters Stuart Davis, Charles Demuth, Georgia O'Keeffe and Ben Shahn began to develop a uniquely American modernist idiom. During the Great Depression, the Mexican muralists José Clemente Orozco, Diego Rivera and David Alfaro Siqueiros influenced a wide assortment of artists working in the Federal Arts Project of the Works Progress Administration (WPA), which produced over 200,000 murals, paintings and posters. For decades before the opening of the Art of this Century gallery, modernist art was happening in America.

Modernist art was also already being institutionalised in New York. In 1929, a young art professor from Wellesley College named Alfred H. Barr, Jr. was hired to become the first director of the newly opened Museum of Modern Art (MoMA) in New York. Barr rationalised the presentation of modernist art by organising exhibitions according to theme and by chronological development (an approach familiar to contemporary museum visitors, but applied at MoMA for the first time to modernism). The 'Cubism and Abstract Art' exhibition in 1936 represented the culmination of Barr's efforts (**Doc. 12, pp. 134–6**). To guide visitors through the exhibition, Barr developed a flowchart that showed the influence of Neo-Impressionism upon Fauvism, Expressionism and Cubism, which in turn affected the development of

Futurism, Dada and Surrealism, Neoplasticism, Constructivism and Bauhaus, and ultimately funnelled all modernist movements into two general camps of Geometrical and Non-Geometrical Abstract Art [Map 1]. Not only was New York establishing itself as an important metropolitan centre to display modern art, MoMA was beginning to institutionalise the canon of modernism.

New York began to emerge as the new centre of modernist art criticism as well, and its chief spokesman was Clement Greenberg. In 1939, Greenberg wrote an article called 'Avant-garde and Kitsch', published in the *Partisan Review*. At the opening of the essay, Greenberg lamented, 'One and the same civilization produces simultaneously two such different things as a poem by T. S. Eliot and a Tin Pan Alley song, or a painting by Braque and a *Saturday Evening Post* cover (Harrison and Wood, 2003: 539).' Greenberg's complaint was not simply that avant-garde and mass culture existed side by side, but that the European artists had lost their avant-garde function. Instead of continuing to produce innovative art, in Greenberg's assessment the European avant-garde had begun to imitate itself. Even worse, he continued, some of the avant-garde had become a rearguard through state-mandated art in Nazi Germany and the Soviet Union. To top it all, the Kitsch of popular commercial art and literature of magazines, pulp fiction, comics, popular jazz tunes, radio shows and Hollywood movies is what the public consumed. In a follow-up article entitled 'Towards a newer Laocoon', published the following year, Greenberg called for a return to 'pure form' in modernist art, and he affirmed the 'superiority of abstract art' in that pursuit.

Greenberg's essays are historically important for a few reasons. First, at a time when more sober voices had been calling for social and political engagement through a return to Realism in art and literature, as advocated by the Popular Front in Europe and the WPA Arts Projects in America, Greenberg reaffirmed the aesthetic mission of the modernist avant-garde to experiment and innovate. Second, he asserted that the European avant-garde had largely become exhausted and stale, and he implicitly suggested that the vanguard of modernism had shifted to America. In the 1950s, Greenberg explicitly affirmed this through the numerous articles he wrote in support of American Abstract Expressionism, giving particular attention to such artists as Jackson Pollock, Hans Hofmann and Willem de Kooning. Second, whether Greenberg was theoretically correct or not in his criticisms of the European avant-garde, by historical circumstance it was increasingly apparent that after the Second World War the centre of modernism had indeed shifted to New York.

As an international centre of commerce and communications, New York was the new image of twentieth-century modernity with such iconic structures as the Brooklyn Bridge, the Rockefeller Center, the Chrysler Building and the skyscraper skyline of Manhattan. The exodus of intellectuals and artists from Europe, first from Nazi Germany and then from France after the war started, helped to secure New York's cosmopolitan status as the new metropolis of modernism. A few 'old guard' modernist artists, such as Henri Matisse, Pablo Picasso, Georges Braque and Pierre Bonnard, continued to live and work in France under the Nazi occupation. Writers such as Louis Aragon, Robert Desnos, Paul Éluard, André Malraux, and Tristan Tzara stayed to fight on the side of the French Resistance. But many European modernists had ended up in America. By 1942, Surrealists André Breton, Max Ernst, André Masson, and Yves Tanguy had arrived in New York, as had Cubist and Abstract artists such as Fernand Léger, Piet Mondrian, Marc Chagall, Jacques Lipchitz and Amédée Ozenfant. Guggenheim's Art of this Century gallery, as well as the 'First papers of Surrealism' installation organised by Marcel Duchamp, provided those exiles with both refuge and venues for public exhibition.

Over the course of the 1940s, European and American avant-garde sensibilities blended in New York. This was due in part to some Europeans who had crossed the Atlantic as young men and subsequently became American modernists. One of the earliest was Arshile Gorky (born Vosdanik Adoian), who had escaped the Turkish genocide of the Armenians as a teenager and immigrated to New York in 1920. One of the foundational painters of American Surrealist and Abstract Expressionist art, as a young man Gorky had studied the works of Cézanne, Giorgio de Chirico, Picasso, Kandinsky and Miró, all on display in New York museums and galleries. The Dutch-born painter Willem de Kooning arrived in the United States as a stowaway in 1926 and made his way to New York shortly thereafter. Influenced by Cubism and Surrealism, and befriended by Gorky, de Kooning developed into one of the leading American Abstract Expressionist painters. The German Abstract Expressionist painter Hans Hofmann immigrated to the United States in 1932, and subsequently became the teacher of the emerging American artists Robert Motherwell and Lee Krasner, who later were the founders of the American Abstract Artists group.

Many of the young and aspiring American artists were benefiting from exchanges with the modernist European masters. Alexander Calder, an art student from Philadelphia, went to Paris in the 1920s, where he was influenced both by the Abstract art of Mondrian and Léger and the Surrealist art of Miró. Returning to New York in the late 1930s, Calder combined geometric designs and fluid forms into the abstract mobiles and large stabiles that would become characteristic of his art. Robert Motherwell, an art history student at Columbia University in 1940, discovered European modernism within New York. Rather than travel to Paris, he befriended members of the Paris Surrealist movement in exile in New York, including Breton, Duchamp, Ernst, Masson and Tanguy. Surrealist ideas about automatism as a path to the unconscious and other European modernist influences are evident in

Motherwell's collages and prints, and especially in the bold and dark series of paintings he produced over the entire course of his adult life, *Elegy to the Spanish Republic* (1948–91).

What eventually distinguished the New York School, however, was the development of a new movement, American Abstract Expressionism. Led by such painters as Jackson Pollock, Barnett Newman and Mark Rothko, and the sculptor David Smith, originally many of these artists studied the works of the European avant-garde and then played with those various styles in their early works. However, the New York School made it a goal to free themselves from the burdens of European history, philosophy and politics, and instead they sought a more direct relationship between the notions 'abstract' and 'expression'. The New York School strove for the immediate expression of powerful emotions and the unconscious through abstract art. The form of the work of art was not based upon preconceived ideas, forms or principles, but emerged from the contact elements – the actual physical quantities and qualities of paint, the size of the canvas or painted surface, the presence or absence of colour, contrast or lack of contrast, and the selection of construction materials. The concrete application of materials determined both the content and form of their art, directly expressing the artist's emotional or psychological state of being. Any meaning derived from the work of art was entirely dependent upon the viewer's subjective ability to interpret it. In these ways, American Abstract Expressionism gave visual expression to issues of freedom and choice that were current in the philosophy of **existentialism**.

Jackson Pollock became perhaps the most celebrated member of the New York School of Abstract Expressionism. The youngest of five sons from a poor farming family in Cody, Wyoming, in 1930 he moved to New York and began to attend classes taught by the muralist Thomas Hart Benton at the Art Students' League. Over the next decade, Pollock studied Baroque and Mannerist art, the Mexican muralists, the works of Picasso and Miró, met the painters Stuart Davis and Arshile Gorky, and he began to develop his own abstract style. In 1943, Peggy Guggenheim provided Pollock with his first solo exhibition at the Art of this Century gallery. As a result, he became associated with the members of what became known as the New York School, which included Barnett Newman, Mark Rothko and Lee Krasner (whom he married).

Influenced by Surrealist ideas about automatism, Pollock sought to develop a non-representational, purely gestural style of painting that allowed for the direct expression of emotions and the psychological unconscious. His early work mostly consisted of doodles and totemic images, but over time this developed into a technique he called 'action painting'. Pollock would drip paint from a brush or pour it directly upon a flat surface, instead

existentialism: A philosophical attitude popular in the immediate post-Second World War era to create one's individual 'essence' despite living in a disorienting, meaningless and absurd world.

of using an upright easel. He guided the paint to form curves, spots and splatters to achieve varying degrees of texture, until a certain rhythm to the overall image had been realised. Pollock believed that action painting was not merely a technique, but an approach to painting that would more fully capture the sensations he felt (which were often dark from bouts of depression and heavy drinking).

In the view of fellow Abstract Expressionist Willem de Kooning, Pollock was an avant-garde genius. 'He busted our idea of a picture all to hell. Then there could be new painting again' (Fineberg, 1995: 86). But the art critics could not agree on the meaning of Pollock's art. Whereas Clement Greenberg extolled action painting as 'pure art', rival art critic Harold Rosenberg denied that it had an aesthetic dimension at all. 'The new American painting is not "pure" art, since the extrusion of the object was not for the sake of the aesthetic. [. . .] What matters always is the revelation contained in the act' (Harrison and Wood, 2003: 589–90). What mattered most for Rosenberg was that the action painter literally pour his emotions on to the canvas, that drama should take precedence over aesthetic form. Pollock was of little help in clarifying such issues, for the remarks he made during interviews about his art often seemed off-the-cuff and contradictory. So even if Pollock had made painting new again, the related issue of 'is it art?' remained a puzzle. Perhaps as a consequence Pollock attracted few direct imitators. Yet there is little doubt that his radical, immediate and emotional approach to art directly inspired the neo-avant-garde, particularly concrete performance artists.

By the 1950s, New York was indisputably the new capital of modernism. The American metropolis boasted numerous corporate and private galleries, in addition to the establishment of institutional modern art museums such as MoMA, the Whitney Museum of American Art and the Museum of Non-Objective Painting (later renamed the Guggenheim Museum). A modernist 'neo-avant-garde' was emerging as well, which included such artists as Robert Rauschenberg, Larry Rivers, Jim Dine, Claes Oldenburg and Jasper Johns. Reacting against Abstract Expressionism, the neo-avant-garde reinvented techniques of figuration and mixed media collage, made assemblages from 'junk' and found objects, and reworked appropriated advertising or media images for unintended artistic purposes. The neo-avant-garde created new modernist art by blending a hodgepodge of materials and images into a pastiche, rather than striving to be 'pure' or 'next stage'. A perceived lack of aesthetic and intellectual rigour led Clement Greenberg to criticise much of the neo-avant-garde for producing 'novelty art', but such criticism had limited impact. Producing 'new' art that both borrowed and was distinct from 'old' European modernism, and its American imitators, was in part what it meant to be 'neo-avant-garde'.

The neo-avant-garde crossed a variety of artistic realms. In music, the composer John Cage, who had studied with Arnold Schoenberg and was inspired by Marcel Duchamp's anti-art ready-mades, emerged as one of the leaders of the American neo-avant-garde. One of Cage's significant musical innovations was the 'prepared piano', a technique for changing the timbre of the instrument by placing objects on or between the piano's strings, hammers and dampers. Cage also experimented with techniques for generating musical compositions, such the *Music of Changes* (1951) which was composed by flipping *I Ching* coins. He also played with the notion of what constituted a musical performance, most notably with *4 minutes 33 seconds* (1952), which designated the length of time during which a musician would sit in silence and the audience heard only the chance ambient sounds occurring within and outside the music hall.

A crowning achievement of Cage's neo-avant-garde efforts was *Theater Piece #1* (1952), also known as 'the event' or the first 'happening'. In this multimedia production, Robert Rauschenberg's *White Paintings* (1951) of panels painted entirely in white were suspended above the stage area. The experimental musician David Tudor performed on the piano, an old phonograph played songs by Edith Piaf and experimental poets Charles Olson and M. C. Richards recited poetry from ladders. Modern dance choreographer Merce Cunningham glided through the audience, and coffee was served by four boys dressed in white suits. Presiding over it all, Cage ascended a stepladder and delivered lectures on the relationship between Zen Buddhism and music, while at other times he sat there silently. Reminiscent of Dadaist anti-art, the performances of Cage and his neo-avant-garde contemporaries created hybrid art that brought playfulness into American modernism, a quality largely missing in Abstract Expressionism.

While New York was the centre of much of this activity, the neo-avant-garde became international in the post-Second World War era as well. In Europe, some of the surviving 'old masters' of modernism such as Matisse, Picasso, Braque, Bonnard and Léger, strove to rekindle the avant-garde flame by pushing into yet new stylistic territories. Yet it was the new artists, like Jean Dubuffet, Alberto Giacometti and Francis Bacon, who established new modernist terrain in the post-war period. Dubuffet, originally a Parisian wine merchant, had started to paint under the Nazi occupation. His post-war works express a profound existentialist pessimism about both the human condition and the material conditions of European society. One of his early paintings, *Childbirth* (1944), more resembles graffiti than a work of art. It is a crudely drawn and painted picture of a naked woman lying on her back upon a white surface, legs spread apart with a head-down baby emerging below and flanked by a clothed woman and man. As his painting developed over the next two decades, Dubuffet pursued a number of primitive painting techniques that he called *art brut* ('raw' art). Such crude art expressed an aesthetic of psychosis through a chaotic jumble of dark shapes and colours, an overabundance of lines or doodles, collage cut-outs from other painted canvases, and an exaggeration of body parts of mouths, eyes and penises. In these ways, Dubuffet's art expressed the existential anxieties of the private world of the individual artist that may or may not be intelligible to viewers beyond general feelings of dissociation, dread and despair.

Existential angst was also predominant in the post-war art of the Swiss sculptor Alberto Giacometti and the British painter Francis Bacon. Giacometti came from a Swiss-Italian family of artists – his father, Giovanni Giacometti, was a Post-Impressionist painter, and his uncle and his godfather, Augusto Giacometti and Cuno Amiet, were Symbolist painters. He received formal training in sculpture in Rome before moving to Paris in the 1920s, where he became friends with some of the Surrealist artists in the 1930s. However, his approach to Surrealism reversed the process of dream work: instead of drawing together disparate images and objects into a complex dreamscape, Giacometti chose to distort real-life bodies into disturbing or nightmarish figures according to his subjective perception of a real-life model, an existential process that left him feeling that his works were always 'unfinished'. His distinctive bronze sculptures, some a few inches high, others several feet tall, were of skinny human figures with puny heads and elongated legs, arms and torsos. Whether displayed individually or in an ensemble, Giacometti's statues conveyed a strong sense of psychological alienation and unbridgeable social distance. Francis Bacon's nightmarish visions were expressed through figurative painting and portraiture. Originally a furniture and interior designer, Bacon had shifted to painting in the 1930s. His paintings expressed an emotionally violent sense of alienation through the use of garish colours, portraiture of pained faces and contorted bodies, and by streaking the canvas with paint or solvent, techniques evident in *Study after Velázquez's Portrait of Pope Innocent X* (1953). In contrast to Giacometti's emotionally cool statues, the aesthetic of Bacon's paintings was one of grotesque horror.

In addition to such figures as Dubuffet, Giacometti and Bacon, who had modernist roots in the pre-war era but rose to prominence afterwards, entirely new neo-avant-garde movements arose in post-war Europe as well, such as **Nouveau Réalisme** (New Realism) in Paris. The *Nouveaux Réalistes* would gather together real objects and then reassemble them into novel images in an effort to force viewers to perceive reality in new ways. Yves Klein, one of the group's founders, was an artist-provocateur who would stage 'happenings' of live painting sessions before an assembled audience accompanied by string quartets. In his performance series *Anthropométries de l'époque bleue* ('Blue Period Anthropometrics', 1960), the naked bodies

Nouveau Réalisme: French phrase meaning 'New Realism', refers to a Parisian neo-avant-garde reaction against abstract modernism by staging concrete performances and creating 'junk art' from recycled advertising images, and industrial and consumer goods.

Plate 1 Pablo Picasso, *Les Demoiselles d'Avignon*, 1907.

Source: Giraudon/ The Bridgeman Art Library/ © DACS

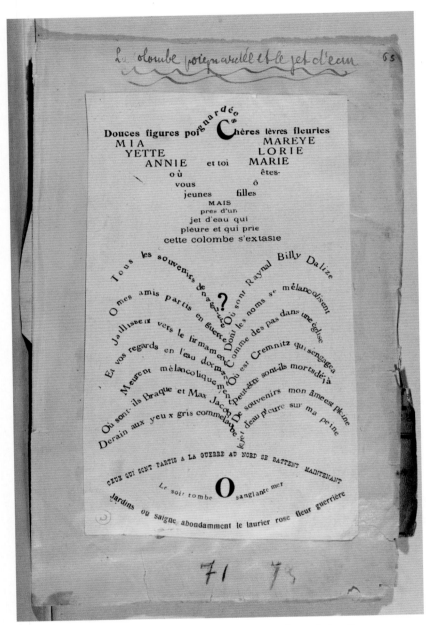

Plate 2 Guillaume Apollinaire, *La colombe poignardée et le jet d'eau*
('The stabbed dove and the water spray') in *Calligrammes: poèmes de la paix et de la guerre, 1913–1916* (Paris: Mercure de France, 1918).

Source: Archives Charmet/ The Bridgeman Art Library Ltd

Plate 3 Joan Miró, *Aidez L'Espagne* ('Help Spain'), 1937. Poster. Miró's handwritten text beneath reads, 'In the current battle, I see obsolete forces on the side of the fascists, and on the other side the people, whose enormous creative resources will give Spain a vital spirit that will astonish the world.'

Source: Giraudon/ The Bridgeman Art Library Ltd/ © DACS

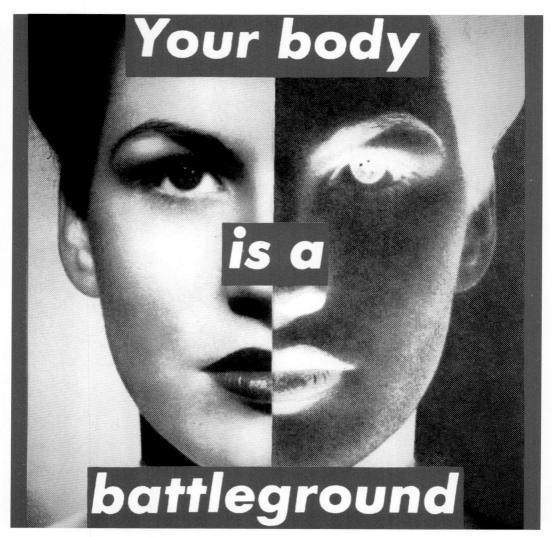

Plate 4 Barbara Kruger, *Untitled (your body is a battleground)*, 1989, photographic silkscreen on vinyl, 112 × 112 inches, The Broad Art Foundation, Santa Monica.

Source: Copyright Barbara Kruger, courtesy: Mary Boone Gallery, New York/ image courtesy of The Broad Art Foundation, Santa Monica

of women were covered with blue paint and then pressed upon, rolled over, or dragged across canvases, leaving a body imprint (anthropometrics refers to the police forensic science techniques of measuring skeletal body parts and fingerprinting). Other *Nouveau Réaliste* artists literally collected garbage and put it on display, such as Arman's 1960 installations *Poubelles* ('Garbage Cans') and *Le Plein* ('Full Up'). Other artists moved installations out of the museum exhibition halls and took them into the streets. One of the earliest projects of Christo and Jeanne-Claude was *Wall of Barrels, Iron Curtain* (1961–62), a barricade of 240 oil barrels clogging the rue Visconti in Paris as a Cold War tribute to the recently constructed Berlin Wall. Over the next forty years, Christo and Jeanne-Claude would continue in this vein of public art, becoming renowned for the colourful fabric wrapping of public monuments such as the Pont Neuf in Paris (1984) and the Reichstag in Berlin (1995), and large-scale environmental projects like the 400-metre *Valley Curtain* in Colorado (1970) and *Wrapped Trees* outside Basel, Switzerland (1989).

The junk aesthetic in *Nouveau Réalisme* was perhaps most fully developed by Jean Tinguely, a welding sculptor who would take cast-off mechanical parts and use them to create makeshift contraptions. Tinguely's triumph was the *Homage à New York*, a massive junk assemblage commissioned by New York MoMA made from a weather balloon, a Klaxon 'ah-ooo-gah' electric horn, a piano, fifty bicycle wheels, putrid-smelling burning chemicals, and mechanical rocker arms, belts and levers. When Tinguely started up the machine in the MoMA sculpture garden on 17 March 1960, the shrieking contraption burst into smoke and flames. After museum officials called in the fire department to put out the flames, the aging Marcel Duchamp rejoiced, 'Maybe Tinguely and a few others . . . are trying to destroy art before it's too late' (Fineberg, 1995: 230). In a spirit sympathetic with the French and British Situationist International movement in avant-garde politics, *Nouveau Réalisme* thrived on outrageous, ironic and anti-establishment provocations.

Neo-avant-garde groups also emerged in Japan during the post-war era of the 1950s. One of the most renowned was the Japanese performance art ensemble **Gutai** *Bijutsu Kyōkai* ('Concrete Art Group'). Influenced by Jackson Pollock's action painting, Gutai sought a direct engagement between media and the human body. As the *Gutai Manifesto* proclaimed,

> Gutai art does not change the material: it brings it to life. Gutai art does not falsify the material. In Gutai art the human spirit and the material reach out their hands to each other . . . If one leaves the material as it is, presenting it just as material, then it starts to tell us something and speaks with a mighty voice.

(Harrison and Wood, 2003: 699)

Gutai: Japanese term for 'concrete' or tangible, an association of neo-avant-garde Japanese artists during the 1950s who, in opposition to modernist abstraction, staged performances where artists interacted with physical materials.

Rejecting aesthetics altogether, Gutai sought modernist understanding through the direct contact of bodies with physical materials.

Performance art was the preferred approach of Gutai, both for the artists and for the audiences who directly witnessed or participated in the performances. One of the more renowned Gutai artists was Kazuo Shiraga, who in October 1955 staged the performance 'composition' *Challenging Mud* by struggling nearly naked in a large pool of mud before an attendant audience. The following year, Saburo Murakami performed *At One Moment Opening Six Holes* by bursting through wooden frames covered with traditional handmade Japanese paper, leaving torn holes where his body had passed through. In a Tokyo exhibition of 1956, Atsuko Tanaka performed *Electric Dress* by wrapping herself in a costume made of incandescent light bulbs and coloured neon tubes.

Although Gutai was a short-lived phenomenon limited to Japan, related neo-avant-garde events occurred worldwide. In Brazil and Argentina, Neo-Concretists encouraged audiences to participate in the construction of sculptures, paintings, and performances as a mode of direct and subjective human experience. A 'Destruction in Art Symposium' of international artists and poets, dedicated to the annihilation of abstract aesthetics, was held in London in 1963. Multiple **Fluxus** ('Flow') performances were staged in New York during the 1960s, carried out by an international entourage of artists, poets and musicians that included Dick Higgins, Robert Morris, Nam June Paik, Yoko Ono, Ben Vautier, Joseph Beuys and Wolf Vostell. Aside from being 'concrete performances' meant to be experienced directly, no common aesthetic united these diverse neo-avant-garde movements.

Fluxus: Latin for 'Flow', refers to neo-avant-garde mixed-media 'happenings' in New York during the 1960s performed by an international network of artists across a variety of disciplines.

By the 1960s, it was apparent that modernism had become international and New York was its new capital. Yet the emergence of the neo-avant-garde had challenged modernism's avant-garde mission. In an effort to settle the meaning of modernism, the New York art critic Clement Greenberg published a short pamphlet entitled *Modernist Painting* in 1960. Later broadcast over the Voice of America radio to a European audience, Greenberg eschewed the social, cultural and political aspirations of modernism to focus exclusively on the refinement of modernist aesthetics. For Greenberg the pursuit of an aesthetic, not liberation from past culture, was the true critical goal of modernism: 'The essence of Modernism lies, as I see it, in the use of the characteristic methods of a discipline to criticize the discipline itself – not in order to subvert it, but to entrench it more firmly in its area of competence' (Harrison and Wood, 2003: 773). The meaning of modernism emerged from processes of further aesthetic development, he concluded, and Abstract Expressionism was its current and most complete expression. Yet by the time of Greenberg's essay, Abstract Expressionism had already passed its heyday and was being challenged by numerous neo-avant-garde movements internationally. With the advent of postmodernism in the subsequent decades, the situation became even more complicated.

Further reading

Barr, Jr., Alfred H., *Cubist and Abstract Art* (rpnt edn), New York: Arno Press, 1996.

Bochloh, Benjamin H. D., *Neo-Avantgarde and Culture Industry: Essays on European and American Art from 1955 to 1975*, Cambridge, MA.: MIT Press, 2001.

Francis Frascina (ed.), *Pollock and After: The Critical Debate* (2nd edn), New York: Routledge, 2000.

Fineberg, Jonathan, *Art since 1940: Strategies of Being*, New York: Harry N. Abrams, 1995.

Greenberg, Clement, *Art and Culture: Critical Essays*, Boston: Beacon Press, 1989.

Guilbaut, Gerge, *How New York Stole the Idea of Modern Art: Abstract Expressionism, Freedom, and the Cold War*, Chicago: University of Chicago Press, 1983.

Hendricks, Jon, *Fluxus Opus*, New York: Harry N. Abrams, 1988.

Neuburger, Susanne (ed.), *Nouveau Réalisme*, Vienna: Verlag für Moderne Kunst, 2006.

Wood, Paul et al., *Modernism in Dispute: Art since the Forties* (Series: 'Modern Art: Practices and Debates'), New Haven and London: Yale University Press/The Open University, 1993.

8

Postmodernism

On 6 May 1968, the National Union of Students of France called for a protest against the Sorbonne and Nanterre university campuses over the mistreatment of students and the unwillingness of administrators to negotiate with student leaders to improve conditions. For the past several weeks, student leaders and protestors had been repeatedly harassed and arrested by the police for trespassing on university grounds. That day, nearly 20,000 students and teachers took to the streets, only to be greeted by battalions of riot police. Responding to the confrontation, the students constructed makeshift barricades and threw paving stones at the police. The police replied by firing canisters of tear gas into the crowds, and several hundred individuals from both sides were injured. Over the next several days the magnitude of the student protests increased, as did the size of the clashes between the students and the police. A week later, French labour unions had joined with the students in a sympathy strike, as well as making some demands of their own upon the French government. By the end of the month, a general strike had brought Paris to a standstill, tens of thousands of people filled the streets, and President de Gaulle fled the capital.

It was a heady time for student leaders of the protest, as in the post-war era few political events had provoked such massive numbers of Parisians into spontaneous action. The event took on a life of its own, with no one in control, and became a kind of revolutionary carnival. Graffiti written throughout the city captured the festive mood, proclaiming 'Poetry is in the streets'. Most of the graffiti was explicitly political, but also playful: 'Workers of all countries, enjoy!' and 'I'm a Groucho Marxist.' A direct linkage was made between the immediacy of desire and the power of revolution, particularly the connection between sexual and political liberation: 'The more I make love, the more I want to make revolution. The more I make revolution, the more I want to make love.' There was an anti-consumerist message in much of the graffiti as well: 'The more you consume, the less you live.' Some of the graffiti contained quotes from leaders from the previous generation of the modernist avant-garde, the Symbolist poet Paul Valéry, 'Every view of things that is not strange is false', and the Surrealist paragon André Breton, 'Imagination is not a gift, it must be conquered.' The spirit of May 1968 was best summed up in the slogan, 'Be realistic, demand the impossible' (Knabb, 2006: 445–57).

Viewed as a neo-avant-garde performance, May 1968 was the ultimate 'happening'. Yet its historical and intellectual legacies are ambiguous, and they bear upon the fate of modernism in the late twentieth century. In terms of political history, May 1968 was a failure. De Gaulle returned to Paris in early June to a hundred thousand cheering French gathered along the Champs Elysées, and the French Fifth Republic, with cosmetic reforms, re-emerged stable and secure. Within the decade, modernism was institutionalised in Paris with the 1977 opening of the Centre Georges Pompidou as the state-authorised modern art research centre and twentieth-century art museum. Revolution in the streets had not overthrown 'the system': rather, the system had absorbed the political and modernist avant-garde, and the state was consolidated. As journalist and host Bernard Pivot ironically commented on the French television programme *Apostrophes* nearly two decades later, 'May '68, we remade the world. May '86, we're redoing the kitchen' (Walz, 2007: 173). Modernist art and literature, far from being perceived as an oppositional avant-garde, were now seen as integral to the system. Even the giddy participants in May 1968 had seen it that way: 'Art is dead, don't consume its corpse.'

On intellectual and cultural levels, however, the long-term implications of May 1968 run deeper than a failed uprising. Over the years leading up to the event, French intellectuals like Louis Althusser and Michel Foucault had been questioning the effectiveness of avant-garde political strategies pursued by the radical Marxist left, coming to the realisation that the organisation of an entire complex of economic, social, political, technological and cultural institutions are not overthrown simply because some group has 'seized power'. This was proving to be a particular problem in a modern society based upon the mass consumption of commodities on a daily basis by the general population. The French intellectual and sociologist Henri Lefebvre called such mass consumption 'terrorism in everyday life' in the sense that individuals were held hostage by the necessity to consume commodities on a daily basis. The Frankfurt School philosopher Herbert Marcuse character-ised such mass consumption as 'desublimation', meaning that the body's desires are only incompletely satisfied by commodities, yet through daily consumption one's actual biology increasingly becomes dependent upon them. Liberation appeared paradoxical, if not impossible, as individuals and the operations of mass society and culture were seen not as distinct from or opposable to each other, but as constitutive of one another.

Such realisations had profound implications for the presumed avant-garde role of modernism. Since the nineteenth century, the European intellectual and cultural elite had been disdainful of commercial mass culture, an attitude largely inherited by the modernist avant-garde in the early twentieth century. Those modernist movements that had incorporated the use of mass-culture materials into their collages and photomontages, such as Cubism, Dada and Constructivism, had appropriated and redirected them for their own avant-garde purposes. In the post-Second World War era, the 'Americanisation' of Western Europe presented a historically unprecedented situation, as entire nations were overwhelmed with US consumer products, commercial advertising, fashion magazines and Hollywood movies. As Frankfurt School intellectuals Max Horkheimer and Theodor Adorno noted in *The Dialectic of Enlightenment* (1944, English translation 1972), the commercial marketing techniques of the American 'culture industry' had the normative effect of reinforcing the status quo while sidelining critical intellectual perspectives to ineffectual margins. The imperative to 'make it new' no longer challenged or transformed culture; instead, artistic experimentation was being actively incorporated into product designs and marketing techniques that reinforced the predominance of mass culture.

Decades earlier, the German–Jewish intellectual Walter Benjamin pondered the implications such developments had for the utopian aims of modernism. In the seminal essay 'The Work of Art in the Age of Mechanical Reproduction' (1935), Benjamin grappled with the challenges to aesthetics presented by technical modes of mass reproduction [**Doc. 13, pp. 136–8**]. In contrast to traditional modes of artistic, literary or musical production, in which copies or performances are based upon an original work, the reproduction techniques of mass culture produce copies *without* an original. In photography, for example, a photographic print is not an original work but is the derivative product of a series of technical processes combining a camera apparatus, a negative celluloid image, light exposure, treated paper and chemical processing. The same applies generally to the industrial production of mass culture, but especially to those forms that involve complex mechanical and electronic processes such as movies, music recordings, and radio and television broadcasting. Any 'aura' attributed to a work of art produced under such conditions, Benjamin noted, is not due to the unique status of an original work of art, but is conferred solely upon its commercial 'cult value' (for example, the value attributed to a 'first edition' publication over its subsequent imprints, a 'limited edition' photograph series, a 'first release' movie or an 'original broadcast' on radio or television). In strictly aesthetic terms, all copies are equal.

In light of these perspectives, the activities of the international neo-avant-garde in the 1950s become more intelligible. Creating pastiches out of commercial images, making assemblages from junk and found objects, staging 'happenings' and concrete art performances: such activities ran against the grain of commercially produced mass culture. The next step along this trajectory was the development of Pop art, whose advent can be traced to 1956 at the 'This is Tomorrow' exhibition at the Whitechapel Art Gallery in London [**Doc. 14, pp. 138–9**]. The exhibition featured works by some of the leading artists from the **Independent Group** of the Institute of Contemporary Arts, such as Richard Hamilton, Edouardo Paolozzi, Nigel Henderson, John McHale and William Turnbull. Collages and assemblages were fashioned from iconic pop culture imagery, like movie stars Marilyn Monroe, Marlon Brando, and Robby the Robot from the science fiction movie *Forbidden Planet*, and included modern commercial products like patio furniture, air freshener, a jukebox and a mammoth bottle of Guinness stout. Richard Hamilton's collage *Just What Is It That Makes Today's Homes So Different, So Appealing?* provides an excellent illustration of the ironic humour that was characteristic of the exhibition. Produced not as an original work of art, but as a poster and catalogue image, Hamilton's collage features a young married couple in their modern apartment living room. The body builder husband holds an oversized Tootsie Pop in front of his underwear briefs, while the naked wife, holding a lampshade on her head and with pasties covering her nipples, cups her left breast in her hand. In the background, a woman on television is talking on the phone, a tinned ham rests on the coffee table, a table lamp bears a Ford motors logo, a woman is cleaning the stairs with an electric vacuum, and a poster of a *Young Romance* magazine is displayed on the back wall. The commodities filling the couple's life are ironically reflected back to the viewer and consumed as a banal and narcissistic image.

It was in America, however, the land of the Hollywood 'dream factory' and of internationally recognisable commercial logos like Coca-Cola, that Pop art had its greatest impact, particularly in the works of Roy Lichtenstein, Andy Warhol and James Rosenquist. Lichtenstein had been raised on modernism and had earned a degree in studio art from Ohio State University. Growing up in Manhattan, he had taken classes at the Art Students' League, had his first Abstract Expressionist solo show exhibited in New York in 1959, and then accepted a teaching position at Rutgers University in 1960. Then Lichtenstein became interested in comics, particularly the use of Ben Day dots to fill in large areas with screened colour. He was also fascinated by the 'language' of comics, the juxtaposition of words or word balloons with an image set within a defined frame, and the way that stereotypic images and the mechanical use of colour could convey powerful emotions. His basic method was to enlarge a single comic's panel to enormous proportions, usually about four metres square, and to reproduce the panel image exactly

Independent Group: An association of painters, sculptors and critics at the Institute of Contemporary Arts in London during the early 1950s who opposed the 'high' status of modernism through the inclusion of 'low' sources of mass culture in artistic productions.

(although he sometimes changed the words or colour values). To do this, he would use an overhead projector to enlarge the comic's panel image directly on to a canvas, trace the lines and dots, and then fill in with colour (a simulation of the actual production of comics, which sequentially orders tasks between the artist, inker and colourer). Reversing the mode of mechanical reproduction described by Benjamin, Lichtenstein retraced the steps of the commercial comic's production process as a painter in order to create an 'original' work of art.

Andy Warhol was also intrigued with art manufactured by mechanical reproduction, but less for its aesthetic value than how it could assist the development of his artistic persona. 'If you want to know all about Andy Warhol,' he claimed, 'just look at the surface of my paintings and films and me, and there I am. There's nothing behind it' (Fineberg, 1995: 250). A commercially successful New York graphic designer, Warhol achieved renown as a Pop artist with such works as *32 Campbell's Soup Cans* (1961–62) and *Marilyn Monroe's Lips* (1962), works that repeated the same image with only minor variations. Employing mechanical printmaking techniques, typically silk-screening, he gave a personal imprint to his works of art by introducing 'errors' into the printing process, such as misalignment of the print screens, or by brushing streaks of paint across the silkscreen images by hand. By the mid-1960s, Warhol had become an industry unto himself, hosting celebrities and sycophants at 'The Factory' where his works were mass-produced. In the 1970s, he specialised in celebrity portraits (including his own) and the reproduction of iconic cultural figures like Mickey Mouse, the Mona Lisa, Richard Nixon and Chairman Mao. He was also a pop culture promoter, making over five dozen short and feature-length 'underground' films, the most successful being *The Chelsea Girls* (1966), and producing the debut record album and cover art for *The Velvet Underground and Nico* (1967). Although Warhol's commercial ventures were never as lucrative as his Pop art, there was really little difference between the two. For Warhol, mass media simply meant there was no limit to artistic production or to sales.

The Pop artist James Rosenquist learned studio art at the University of Minnesota and the production techniques for his large-scale creations as a billboard painter. Rosenquist arrived in New York in 1955 to study at the Art Students' League, but continued to earn his living painting billboards in Times Square of movie stars and commercial products. Under this training, he learned how 'detail' at the large scale is an illusion produced by the effect of the calculation of the size and relationship of painted surfaces and open spaces to viewing distance. He also began to gather an extensive collection of advertising, magazine and photo images, which he would assemble as montage fragments in his compositions. One of the earliest, *White Cigarette* (1961), was a montage nearly one and a half metres high of a burning cigarette, the mouth of a bottle, a drinking glass at a diagonal angle, and a woman's bare knees exposed at her dress line. Over the next few years, the scale of his compositions became increasingly large, culminating in *F-111* (1965). Three metres tall and twenty-six metres wide, the massive painting superimposed images of a tube cake, a Firestone rubber tyre, incandescent light bulbs, a young girl under a beauty shop hairdryer, an atomic mushroom cloud capped by a multi-coloured umbrella, underwater air bubbles from a scuba diver and spaghetti noodles in sauce upon the profile of a US Air Force F-111 fighter plane. The antithesis of 'pure' modernism, American Pop art elevated the most banal images of mass commercial culture and extolled them as art.

While it was unclear whether Pop art constituted an avant-garde, there was little doubt that these artists were experimental, innovative, and sometimes they managed to shock and offend highbrow artistic sensibilities. By this point in time, modernism had been thoroughly institutionalised in art museums and was becoming part of the standard university curriculum. This presented a historically unprecedented problem: as modernism becomes canonised, what happens to the avant-garde? In *The Theory of the Avant-Garde* (1974), critical theorist Peter Bürger distinguished between two avant-gardes, the 'historical avant-garde' before the Second World War and the 'neo-avant-garde' afterwards [**Doc. 15, pp. 140–2**]. According to Bürger, earlier avant-gardes such as Cubism, Dada, Constructivism and Surrealism, had made the critique of the autonomy of bourgeois art – 'art for art's sake' – its central project. The post-war neo-avant-garde, by contrast, critiqued the modernist avant-garde. Also, the works of the modernist avant-garde were largely exhibited in modern art museums, exclusive galleries and authorised performance venues, and then were endlessly discussed in high-brow art magazines and university seminars. As a result, the neo-avant-garde critique of the modernist avant-garde did not seriously challenge either the institutionalised museum or the mass media produced and distributed by the culture industry; on the contrary, more often the neo-avant-garde provided new material for the modern art museum and stylistic innovations that further advanced commercial culture.

The emergence of Pop art presented a related challenge: if the neo-avant-garde had lost the capacity to direct art towards critiques of society and culture, what happens to modernism after 'the great divide' that formerly distinguished elite from popular culture? That is, once 'high' modern art and 'low' mass culture are no longer seen strictly in opposition to each other, but as inexorably intertwined, do contemporary artists, writers, musicians and performers continue to have an avant-garde aesthetic, or a social or political function, beyond supplying the culture industry with new material? Since the 1970s, artists and critics have variously grappled with these issues under the somewhat nebulous category of 'postmodernism'. Perhaps the easiest way to understand the term is simply as 'art after modernism'. In this conception, 'Pomo Art' is a kind of 'anything goes' approach to artistic experimentation that yields a pastiche or parody of previous styles, drawn not only from modernism but the entire canon of art history. This type of postmodernism is most readily seen in corporate architecture, commercial advertising, product design and 'virtual reality' production techniques of film, video, digital imaging, electronica music and studio recordings. As a result, some scholars and critics have criticised this type of postmodernism as conservative in the sense that it adheres closely to marketing strategies and the circulation of consumer capitalism.

Another way to understand postmodernism is in terms of the 'crisis of the referent'. An extension of **structuralism** and **post-structuralism** in linguistics, anthropology and critical theory, this approach to postmodernism separates out how language functions as a self-perpetuating cultural system that may or may not have a referential correspondence to reality. The early twentieth-century Swiss linguist Ferdinand de Saussure first explored this issue in a series of lectures published posthumously as *Course in General Linguistics* (1916). Saussure was a pioneer in the field of semiotics, or the study of language 'signs' – the combination of the signifier (a sound utterance or graphic shape), the signified (combinations of utterances or graphics that are recognisably distinct from one another, such as aural or typographic differences in the composition of words) and the referent (the thing the word refers to). In semiotic theory, signs depend less on their correspondence to things in the real world than upon their relationship to each other as embedded in deeper language structures, such as grammar and syntax. On a superficial level, the arbitrary composition of signs becomes specific within their particular language system; dog, *chien* and *perro* may all refer to the same four-legged animal, but as signs they are only intelligible within their respective English, French and Spanish language systems. Structural linguists remain divided on whether deep language structures are universal across cultures (structuralism) or are self-referentially constituted by the cultural system itself (post-structuralism).

As early as the 1920s, Russian Formalism and Prague Structuralism explored the uses of semiotics in the critical analysis of literature and poetry. But it was in the post-May 1968 era that literary and critical theorists began to generally apply semiotics to theories of modernism, commercial mass culture and the avant-garde. A landmark work in this development was *Mythologies* (1957) by the French literary critic Roland Barthes. The individual essays in that collection demystified various aspects of mass culture, such as TV wrestling, the *Blue Guides* to France, wine tasting, burlesque dancing and Bridgette Bardot as a pop icon. In the postscript 'Myth Today',

structuralism: An approach to 'semiotics' or the study of linguistic signs that establishes the meaning of a particular work of literature or art by relating it to underlying rules of language or aesthetic principles.

post-structuralism: An approach to art, literature and philosophy that questions the specific meaning of a work in relation to shifts in underlying structures of language and aesthetics.

Barthes recognised that ideology critique as demystification, revealing the class or political interests behind cultural systems, provided an insufficient explanation of how mass media communicates. After reading Saussure, Barthes also recognised how signs in mass culture may operate as 'second order semiotics', that is, as derivative and spin-off language systems having the power to communicate at their own level, generated solely on the basis of language structures. Further, detached from concrete references, such second-order mythologies only referred back to themselves. The post-structural philosopher Michel Foucault further complicated this issue by arguing that the cultural logic that organises the totality of cultural discourses, which he called an *episteme*, may actually shift between one historical epoch and another. Thus, even the deep structures that organise cultural systems are susceptible to change.

In a continuation of this trajectory, postmodern philosophers suggested that in late twentieth-century culture the referent has been lost altogether. Two key French theorists, François Lyotard and Jean Baudrillard, pursued this issue from somewhat different directions. In *The Postmodern Condition: A Report on Knowledge* (1979), Lyotard grappled with implications of the reduction of knowledge to binary-based information systems. With the advent of computer processing, Lyotard observed, for the first time in history the human mind is not required for information analysis. Simply put, the system runs itself. The catch is that only those things that can be binary coded are permitted into the system in the first place. As a consequence, anything outside the binary code system remains outside; even if something is real, from the perspective of the system it does not exist. Yet given the predominance of data-processing systems in everyday life, for many people this postmodern condition passes unnoticed. An obvious avant-garde response would be to challenge the system with alternate perspectives. Yet as Baudrillard argued in *Simulations* (1981), this may be more easily said than done [**Doc. 16, pp. 142–4**]. The extent and pervasiveness of visually based commercial mass-media culture, Baudrillard argued, renders everything as simulacra, that is, as a 'hyper-reality' of an endless succession of images. For example, no matter how catastrophic natural or human disasters really are, recorded images are what end up on the television news. Disaster images, not the reality of the disaster itself, are what viewers experience and respond to. These images do not challenge or provide alternative perspectives on the news media, because they are the news media. Seemingly everything is recuperated by the system, and reality lies elsewhere.

Some artists and performers, however, strove to put this postmodern 'crisis of the referent' to avant-garde uses. An early example of this is **minimalism**, which draws attention to the instability of signs by reducing the number of elements to such a degree that the composition of signs and their

minimalism: Movement in art and music after the mid twentieth century that reveals the essence of a work by eliminating all non-essential features of the medium.

operations form a self-referential system. This is apparent in the minimalist paintings in the late 1950s and early 1960s, such as Ad Reinhardt's *Abstract Painting, No. 5* (1962) of a canvas painted entirely black. In *Leaf* (1965) by Agnes Martin, the painting is a large square sheet composed entirely of lined scientific quadrangles. In Robert Ryman's *VIII* (1968), a large piece of cardboard is insufficiently covered with paint so that the under surface periodically shows through. Such types of minimalist works present themselves as nothing more or less than painting. Not only is such art non-representational, it is not even abstract or expressionist. Further, the scale of these minimalist paintings tends to be large, around four metres square or greater, which renders their sheer presence as a painting unavoidable. These paintings form their own visual signs without an outside reference.

In the 1960s, minimal music composers like Terry Riley, Steve Reich and Philip Glass explored structural approaches to musical composition that rendered sound and its form synonymous through duration, repetition and the gradual alteration of rhythms or melodic motifs. In the performance of Terry Riley's *In C* (1965), for example, one musician repeats a C-note on the piano at a steady beat while other musicians randomly join in with any of fifty-three one-measure 'modules' composed by Riley, repeating the module until the overall ensemble sound has achieved some kind of coherence. Then, one of the musicians switches modules or another musician adds to the ensemble in order to keep the development of the composition going for the duration of the performance, another variable also left up to the musicians. Steve Reich's minimal music features an ensemble of percussionists or melodic instrument players playing repeated rhythmic motifs. The ensemble begins in unison and then changes 'phases' as the individual musicians alter rhythms one beat or motif at a time. Gradually, this shifts both the underlying pattern of the music and the discrete sub-rhythms, effects most notable in Reich's compositions *Piano Phase* (1967), *Drumming* (1971), *Music for Mallet Instruments, Voices and Organ* (1973), and *Music for 18 Musicians* (1976). In these approaches to minimal music, the sounds (signifiers), discrete sound combinations (the signified), and patterns (completed signs as rhythms or motifs) complete the composition or performance without any outside reference.

Composer Philip Glass and stage director Robert Wilson achieved a kind of minimalist *Gesamtkunstwerk* with *Einstein on the Beach* (1976). This postmodern opera in four acts combines spoken voice, chorus, dancers, instrumental ensemble and solo violin, placed upon a stage that is alternately bare, constructed of cubicles and neon lights, or a courtroom set, and is periodically traversed by massive locomotive, bus and spaceship props. The opera has no plot, and instead is organised by themes of 'Train', 'Trial' and 'Spaceship', with 'Knee Plays' that introduce, connect, and conclude the four acts. An amplified musical ensemble of keyboards, winds, voices and solo violin play repetitive four-note progressions in various combinations of rhythms in 3, 4, 6, 7 (4 + 3), 8 and 9 (4 + 3 + 2), while the actors and dancers perform on stage. Performed in the high culture venue of the New York Metropolitan Opera House in November 1976, the performance lasted over five hours without intermission. The programme notes encouraged the audience to enter, leave, and re-enter the auditorium at will. Taken together, *Einstein on the Beach* was an unparalleled oversaturated minimalist pastiche of words, music styles, spoken voice, movement, constructions, audio amplification and visual projections. Glass continued to compose other large scale operas as well, *Satyagraha* (1980), *Akhnaten* (1984) and *CIVIL warS* (1984, again in collaboration with Robert Wilson), as well as symphonies and chamber music for a classical music audience. Glass also bridged the 'great divide' by scoring music for over two dozen feature and documentary films, and he includes pop musicians among his musical influences. Throughout his career, Glass has pursued a postmodern art through a nearly endless pastiche and recycling of musical signs and visual images, past and present.

In the 1970s and 1980s, postmodernism emerged as a critical visual aesthetic, particularly in the field of photography. Inspired by notions about the loss of the referent, photographers like Sarah Charlesworth, Richard Prince, James Welling and James Casebere displayed photographic images drawn from magazines and advertising copy in successive series that played with the images sequence toward the goal of creating visual ambiguities that emphasise uncertain meaning. Other postmodern photographers would 'pirate' or appropriate canonical art or photographic images and then crop or montage them in order to question their presumed meaning. This kind of agenda is at work in Cindy Sherman's series *Untitled Film Still* (1978) and Sherrie Levine's series *Untitled, After Edward Weston* (1980). These avant-garde artists pursue a critical postmodernism by calling the meaning of art into question by 'deconstructing' the 'visual language' of photographic images themselves, rather than looking for a gap between the image and its supposed relation to something in reality. Since imagistic mass culture pervades postmodern culture so thoroughly, such critical visual practices help to crack open the virtual seamlessness of hyper-reality.

Postmodernism is most monumentally visible, however, in architecture. In reaction against the extreme rationality of form and function in modernist architecture, late twentieth-century postmodern architects such as Robert Venturi, Charles Willard Moore and Michael Graves designed large-scale steel, glass, and brick architectural projects of 'impure forms' by combining asymmetrical exterior designs with a pastiche of ornamental decorations drawn from diverse styles. Frank Gehry may be perhaps the most prolific of these postmodern architects, who achieved renown by deconstructing the forms of modernist architecture and reassembling them in fluid and unexpected ways – such as the Gehry Tower in Hanover, Germany (2001) and the Eight Spruce Street skyscraper in Manhattan, New York (2011). In addition to his novel and innovative postmodern designs, however, Gehry's architecture has also become emblematic of what art critic Hal Foster has called postmodern 'corporate branding', through government-sponsored projects such as the Olympic Village in Barcelona, Spain (1992), the Guggenheim Museum in Bilbao, Spain (1997) and other modern art museums internationally, as well as through commissions by private corporations such as Novartis Pharma International AG and Disney.

In this sense, postmodern architecture perhaps best illustrates the 'end of modernism' in terms of the revolutionary aspirations of the early twentieth-century modernist avant-garde. In a manner similar to critical theorist Peter Bürger's conception of the neo-avant-garde, the critical role of postmodernism may lie in its ability to critique modernism. But as Frederic Jameson has observed, the chief effect of postmodern pastiche seems to be the creation of an ersatz nostalgia for a past that never was, consolidated through the corporate power of late capitalism [**Doc. 17, pp. 144–6**]. What remains for the future is a continuing assessment of the ways in which postmodernism may or may not have contributed to the aims, accomplishments, and detours of modernism.

Further reading

Foster, Hal and Mark Francis, *Pop*, London: Phaidon Press, 2005.

Harvey, David, *The Condition of Postmodernity*, Oxford: Blackwell, 1990.

Huyssen, Andreas, *After the Great Divide: Modernism, Mass Culture, Postmodernism*, Bloomington: Indiana University Press, 1986.

Jameson, Fredric, *Postmodernism, or The Cultural Logic of Late Capitalism*, Durham: Duke University Press, 1991.

Robbins, David (ed.), *The Independent Group: Postwar Britain and the Aesthetics of Plenty*, Cambridge, MA: MIT Press, 1990.

Varnedoe, Kirk and Adam Gopnik, *High & Low: Modern Art, Popular Culture*, New York: The Museum of Modern Art, 1991.

Wallis, Brian (ed.), *Art After Modernism: Rethinking Representation*, New York: The New Museum of Contemporary Art, 1984.

Whiting, Cecile, *A Taste for Pop: Pop Art, Gender, and Consumer Culture*, Cambridge: Cambridge University Press, 1997.

Part 5

CONCLUSION

9

Assessment

In the early twentieth century, a self-conscious modernist avant-garde across the arts set out to transform European consciousness and society. A century later, that endeavour has lost much of its originality and radical edge. Modernist art and literature no longer challenge the establishment; rather, modernism has become institutionalised in modern art museums and canonised in the literature and art history departments of major universities. Techniques of abstraction and montage, as well as the creative impulses to innovate and shock, are no longer the domains of an artistic elite, but have become the stock-in-trade of commercial advertising, feature films, television and computer-generated graphics. Modernism has been infused throughout the contemporary culture we consume on an everyday basis.

Yet the fact that modernism has been woven extensively throughout the fabric of both official and commercial culture suggests that, in some sense, the goal of transforming Western civilisation, and the world, was accomplished. Whether modernism has transformed human consciousness on a wide scale as a result seems more debatable. And from a historical perspective, it appears that the socially and politically revolutionary aspirations of the modernist avant-garde were largely situational, contributing a flurry of experimental and provocative artistic activity in the moment, but falling short of large-scale transformations. In these ways, the results of the modernist avant-garde appear mixed in terms of its historical aspirations. And if we accept that contemporary life constitutes a 'postmodern condition', circumscribed by virtual technologies and high-end consumer culture, we may have reached the end of modernism, if not history, altogether.

However, some contemporary artists and writers have responded to the challenges of postmodernism by asking, 'crisis of the referent for whom?' The emergence of feminism and queer theory in art provide two examples of how we might go about re-evaluating the legacies of modernism and how new artistic avant-gardes may be emerging in the twenty-first century. With the development of the Women's Liberation Movement and the establishment of Women's Studies programmes at universities in the 1970s, feminist scholars began to critique the modernist canon as male dominated. Ever since the publication of Simone de Beauvoir's *The Second Sex* (1949), it has been axiomatic that woman is the 'other' of male identity, an object formulated by his gaze. In the 1970s, feminist critiques used this insight to question the assumption that modernism can be gender neutral. Historically, famous men have predominated in Western civilisation, including modernism, and the contributions of women have been obscured. At the level of audience reception, this means that the viewer or consumer of works of art and literature has a presumed male identity, a critique powerfully articulated by British feminist film theorist Laura Mulvey in her foundational essay 'Visual Pleasure and Narrative Cinema' (1975).

In response, feminist scholars have striven to recover the lives and works of neglected yet important modernist women artists and writers, and feminist perspectives have been worked into contemporary art criticism. While a few literary authors such as H. D., Gertrude Stein and Virginia Woolf, and visual artists like Hannah Höch and Lee Krasner, secured a place in the modernist canon early on, many other influential women modernists have been subsequently added as a direct consequence of feminist studies. The current canon of British and American modernist literature, for example, now typically includes such authors as Marianne Moore, Djuna Barnes, Nancy Cunard, Jean Rhys, Rebecca West and Edith Wharton, who were recognised as important authors in their time, but were neglected in the early canonisation of literary modernism. In the visual arts, the contribution of important women artists to Surrealism, such as Valentine Hugo, Meret Oppenheim, Claude Cahun, Lee Miller, Leonora Carrington, Gala Dalí, Remedios Varo and Frida Kahlo, have been critical to expanding both our understanding of the Surrealist muse and to the portrayal of female desire.

The contributions of contemporary feminist artists and writers also began to receive increased attention at the end of the twentieth century. In 1975, American feminist artist Judy Chicago gained renown with *The Dinner Party*. The installation featured a large triangular table set with placemats and ceramic plate vulvas of thirty-nine important women 'missing from the historical record', from the Primordial Goddess of prehistory to Georgia O'Keefe. The names of an additional 999 'Women of Achievement' were imprinted on the floor tiles. In France during the 1980s, *l'écriture féminine*, or 'writing the female body', became a feminist practice in the experimental fiction, poetry and critical theory in the writings of Monique Wittig, Hélène Cixous, Luce Irigaray and Julia Kristeva. In the United States, collage artist Barbara Kruger appropriated images from women's magazines and critically redirected them with feminist messages by giving them her own captions, such as *Your Gaze Hits the Side of My Face* (1981), *We Won't Play Nature to Your Culture* (1983), and *Your Body is a Battleground* (1989) (*see* Plate 4). In various ways, feminist art and literature, both past and present, have made their imprint on contemporary culture. While some feminist artists and authors have engaged in critiques of the postmodern condition, this has not necessarily been the prime motive. Most often, their avant-garde engagement as artists primarily has to do with the pursuit of a feminist social and political agenda that is keenly aware of the intersections of race, class and gender [**Doc. 18, pp. 146–8**].

The emergence of 'queer theory' in late twentieth-century art criticism reveals how gay and lesbian artists have similarly pursued avant-garde art-istic agendas without being overly concerned about the postmodern crisis of the referent. In terms of art criticism, this has led to the reinterpretation of the works of such prominent neo-avant-garde figures as John Cage, Merce Cunningham, Jasper Johns, Robert Rauschenberg, Larry Rivers and Agnes Martin, in terms of the 'silences' and 'out' elements in their art. At other times, the meaning of queer art has been explicitly political. In the mid-1980s, New York artists in ACT-UP (AIDS Coalition To Unleash Power) began to make subversive posters, take out newspaper advertisements and produce videos about police brutality and media misrepresentations of ACT-UP demonstrations, in order to raise public consciousness about the burgeoning AIDS crisis. This led to the emergence of a new avant-garde of gay and lesbian artists, such as Robert Gober, Robert Mapplethorpe, Donald Moffet, Jack Pierson, David Wojnarowicz, Felix Gonzalez-Torres and Zoe Leonard, who began to explore the shifting cultural and historical meanings of sexuality in their art. The Pop artist Keith Haring was a key cross-over figure in making gay themes in art accessible to a general population, through his Pop Shop boutique that marketed his art as clothing and gifts, the Keith Haring Foundation to assist AIDS-related and children's charities, and the Haring Kids website for children to participate in making art. What feminist studies and queer art bring to this assessment is the critical perspec-tive that while the modernist avant-garde may have run its course, contem-porary society, culture and politics create conditions that may foster the rise of new forms of artistic production and avant-garde movements.

As the cultural critic Raymond Williams has observed, a historical assessment of modernism might be best addressed by asking, 'When was Modernism?' [**Doc. 19, pp. 149–50**]. Canonising modernism according to movements, styles and aesthetics, he emphasised, drains the avant-garde of its historical functions and power. Overcoming the 'non-historical fixity of *post*-modernism,' Williams insisted, may be best accomplished by situating the modernist avant-garde within the actual conditions of history, past and present. Just as 'high modernism' developed in Europe under specific historical conditions in the early twentieth century, so too circumstances in the late twentieth century may provide the impetus and materials for entirely new modes of artistic expression and avant-garde aspirations in the twenty-first century. Postmodernism is just one of the latter-day responses to modernism, and it was by no means the only one. By bringing explicit social and political agendas to their work, contemporary artists and writers may reconstitute the historical mission of the avant-garde by rejecting the presumed cultural supremacy of twentieth-century modernism, or its afterlife as postmodernism. The legacy of modernism, like history itself, remains an unfinished project.

Further reading

Brown, Betty Ann, *Gradiva's Mirror: Reflections on Women, Surrealism and Art History*, New York: Midmarch Arts Press, 2002.

Butt, Gavin, 'How New York Queered the Idea of Modern Art', in Paul Wood (ed.), *Varieties of Modernism*, New Haven and London: Yale University Press/The Open University, 2004.

Caws, Marianne, Rudoph Kuenzli and Gwen Raab (eds), *Surrealism and Women*, Cambridge, MA: MIT Press, 1991.

Chadwick, Whitney, *Women Artists and the Surrealism Movement*, New York: Thames & Hudson, 1991.

Crimp, Douglas and Adam Rolston (eds), *AIDS DEMOgraphics*, Seattle: Bay Press, 1988.

Perry, Gill and Paul Wood (eds), *Themes in Contemporary Art*, New Haven and London: Yale University Press/The Open University, 2000.

Pollock, Griselda, *Vision and Difference: Feminism, Femininity and Histories of Art* (revd edn), New York: Routledge, 2003.

Summers, Claude J. (ed.), *The Queer Encyclopedia of the Visual Arts*, Berkeley: Cleis Press, 2004.

Williams, Raymond, *The Politics of Modernism: Against the New Conformists*, London: Verso, 1989.

Part 6

DOCUMENTS

Document 1   CHARLES BAUDELAIRE, 'THE PAINTER OF MODERN LIFE'

While Charles Baudelaire (1821–1867) was considered a minor literary figure during his life, the Symbolists and Surrealists later recognised him as a poetic genius. In 'The Painter of Modern Life' (1863), Baudelaire calls for a new kind of art, one that captures the spirit of modernity in an objective manner that is simultaneously ephemeral and eternal. Such art, he mused, would not be produced by 'great masters', but by the likes of M.C.G. (Monsieur Constantin Guys), an obscure watercolourist and illustrator whose contemporary subjects included scenes from the Crimean War, military parades, and boulevard landscapes populated with elegantly dressed dandies, fashionable women and prostitutes.

Today I want to talk to my readers about a singular man, whose originality is so powerful and clear-cut that it is self-sufficing, and does not bother to look for approval. None of his drawings is signed, if by signature we mean the few letters, which can be so easily forged, that compose a name, and that so many other artists grandly inscribe at the bottom of their most carefree sketches. But all his works are signed with his dazzling soul, and art-lovers who have seen and liked them will recognize them easily from the description I propose to give them. M. C. G. loves mixing with the crowds, loves being incognito, and carries his originality to the point of modesty. M. Thackeray, who, as is well known, is very interested in all things to do with art, and who draws the illustrations for his own novels, one day spoke of M. G. in a London review, much to the irritation of the latter who regarded the matter as an outrage to his modesty. And again quite recently, when he heard that I was proposing to make an assessment of his mind and talent, he begged me, in a most peremptory manner, to suppress his name, and to discuss his works only as though they were the works of some anonymous person. I will humbly comply with this odd request. The reader and I will proceed as though M. G. did not exist, and we will discuss his drawings and his water-colours, for which he professes a patrician's disdain, in the same way as would a group of scholars faced with the task of assessing the importance of a number of precious historical documents which chance has brought to light, and the author of which must for ever remain unknown. And even to reassure my conscience completely, let my readers assume that all the things I have to say about the artist's nature, so strangely and mysteriously dazzling, have been more or less accurately suggested by the works in question; pure poetic hypothesis, conjecture, or imaginative reconstructions.

[. . .]

And so, walking or quickening his pace, he goes his way, for ever in search. In search of what? We may rest assured that this man, such as I have described him, this solitary mortal endowed with an active imagination, always roaming the great desert of men, has a nobler aim than that of the

pure idler [*flaneur*], a more general aim, other than the fleeting pleasure of circumstance. He is looking for that indefinable something we may be allowed to call 'modernity', for want of a better term to express the idea in question. The aim for him is to extract from fashion the poetry that resides in its historical envelope, to distil the eternal from the transitory. [. . .] Modernity is the transient, the fleeting, the contingent; it is one half of art, the other being the eternal and the immovable. There is a form of modernity for every painter of the past; the majority of the fine portraits that remain to us from former times are clothed in the dress of their own day. They are perfectly harmonious works because the dress, the hairstyle, and even the gesture, the expression and the smile (each age has its carriage, its expression and its smile) form a whole, full of vitality. You have no right to despise this transitory fleeting element, the metamorphoses of which are so frequent, nor to dispense with it. If you do, you inevitably fall into the emptiness of an abstract and indefinable beauty, like that of the one and only woman of time before the Fall. If for the dress of the day, which is necessarily right, you substitute another, you are guilty of a piece of nonsense that only a fancy-dress ball imposed by fashion can excuse. Thus the goddesses, the nymphs, and sultans of the eighteenth century are portraits in the spirit of their day.
   [. . .]

We are betting on a certainty when we say that in a few years drawings of M. G. will become precious archives of civilized life. His works will be sought after by discerning collectors. . . . M. G. retains a profound merit, which is all his own; he has deliberately fulfilled a function which other artists disdain, and which a man of the world above all others could carry out. He has gone everywhere in quest of the ephemeral, fleeting forms of beauty in the life of our day, the characteristic traits of what, with the reader's permission, we have called 'modernity.' Often bizarre, violent and excessive, but always full of poetry, he has succeeded, in his drawings, in distilling the bitter and heady flavour of the wine of life.

Source: Baudelaire, Charles, 'The Painter of Modern Life', in *Selected Writings on Art and Literature* (trans. and intro. P. R. Charvet), London: Penguin, 1992, pp. 395, 402–403, 435.

VIRGINIA WOOLF, 'MR. BENNETT AND MRS. BROWN'   **Document 2**

Virginia Woolf (1882–1941) was one of the leading literary modernists in early twentieth-century Britain. Dissatisfied with the kinds of popular post-Victorian novels being written by Arnold Bennett, John Galsworthy, and H. G. Wells, Woolf sought to infuse modern prose fiction with a more lyrical and poetic style, one that expressed the stream of consciousness ebb and flow of an inner psychology. In 'Mr. Bennett and Mrs. Brown', Woolf urges authors to cultivate a subjective and multi-perspective imagination that resonated with the 'perceptual revolution' of the early twentieth century.

My belief that men and women write novels because they are lured on to create some character which has thus imposed itself upon them has the sanction of Mr. Arnold Bennett. In an article from which I quote, he says, 'The foundation of good fiction is character-creating and nothing else . . . Style counts; plot counts; originality of outlook counts. But none of these counts anything like so much the convincingness of the characters. If the characters are real the novel will have a chance; if they are not, oblivion will be its portion . . .' And he goes on to draw the conclusion that we have no young novelists of first-rate importance at the present moment, because they are unable to create characters that are real, true, and convincing.

[. . .]

My first assertion is one that I think you will grant – that everyone in this room is a judge of character. Indeed it would be impossible to live for a year without disaster unless one practised character-reading and had some skill in the art. Our marriages, our friendships depend on it; our business largely depends on it; every day questions arise which can only be solved by its help. And now I will hazard a second assertion, which is more disputable perhaps, to the effect that in or about December, 1910, human character changed.

I am not saying that one went out, as one might into a garden, and there saw that a rose had flowered, or that a hen had laid an egg. The change was not sudden and definite like that. But a change there was, nevertheless; and since one must be arbitrary, let us date it about the year 1910. [. . .] All human relations have shifted – those between masters and servants, husbands and wives, parents and children. And when human relations change there is at the same time a change in religion, conduct, politics, and literature. Let us agree to place one of these changes about the year 1910.

[. . .]

One night some weeks ago, then, I was late for the train and jumped into the first carriage I came to. As I sat down I had the strange and uncomfortable feeling that I was interrupting a conversation between two people who were already sitting there. [. . .] They were sitting opposite each other, and the man, who had been leaning over and talking emphatically to judge by his attitude and the flush on his face, sat back and became silent. I had disturbed him and he was annoyed. The elderly lady, however, whom I will call Mrs. Brown, seemed rather relieved. She was one of those clean, threadbare old ladies whose extreme tidiness – everything buttoned, fastened, tied together, mended and brushed up – suggests more extreme poverty than rags and dirt. There was something pinched about her – a look of suffering, of apprehension, and, in addition, she was extremely small. Her feet, in their clean little boots, scarcely touched the floor. I felt she had nobody to support her; that she had to make up her mind for herself; that, having been deserted, left a widow, years ago, she had led an anxious, harried life, bringing up an only son, who, as likely as not, was by this time beginning to go to the bad. All this shot through my mind as I sat down . . .

[. . .]

Mrs. Brown and I were left alone together. She sat in her corner opposite, very clean, very small, rather queer, and suffering intensely. The impression she made was overwhelming. It came pouring out like a draught, like a smell of burning. What was it composed of – that overwhelming and peculiar impression? Myriads of irrelevant and incongruous ideas crowd into one's head on such occasions; one sees the person, one sees Mrs. Brown, in the centre of all sort of different scenes. I thought of her in a seaside house, among queer ornaments: sea-urchins, models of ships in glass cases. Her husband's medals were on the mantelpiece. She popped in and out of the room, perching on the edges of chairs, picking meals out of saucers, indulging in long silent stares. The caterpillars and the oak-trees seemed to imply all that. And then, into this fantastic and secluded life, in broke Mr. Smith. I saw him blowing in, so to speak, on a windy day. He banged, he slammed. His dripping umbrella made a pool in the hall. They sat closeted together.

And then Mrs. Brown faced the dreadful revelation. She took her heroic decision. Early, before dawn, she packed her bag and carried it to the station . . . The important thing was to realize her character, to steep oneself in her atmosphere. I had no time to explain why I felt it somewhat tragic, heroic, yet with a dash of the flighty, the fantastic, before the train stopped, and I watched her disappear, carrying her bag, into the vast blazing station. She looked very small, very tenacious; at once very frail and very heroic. And I have never seen her again, and I shall never know what became of her.

[. . .]

Your part is to insist that writers shall come down off their plinths and pedestals, and describe beautifully if possible, truthfully at any rate, our Mrs. Brown. You should insist that she is an old lady of unlimited capacity and infinite variety; capable of appearing in any place; wearing any dress; saying anything and doing heaven knows what. But the things she says and the things she does and her eyes and her nose and her speech and her silence have an overwhelming fascination, for she is, of course, the spirit we live by, life itself.

Source: Virginia Woolf, 'Mr. Bennet and Mrs. Brown', in *Collected Essays*, Vol. 1, New York: Harcourt, Brace & World, 1967, pp. 319–324, 336–337. Reprinted in the US courtesy of Houghton Mifflin, and in the rest of the world courtesy of The Random House Group Limited.

Document 3   HENRI MATISSE, 'NOTES OF A PAINTER'

A leading member of the Fauves *('wild beasts') group of early modernist painters,
Henri Matisse (1869–1954) was influenced by the Impressionists and the
Neo-Impressionists, most particularly Paul Cézanne. For Matisse, the form
and meaning of paintings was conveyed more through the compositional elements of brushstroke, intensities of colour, and the harmony of elements upon
the canvas, than upon the figurative or representational image. 'Notes of a
Painter' (1908) articulates his theory of expressionism, or the ability of an
artist to manipulate the elements of the paint medium to evoke a strong emotional impact within a viewer.*

Expression, for me, does not reside in passions glowing in a human face or
manifested by violent movement. The entire arrangement of my picture is
expressive: the place occupied by the figures, the empty spaces around them,
the proportions, everything has its share. Composition is the art of arranging
in a decorative manner the diverse elements at the painter's command to
express his feelings. In a picture every part will be visible and will play its
appointed role, whether it be principal or secondary. Everything that is not
useful in the picture is, it follows, harmful. A work of art must be harmonious in its entirety: any superfluous detail would replace some other essential
detail in the mind of the spectator.

Composition, the aim of which should be expression, is modified according to the surface to be covered. If I take a sheet of paper of a given size, my
drawing will have a necessary relationship to its format. I would not repeat
this drawing on another sheet of different proportions, for example, rectangular instead of square. Nor should I be satisfied with a mere enlargement,
had I to transfer the drawing to a sheet the same shape, but ten times larger.
A drawing must have an expansive force which gives life to the thing around
it. An artist who wants to transpose a composition from one canvas to
another larger one must conceive it anew in order to preserve its expression;
he must alter its character and not just square it up onto the larger canvas.

[. . .]

Both harmonies and dissonances of colour can produce agreeable effects.
Often when I start to work I record fresh and superficial sensations during
the first session. A few years ago I was sometimes satisfied with the result.
But today if I were satisfied with this, now that I think I can see further, my
picture would have a vagueness in it: I should have recorded the fugitive
sensations of a moment which could not completely define my feelings and
which I should barely recognize the next day.

I want to reach that state of condensation of sensations which makes a
painting. I might be satisfied with a work done at one sitting, but I would
soon tire of it; therefore, I prefer to rework it so that later I may recognize it

as representative of my state of mind. There was a time when I never left my paintings hanging on the wall because they reminded me of moments of over-excitement and I did not like to see them again when I was calm. Nowadays I try to put serenity into my pictures and to rework them as long as I have not succeeded.

[. . .]

The chief function of colour should be to serve expression as well as possible. I put down my tones without a preconceived plan. If at first, and perhaps without my having been conscious of it, one tone has particularly seduced or caught me, more often than not once the picture is finished I will notice that I have respected this tone while I progressively altered and transformed all the others. The expressive aspect of colours imposes itself on me in a purely instinctive way. To paint an autumn landscape I will not try to remember what colours suit this season, I will be inspired only by the sensation that the season arouses in me: the icy purity of the sour blue sky will express the season just as well as the nuances of foliage. My sensation itself may vary, the autumn may be soft and warm like a continuation of summer, or quite cool with a cold sky and lemon-yellow tress that give a chilly impression and already announce winter.

My choice of colours does not rest on any scientific theory; it is based on observation, on sensitivity, on felt experiences. Inspired by certain pages of Delacroix, an artist like Signac is preoccupied with complementary colours, and the theoretical knowledge of them will lead him to use a certain tone in a certain place. But I simply try to put down colours which render my sensation. There is an impelling proportion of tones that may lead me to change the shape of a figure or to transform my composition. Until I have achieved this proportion in all parts of the composition I strive towards it and keep on working. Then a moment comes when all the parts have found their definite relationships, and from then on it would be impossible for me to add a stroke to any picture without having to repaint it entirely.

In reality, I think that the very theory of complementary colours is not absolute. In studying the paintings of artists whose knowledge of colours depends upon instinct and feeling, and on a constant analogy with their sensations, one could define certain laws of colour and so broaden the limits of colour theory as it is now defined.

Document 4   WASSILY KANDINSKY, *CONCERNING THE SPIRITUAL IN ART*

The career of the Russian painter Wassily Kandinsky (1866–1944) corresponds with the era of 'high modernism' in art. He was an influential figure in numerous modernist art movements, including Der Blaue Reiter (the 'Blue Rider' Group), the Bauhaus, and Abstract Expressionism. In Concerning the Spiritual in Art *(1911), Kandinsky explores the psychology of modern art as a universal mode of communication that speaks directly to the 'inner need' of the human soul. Through the simile of an ascending triangle, Kandinsky also attributes an avant-garde role to artists, whose works of art, although often scorned, lead the rest of society towards future enlightenment.*

Every work of art is the child of its age and, in many cases, the mother of our emotions. It follows that each period of culture produces an art of its own which can never be repeated. Efforts to revive the art-principles of the past will at best produce an art that is still-born. It is impossible for us to live and feel, as did the ancient Greeks. In the same way those who strive to follow the Greek methods in sculpture achieve only a similarity of form, the work remaining soulless for all time. Such imitation is mere aping. Externally the monkey completely resembles a human being; he will sit holding a book in front of his nose, and turn the pages with a thoughtful aspect, but his actions have for him no real meaning.

There is, however, in art another kind of external similarity which is founded on a fundamental truth. When there is a similarity in inner tendency in the whole moral and spiritual atmosphere, a similarity of ideals, at first closely pursued but later lost to sight, a similarity in the inner feeling of any one period to that of another, the logical result will be a revival of the external forms which served to express those inner feelings in an earlier age. An example of this today is our sympathy, our spiritual relationship, with the Primitives. Like ourselves, these artists sought to express in their work only internal truths, renouncing in consequence all consideration of external form.

This all-important spark of inner life today is at present only a spark. Our minds, which are even now only just awakening after years of materialism, are infected with the despair of unbelief, of lack of purpose and ideal. The nightmare of materialism, which has turned the life of the universe into an evil, useless game, is not yet past; it holds the awakening soul still in its grip. Only a feeble light glimmers like a tiny star in a vast gulf of darkness. This feeble light is but a presentiment, and the soul, when it sees it, trembles in doubt whether the light is not a dream, and the gulf of darkness a reality. This doubt, and the still harsh tyranny of the materialistic philosophy, divide our soul sharply from that of the Primitives . . .

These two possible resemblances between art forms of today and those of the past will be at once recognized as diametrically opposed to one another. The first, being purely external, has no future. The second, being internal, contains the seed of the future within itself. After the period of materialist effort, which held the soul in check until it was shaken off as evil, the soul is emerging, purged by trials and sufferings. Shapeless emotions such as fear, joy, grief, etc., which belonged to this time of effort, will no longer greatly attract the artist. He will endeavour to awake subtler emotions, as yet unnamed. Living himself a complicated and comparatively subtle life, his work will give to those observers capable of feeling them lofty emotions beyond the reach of words.

[. . .]

The life of the spirit may be fairly represented in diagram as a large acute-angled triangle divided horizontally into unequal parts with the narrowest segment uppermost. The lower the segment the greater it is in breadth, depth, and area.

The whole triangle is moving slowly, almost invisibly forwards and upwards. Where the apex was today the second segment is tomorrow; what today can be understood only by the apex and to the rest of the triangle is an incomprehensible gibberish, forms tomorrow the true thought and feeling of the second segment.

At the apex of the top segment stands often one man, and only one. His joyful vision cloaks a vast sorrow. Even those who are nearest to him in sympathy do not understand him. Angrily they abuse him as charlatan or madman. So in his lifetime stood Beethoven, solitary and insulted. How many years will it be before the greater segment of the triangle reaches the spot where he once stood alone? Despite memorials and statues, are they really many who have risen to his level?

In every segment of the triangle are artists. Each one of them who can see beyond the limits of his segment is a prophet to those about him, and helps the advance of the obstinate whole. But those who are blind, or those who retard the movement of the triangle for baser reasons, are fully understood by their fellows and acclaimed for their genius. The greater the segment (which is the same as saying the lower it lies in the triangle) so the greater the number who understand the words of the artist. Every segment hungers consciously or, much more often, unconsciously for their corresponding spiritual food. This food is offered by the artists, and for this food the segment immediately below will tomorrow be stretching out eager hands.

Source: Wasilly Kandinskky, *Concerning the Spiritual in Art* (trans. and intro. M. T. H. Sadler), New York: Dover Publications Inc., 1977, pp. 1–9.

Document 5   PIET MONDRIAN, 'NEO-PLASTICISM: THE GENERAL PRINCIPLE OF PLASTIC
EQUIVALENCE'

*Originally a student of Cubism, in the post-World War I era Dutch painter Piet
Mondrian (1872–1944) developed a new theory and practice of abstract art
known as Neo-Plasticism. In this essay, first published in conjunction with the
'Masters of Cubism' exhibition in Paris in 1921, Mondrian extends the notion
of plastic arts beyond customary three-dimensional media such as sculpture
and ceramics to invoke 'the plastic' as a universal principle of consciousness
and the objective realisation of unconscious and subjective realms occurring
within the artist, which he believed could be applied across all the arts, literary and musical as well as visual and architectural.*

Although art is the plastic expression of *our* aesthetic emotion, we cannot
therefore conclude that art is only 'the aesthetic expression of our subjective
sensations.' Logic demands that art be the *plastic expression of our whole being*:
therefore, it must be equally the plastic appearance of the *nonindividual*, the
absolute and annihilating opposition of subjective sensations. That is, it must
also be the *direct expression of the universal in us* – which is the *exact appearance of the universal outside us*.

The universal thus understood is that which *is* and *remains constant*: the
more or less *unconscious* in us, opposed to the more or less *conscious* – *the
individual*, which is repeated and renewed.

Our whole being is as much the one as the other: *the unconscious and the
conscious, the immutable and the mutable, emerging and changing form through
their reciprocal action.*

This action contains all the misery and all the happiness of life: misery is
caused by *continual separation*, happiness by perpetual rebirth of *the change-
able*. The immutable is beyond all misery and all happiness: it is *equilibrium*.

Through the immutable in us, we are united with all things; the mutable
destroys our equilibrium, limits us, and separates us from all that is other
than us. It is from this equilibrium, from *the unconscious*, from *the immutable*
that art comes. It attains its *plastic expression* through *the conscious*. In this
way, *the appearance of the art* is the plastic expression of *the unconscious and
the conscious*. It shows *the relationship* of each to the other: its appearance
changes, but *art* remains immutable.

In 'the totality of our being' the individual or the universal may dominate,
or equilibrium between the two may be approached. This latter possibility
allows us *to be universal as individuals: to exteriorize the unconscious consciously*.
Then we see and hear *universally*, for we have transcended the domination of
the most external. The forms of external appearance we see, the noises,
sounds, and words we hear, appear to us otherwise than through our universal vision and hearing. What we *really* see or hear is the *direct manifestation*

of the universal, whereas what we perceive outside ourselves as form or sound shows itself weakened and veiled. In seeking plastic expression we express our *universal perception* and thus our *universal beings as individuals*: therefore, the one and the other *in equivalence*. To transcend the limitations of form and nevertheless to use limited form and descriptive word is not a true manifestation of our being, is not its *pure plastic expression: a new plastic expression is inevitable, an equivalent appearance of these opposites, therefore plastic expression in equilibrated relationship*.

[. . .]

In the New Plastic, painting no longer expresses itself through the *corporeality* of appearance that gives it a naturalistic expression. To the contrary, painting is expressed plastically by *plane within plane*. By reducing three-dimensional corporeality to a single plane, *it expresses pure relationship*.

However, the plastic means of architecture as well as sculpture have an advantage over painting through their other possibilities.

By its plastic means, *architecture* has an aesthetic and mathematical appearance, which is therefore *exact* and *more or less* abstract. *Being a composition of contrasting and self-neutralizing planes, architecture is the exact plastic expression of aesthetic relationship equilibrated in space*. The New Plastic does not regard architecture, any more than painting, as *morphoplastic*. That was the old view. Although form does appear in architectural plastic, it is not closed and limited form – any more than is the composition of rectangular color planes in the New Plastic of painting. *Real* form *is closed or round or curved* in opposition to the apparent form of the rectangle, where lines *intersect, touch at tangent, but continue uninterrupted*.

Seen as *equilibrated opposition of expansion and limitation in plane composition*, architectural expression (in spite of its third dimension) ceases to exist *as corporeality and as object*. Its abstract expression appears even more directly than in painting.

[. . .]

In any case, *the new spirit* must be manifested in *all the arts without exception*. That there are differences between the arts is no reason that one should be valued less than the other; that can lead to *another* appearance but not to an *opposed* appearance. As soon as one art becomes plastic expression of the abstract, the others can no longer remain plastic expressions of the natural. The two do not go together: from this comes their mutual hostility down to the present. The New Plastic abolishes this antagonism: *it creates the unity of all the arts*.

Source: From Piet Mondrian, *The New Art—The New Life: The Collected Writings of Piet Mondrian* (ed. and trans. Harry Holtzman and Martin S. James), London: Thames & Hudson Ltd, 1987, pp. 134–140.

Document 6   EMIL NOLDE, *'ON PRIMITIVE ART'*

During the 'Age of Imperialism', and the attendant emergence of ethnography, some early modernists found aesthetic correspondences between their works and the 'primitive' art produced by the indigenous peoples of Africa, the Americas, and Oceania. For members of the Brücke group of German Expressionist painters, including Emil Nolde (1867–1956), the artefacts of non-Western cultures and artisanal techniques of pre-industrial crafts provided materials for creating an entirely new and modernist art. In 'On Primitive Art' (1912), Nolde rejects the heritage of Western civilisation to pursue the creation of a modernism infused with primitive imagery and craft methods.

1. 'The most perfect art was Greek art. Raphael is the greatest of all masters in painting.' Such were the doctrines of every art teacher only twenty or thirty years ago.

2. Since then, much has changed. We do not care for Raphael, and are less enthusiastic about the statues of the so-called golden age of Greece. Our predecessors' ideas are not ours. Works signed by great names over the centuries appeal to us less. In the hurry and bustle of the times, wordly-wise artists created works for Popes and palaces. It is the ordinary people who laboured in their workshops and of whose lives scarcely anything is now known, whose very names have not come down to us, that we love and respect today in their plain, large-scale carvings in the cathedrals of Naumburg, Magdeburg and Bamberg.

3. Our museums are getting large and crammed and are growing rapidly. I am not keen on these vast collections, deadening by virtue of their sheer mass. A reaction against such excess must surely come soon.

4. Not long ago only a few artistic periods were thought suitable for museums. Then they were joined by exhibitions of Coptic and early Christian art, Greek terracottas and vases, Persian and Islamic art. But why is Indian, Chinese and Javanese art still classified under ethnology or anthropology? And why is the art of primitive peoples not considered art at all?

5. What is it about these primitive forms of expression that appeals so much to us artists?

6. In our own time, every earthenware vessel or piece of jewellery, every utensil or garment, has to be designed on paper before it is made. Primitive peoples, however, create their works with the material itself in the artist's hand, held in his fingers. They aspire to express delight in form and the love of creating it. Absolute originality, the intense and often grotesque expression of power and life in very simple forms – that may be why we like these works of native art.

Source: From *Jahre der Kämpfe, 1912–1914*, Berlin: Rembrandt, 1934, English translation in Charles Harrison and Paul Wood, *Art in Theory 1900–2000* (new edn), Oxford: Blackwell, 2003, p. 97.

F. T. MARINETTI, 'THE FOUNDING AND THE MANIFESTO OF FUTURISM'   **Document 7**

Poet and provocateur, Filippo Tommaso Marinetti (1876–1944) was the founder of Futurism, an Italian modernist avant-garde movement across the arts that encompassed literature, poetry, painting, sculpture, music, architecture and design. One of the few modernist movements to bridge the experience of World War I, and briefly embraced by Italian Fascism, Futurism influenced multiple modernist movements across Europe, including Cubo-Futurism in Russia, Vorticism in Britain, and late-Cubism, Dada, and Surrealism in France. In this excerpt from the 'Manifesto of Futurism' (1909), Marinetti openly embraces industrial production, technological innovation, mass culture, masculine militarism, revolutionary violence and apocalyptic destruction as bases for Futurist aesthetics and artistic production.

We had stayed up all night – my friends and I – beneath mosque lamps hanging from the ceiling. Their brass domes were filigreed, starred like our souls; just as they were illuminated, again like our souls, by the imprisoned brilliance of an electric heart. On the opulent oriental rugs, we had crushed our ancestral lethargy, arguing all the way to the final frontiers of logic and blackening reams of paper with delirious writings.

Our chests swelled with immense pride, for we alone were still awake and upright at that hour, like magnificent lighthouses or forward sentries facing an army of enemy stars, eyeing us from their encampments in the sky. Alone with the stokers who bustle in front of the boilers' hellish fires in massive ships; alone with the black specters who grope before the red-hot bellies of locomotives launched on insane journeys; alone with drunkards who feel their way against the city walls, with the beating of uncertain wings.

Suddenly we jumped at the tremendous noise of the large double-decker trams which jolted along outside. . . .

'Let's go!' I said. 'Let's go, my friends! Let's leave! At last mythology and the mystical ideal have been superseded. We are about to witness the birth of the Centaur, and soon we shall see the first Angels fly! . . . We have to shake the doors of life to test their hinges and bolts! . . . Let's leave! Look! There, on the earth, the earliest dawn! Nothing can match the splendor of the sun's red sword, skirmishing for the first time with our thousand-year-old shadows."

[. . .]

The Manifesto of Futurism

1. We intend to sing to the love of danger, the habit of energy and fearlessness.
2. Courage, boldness, and rebelliousness will be the essential elements of our poetry.
3. Up to now literature has exalted contemplative stillness, ecstasy, and sleep. We intend to exalt movement and aggression, feverish insomnia, the racer's stride, the mortal leap, the slap and the punch.
4. We affirm that the beauty of the world has been enriched by a new form of beauty: the beauty of speed. A racing car with a hood that glistens with large pipes resembling a serpent with explosive breath . . . a roaring automobile that rides on grape-shot – that is more beautiful than the [Hellenistic statue] *Victory of Samothrace*.
5. We intend to hymn man at the steering wheel, the ideal axis of which intersects the earth, itself hurled ahead in its own race along the path of its orbit.
6. Henceforth poets must do their utmost, with ardor, splendor, and generosity, to increase the enthusiastic fervor of the primordial elements.
7. There is no beauty that does not consist of struggle. No work that lacks an aggressive character can be considered a masterpiece. Poetry must be conceived as a violent assault launched against unknown forces to reduce them to submission under man.
8. We stand on the last promontory of the centuries! . . . Why should we look back over our shoulders, when we intend to breach the mysterious doors of the Impossible? Time and space died yesterday. We already live in the absolute, for we have already created velocity which is eternal and omnipotent.
9. We intend to glorify war – the only hygiene of the world – militarism, patriotism, the destructive gesture of emancipators, beautiful ideas worth dying for, and contempt for woman.
10. We intend to destroy museums, libraries, academies of every sort, and to fight against moralists, feminism, and every utilitarian or opportunistic cowardice.
11. We shall sing the great masses shaken with work, pleasure, or rebellion: we shall sing the multicoloured and polyphonic tidal waves of revolution in the modern metropolis; shall sing the vibrating nocturnal fervor of factories and shipyards burning under violent electrical moons; bloated railway stations that devour smoking serpents; factories hanging from the sky by the twisting threads of spiraling smoke; bridges like gigantic gymnasts who span rivers, flashing at the sun with the gleam of a knife; adventurous steamships that scent the horizon, locomotives with their swollen chests, pawing the tracks like massive steel horses bridled with pipes, and the oscillating flight of airships, whose propeller flaps at the wind like a flag and seems to applaud like a delirious crowd.

[. . .]

I declare, in all truth, that a daily visit to museums, libraries, and academies (cemeteries of futile efforts, Calvaries of crucified dreams, record books of broken assaults! . . .) is as dangerous for artists as a prolonged guardianship under the thumb of one's family is for certain young talents intoxicated with their own genius and ambitious aims. For the sickly, the ill, or the imprisoned – let them go and visit: the admirable past is perhaps a solace for their troubles, since the future is now closed to them. . . . But we intend to know nothing of it, nothing of the past – we strong and youthful *Futurists*!

And so, let the glad arsonists with charred fingers come! Here they are! Here they are! . . . Go ahead! Set fire to the shelves of the libraries! . . . Turn aside the course of the canals to flood the museums! . . . Oh, the joy of seeing all the glorious old canvasses floating adrift on the waters, shredded and discolored! . . . Grasp your pickaxes, axes, and hammers, and tear down, pitilessly tear down the venerable cities!

Source: From Lawrence Rainey (ed. and trans.), *Modernism: An Anthology*, John Wiley & Sons, 2005, pp. 3–5.

TRISTAN TZARA, 'DADA MANIFESTO 1918'   **Document 8**

Romanian poet Tristan Tzara (1896–1963) was one of the founders of Dada at the Cabaret Voltaire in Zurich in 1916. A radical anti-art movement created by an international assembly of European artists, poets, musicians and performers who had fled to neutral Switzerland during World War I, Dada subsequently spread to Berlin and Paris in the immediate post-war era. This excerpt from a 'Dada Manifesto,' recited by Tzara in Zurich in 1918, was reprinted in the Dada Almanac, *published in conjunction with the First International Dada Fair in Berlin in 1920.*

To launch a manifesto you have to want: A, B & C, and fulminate against 1, 2 & 3,
work yourself up and sharpen your wings to conquer and circulate lower and upper case As, Bs & Cs,
sign, shout, swear, organise prose into a form that is absolutely and irrefutably obvious, prove its ne plus ultra and maintain that novelty resembles life in the same way as the latest apparition of a harlot proves the essence of God. His existence has already been proved by the accordion, the landscape and soft words. ■ To impose one's A.B.C. is only natural – and therefore regrettable. Everyone does it in the form of a crystalbluff-madonna, or a monetary

system, or pharmaceutical preparations, a naked leg being the invitation to an ardent and sterile Spring. The love of novelty is a pleasant sort of cross, it's evidence of a native don't-give-a-damn attitude, a passing, positive, sign without rhyme or reason. But this need is out of date, too. By giving art the impetus of supreme simplicity – novelty – we are being human and true in relation to innocent pleasures; impulsive and vibrant in order to crucify boredom. At the lighted cross-roads, alert, attentive, lying in wait for years, in the forest. ■

[. . .]

Dada does not mean anything

If we consider it futile, and if we don't waste our time over a word that doesn't mean anything . . . The first thought that comes to these minds is of a bacteriological order: at least to discover its etymological, historical or psychological meaning. We read in the papers that the negroes of the Kroo race call the tail of a sacred cow: **DADA**. A cub, and a mother, in a certain region of Italy, are called: **DADA**. The word for a hobby-horse, a children's nurse, a double affirmative in Russian and Romanian, is also: **DADA**. Some learned journalists see it as an art for babies, others Jesuscallingthelittle childrenuntohim saints see it as a return to an unemotional and noisy primitivism – noisy and monotonous. A sensitivity cannot be built on the basis of a word; every sort of construction converges into a boring sort of perfection, a stagnant idea of a golden swamp, a relative human product. A work of art shouldn't be beauty *per se*, because it is dead; neither gay nor sad, neither light nor dark; it is to rejoice or maltreat individualities to serve them up as the cakes of sainted haloes or the sweat of a meandering chase through the atmosphere. A work of art is never beautiful, by decree, objectively, for everyone. Criticism is, therefore, useless; it only exists subjectively, for every individual, and without the slightest general characteristic. Do people imagine they have found the psychic basis common to all humanity? The attempt of Jesus, and the Bible, conceal, under their ample, benevolent wings: shit, animals and days. How can anyone hope to order the chaos that constitutes that infinite, formless variation: man? The principle: "Love they neighbour" is hypocrisy. "Know thyself" is utopian, but more acceptable because it includes malice. No pity. After the carnage we are left with the hope of a purified humanity.

[. . .]

Dadaist disgust

Every product of disgust that is capable of becoming a negation of the family is Dada; protest with the fists of one's whole being in destructive action: **DADA**; acquaintance with all the means hitherto rejected by the sexual prudishness of easy compromise and good manners: **DADA**; abolition of logic, dance of those who are incapable of creation: **DADA**; every hierarchy and social equation established for values by our valets: **DADA**; every object, all objects, feelings and obscurities, every apparition and the precise shock of parallel lines, are means for the battle of: **DADA**; the abolition of memory: **DADA**; the abolition of archaeology: **DADA**; the abolition of prophets: **DADA**; the abolition of the future: **DADA**; the absolute and indisputable belief in every god that is an immediate product of spontaneity: **DADA**; the elegant and unprejudiced leap from one harmony to another sphere; the trajectory of a word, a cry, thrown into the air like an acoustic disc; to respect all individualities in their folly of the moment, whether serious, fearful, timid, ardent, vigorous, decided or enthusiastic; to strip one's church of every useless and unwieldy accessory; to spew out like a luminous cascade any offensive or loving thought, or to cherish it – with the lively satisfaction that it's all precisely the same thing – with the same intensity in the bush, which is free of insects for the blue-blooded, and gilded with the bodies of archangels; with one's soul. Liberty: **<u>DADA DADA DADA</u>**; – the roar of contorted pains, the interweaving of contraries and of all contradictions, freaks and irrelevancies: **LIFE**.

Source: In *The Dada Almanac*, Richard Huelsenbeck (ed.) (English edn, Malcolm Green, trans.) Malcolm Green et al., London: Atlas Press, 1993, pp. 121–132. Originally printed in T. Tzara, *Seven Dada Manifestoes and Lampisteries* (Calder Publications Ltd, 1981) © Alma Classics Ltd, 2011. Reprinted with permission of Alma Classics.

ANDRÉ BRETON, "THE MANIFESTO OF SURREALISM"   **Document 9**

The 'magus of Surrealism,' André Breton (1896–1966) was the chief spokesman for the movement throughout his life. Breton founded the Paris Dada group in the aftermath of World War I, and then subsequently transformed the anti-art stance of that movement into Surrealism. 'The Manifesto of Surrealism' (1924), published in the first issue of La Révolution Surréaliste, *is a panegyric to the power of the imagination and provides preliminary definitions toward the movement's aims and methods.*

We are still living under the reign of logic: this, of course, is what I have been driving at. But in this day and age logical methods are applicable only to solving problems of secondary interest. The absolute rationalism that is in vogue allows us to consider only facts relating directly to our experience. Logical ends, on the contrary, escape us. It is pointless to add that experience itself has found itself increasingly circumscribed. It paces back and forth in a cage from which it is more and more difficult to make it emerge. It too leans for support on what is most immediately expedient, and it is protected by the sentiments of common sense. Under the pretense of civilization and progress, we have managed to banish from the mind everything that may rightly or wrongly be termed superstition or fancy; forbidden is any kind of search for truth which is not in conformance with accepted practices. It was, apparently, by pure chance that a part of our mental world which we pretended not to be concerned with any longer – and, in my opinion by far the most important part – has been brought back to light. For this we must give thanks to the discoveries of Sigmund Freud. On the basis of these discoveries a current of opinion is finally forming by means of which the human explorer will be able to carry his investigations much further, authorized as he will henceforth be not to confine himself solely to the most summary realities. The imagination is perhaps on the point of reasserting itself, of reclaiming its rights. If the depths of our mind contain within it strange forces capable of augmenting those on the surface, or of waging a victorious battle against them, there is every reason to seize them – first to seize them, then, if need be, to submit them to the control of reason. The analysts themselves have everything to gain by it. But it is worth noting that no means has been designated a priori for carrying out this undertaking, that until further notice it can be construed to be the province of poets as well as the scholars, and that its success is not dependent upon the more or less capricious paths that will be followed.

    [. . .]

Those who might dispute our right to employ the term SURREALISM in the very special sense that we understand it are being extremely dishonest, for there can be no doubt that this word had no currency before we came along. Therefore, I am defining it once and for all:

    SURREALISM, n. Psychic automatism in its pure state, by which one proposes to express – verbally, by means of the written word, or in any other manner – the actual functioning of thought. Dictated by thought, in the absence of any control exercised by reason, exempt from any aesthetic or moral concern.

    ENCYCLOPEDIA. *Philosophy*. Surrealism is based on the belief in the superior reality of certain forms of previously neglected associations, in the omnipotence of dream, in the disinterested play of thought. It tends to ruin once and for all other psychic mechanisms and to substitute itself for them in solving all the principal problems of life . . .

    [. . .]

I would like to stress the point: they [visionary poets, writers and artists, both past and present] are not always Surrealists, in that I discern in each of them a certain number of preconceived ideas to which – very naively! – they hold. They hold to them because they had not *heard the Surrealist voice*, the one that continues to preach on the eve of death and above the storms, because they did not want to orchestrate the marvellous score. They were instruments too full of pride, and this is why they have not always produced a harmonious sound.

But we, who have made no effort whatsoever to filter, who in our works have made ourselves into simple receptacles of so many echoes, modest *recording instruments* who are not mesmerized by the drawings we are making, perhaps we serve an even nobler cause. Thus do we render with integrity the 'talent' which has been lent to us. You might as well speak of the talent of this platinum ruler, this mirror, this door, and of the sky, if you like.

[. . .]

Surrealism, such as I conceive it, asserts our complete *nonconformism* clearly enough so that there can be no question of translating it, at the trial of the real world, as evidence for the defense. It could, on the contrary, only serve to justify the complete state of distraction which we hope to achieve here below. Kant's absentmindedness regarding women, Pasteur's absentmindedness about 'grapes,' Curie's absentmindedness with respect to vehicles, are in this regard profoundly symptomatic. This world is only very relatively in tune with thought, and incidents of this kind are only the most obvious episodes of a war in which I am proud to be participating. Surrealism is the 'invisible ray' which will one day enable us to win out over our opponents. 'You are no longer trembling, carcass.' This summer the roses are blue; the wood is of glass. The earth, draped in its verdant cloak, makes as little impression upon me as a ghost. It is living and ceasing to live that are imaginary solutions. Existence is elsewhere.

Source: From André Breton, *Manifestoes of Surrealism* (trans. Richard Seaver and Helen R. Lane), Ann Arbor: University of Michigan Press, 1972, pp. 3–47.

LE CORBUSIER AND AMÉDÉE OZENFANT, 'PURISM'   **Document 10**

In the 1920s, Swiss draftsman Le Corbusier (pseudo. Charles Édouard Jean-neret, 1887–1965) and French Cubist painter Amédée Ozenfant (1886–1966) called for a 'return to order' in art and architecture. In contrast to the celebration of irrationality in Futurism, Dada and Surrealism, Purism expressed a modernist impulse toward complete rationality. In 'Purism' (1920), Le Corbusier and Ozenfant argue that works of art and architecture that conform to a hierarchy of order based upon mathematics and optimal design provide universal keys to human happiness.

The Work of Art

The work of art is an artificial object which permits the creator to place the spectator in the state he wishes; later we will study the means the creator has at his disposal to attain this result. With regard to man, esthetic sensations are not all of the same degree of intensity of quality; we might say that there is a hierarchy.

The highest level of this hierarchy seems to us to be that special state of a mathematical sort to which we are raised, for example, by the clear perception of a great general law (the state of mathematical lyricism, one might say); it is superior to the brute pleasure of the senses; the senses are involved, however, because every being in this state is as if in a state of beatitude.

The goal of art is not simple pleasure, rather it partakes of *the nature of happiness*.

It is true that plastic art has to address itself more directly to the senses than pure mathematics which only acts by symbols, these symbols sufficing to trigger in the mind consequences of a superior order; in plastic art, the senses should be strongly moved in order to predispose the mind to the release into play of subjective reactions without which there is no work of art. But there is no art worth having without this excitement of an intellectual order, of a mathematical order; architecture is the art which up until now has most strongly induced the states of this category. The reason is that everything in architecture is expressed by order and economy.

The means of executing a work of art is a transmittable and universal language.

One of the highest delights of the human mind is to perceive the order of nature and to measure its own participation in the scheme of things; the work of art seems to us to be a labor of putting into order, a masterpiece of human order.

Now the world only appears to man from the human vantage point, that is, the world seems to obey the laws man has been able to assign to it; when man creates a work of art, he has the feeling of acting as a 'god.'

Now a law is nothing other than the verification of an order.

In summary, a work of art should induce a sensation of a mathematical order, and the means of inducing this mathematical order should be sought among universal means.

[. . .]

System

Man and organized beings are products of *natural selection*. In every evolution on earth, the organs of beings are more and more adapted and purified, and the entire forward march of evolution is a form of purification. The human body seems to be the highest product of natural selection.

When examining these selected forms, one finds a tendency toward certain identical aspects, corresponding to constant functions, functions which are of maximum efficiency, maximum strength, maximum capacity, etc., that is, maximum economy. ECONOMY is the law of natural selection.

It is easy to calculate that it is also the great law which governs what we will call 'mechanical selection.'

Mechanical selection began with the earliest times and from those times provided objects whose general laws have endured; only the means of making them changed, the rules endured.

In all ages and with all people, man has created for his use objects of prime necessity which responded to his imperative needs; these objects were associated with his organism and helped complete it. In all ages, for example, man has created containers: vases, glasses, bottles, plates, which were built to suit the needs of maximum capacity, maximum strength, maximum economy of materials, maximum economy of effort. In all ages, man has created objects of transport: boats, cars; objects of defense: arms; objects of pleasure: musical instruments, etc., all of which have always obeyed the law of selection: economy.

[. . .]

Purism

The highest delectation of the human mind is the perception of order, and the greatest human satisfaction is the feeling of collaboration or participation in this order. The work of art is an artificial object which lets the spectator be placed in the state desired by the creator. The sensation of order is of a mathematical quality. The creation of a work of art should utilize means for specified results. Here is how we have tried to create a language possessing these means:

Primary forms and colors have standard properties (universal properties which permit the creation of a transmittable plastic language). But the utilization of primary forms does not suffice to place the spectator in the sought-for state of mathematical order. For that one must bring to bear the associations of natural or artificial forms, and the criterion for their choice is the degree of selection at which certain elements have arrived (natural selection and mechanical selection). The Purist element issued from the purification of standard forms is not a copy, but a creation whose end is to materialize the object in all its generality and its invariability. Purist elements are thus comparable to words of carefully defined meaning; Purist syntax is the application of constructive and modular means; it is the application of the laws which control pictorial space. A painting is a whole (unity); a painting is an artificial formation which, by appropriate means, should lead to the objectification of an entire 'world.' One could make an art of allusions, an art of fashion, based upon surprise and the conventions of the initiated. Purism strives for an art free of conventions which will utilize plastic constants and address itself above all to the universal properties of the senses and the mind.

Source: From Robert L. Herbert (ed. and trans.), *Modern Artists on Art* (2nd edn), Mineola, NY: Dover Publications, Inc., 2000, pp. 53–65.

Document 11   WALTER GROPIUS, 'THE THEORY AND ORGANISATION OF THE BAUHAUS'

Walter Gropius (1883–1969) was a Berlin architect who founded the Bauhaus School in Weimar, and later Dessau, under the short-lived Weimar Republic. In contrast to Le Corbusier's analytical and hierarchical Purism, the Bauhaus pursued a creative and dynamic approach to architecture and design that drew together the multiple modernist movements of Neo-Plasticism, Constructivism, Cubism, Expressionism and Abstract Expressionism. In 'The Theory and Organisation of the Bauhaus' (1923), Gropius details a workshop-based educational curriculum of industrial design and production in which students, individually and collectively, receive multifaceted training in aesthetic theory and practical application.

The dominant spirit of our epoch is already recognizable although its form is not yet clearly defined. The old dualistic world-concept which envisaged the ego in opposition to the universe is rapidly losing ground. In its place is rising the idea of a universal unity in which all opposing forces exist in a state of absolute balance. This dawning recognition of the essential oneness of all things and their appearances endows creative effort with a fundamental inner meaning. No longer can anything exist in isolation. We perceive every form as the embodiment of an idea, every piece of work as a manifestation of our innermost selves. Only work which is the product of inner compulsion can have spiritual meaning. Mechanized work is lifeless, proper only to the lifeless machine. So long, however, as machine-economy remains an end in itself rather than a means of freeing the intellect from the burden of mechanical labor, the individual will remain enslaved and society will remain disordered. The solution depends on change in the individual's attitude toward his work, not on the betterment of his outward circumstances, and the acceptance of this new principle is of decisive importance for new creative work.
[. . .]

The 'academy'

The tool of the spirit of yesterday was the 'academy.' It shut off the artist from the world of industry and handicraft, and thus brought about his complete isolation from the community. In vital epochs, on the other hand, the artist enriched all the arts and crafts of a community because he had a part in its vocational life, and because he acquired through actual practice as much adeptness and understanding as any other worker who began at the bottom and worked his way up. But lately the artist has been misled by the fatal and arrogant fallacy, fostered by the state, that art is a profession which can be mastered by study. Schooling alone can never produce art! Whether the finished product is an exercise in ingenuity or a work of art depends on the talent of the individual who creates it. This quality cannot be taught and cannot be learned. On the other hand, manual dexterity and the thorough knowledge which is a necessary foundation for all creative effort, whether the workman's or the artist's, can be taught and learned.

[. . .]

The Bauhaus at Weimar

Every factor that must be considered in an education system to produce actively creative human beings is implicit in such an analysis of the creative process. At the 'State Bauhaus at Weimar' the attempt was made for the first time to incorporate all of these factors in a consistent program.

. . . The theoretical curriculum of an art academy combined with the practical curriculum of an arts and crafts school was to constitute the basis of a comprehensive for gifted students. Its credo was: 'The Bauhaus strives to coordinate all creative effort, to achieve, in a new architecture, *the unification of all training in art and design*. The ultimate, if distant, goal of the Bauhaus is the *collective work of art*—the Building—in which no barriers exist between the structural and the decorative arts.'

The guiding principle of the Bauhaus was therefore the idea of creating a new unity through the welding together of many 'arts' and 'movements' a unity having its basis in Man himself and significant only as a living organism.

Human achievement depends on the proper coordination of all the creative faculties. It is not enough to school one or another of them separately: they must all be thoroughly trained at the same time. The character and scope of the Bauhaus teachings derive from the realization of this.

[. . .]

The goal of the Bauhaus curriculum

Thus the culminating point of the Bauhaus teaching is a demand for a new and powerful working correlation of all the processes of creation. The gifted student must regain a feeling for the interwoven strands of practical and formal work. The joy of building, in the broadest meaning of that word, must replace the paper work of design. Architecture unites in a collective task all creative workers, from the simple artisan to the supreme artist.

For this reason, the basis of collective education must be sufficiently broad to permit the development of every kind of talent. Since a universally applicable method for the discovery of talent does not exist, the individual in the course of his development must find for himself the field of activity best suited to him within the circle of the community. The majority become interested in production; the few extraordinarily gifted ones will suffer no limits to their activity. After they have completed the course of practical and formal instruction, they undertake independent research and experiment.

Modern painting, breaking through old conventions, has released countless suggestions which are still waiting to be used by the practical world. But when, in the future, artists who sense new creative values have had practical training in the industrial world, they will themselves possess the means for realizing those values immediately. They will compel industry to serve their idea and industry will seek out and utilize their comprehensive training.

Source: English translation of *Idee und Aufbau des Staatlichen Bauhauses Weimar* in Herbert Bayer, Walter Gropius and Ise Gropius (eds), *Bauhaus, 1919–1928,* New York: Museum of Modern Art, 1938, pp. 20–29.

Document 12   ALFRED H. BARR, JR., *CUBISM AND ABSTRACT ART*

The first director of the Museum of Modern Art in New York, Alfred H. Barr, Jr. was the first art critic to try to synthesise modernist art into a comprehensive system, arranged chronologically. For Barr, the concept of the 'abstract' best encompassed the diversity of modernist art movements in twentieth-century Europe and America. The following passages are excerpted from the catalogue Barr prepared for MoMA's 'Cubism and Abstract' exhibit in 1936 (see Map 1).

The Early Twentieth Century

Sometimes in the history of art it is possible to describe a period or a generation of artists as having been obsessed by a particular problem. The artists of the early fifteenth century for instance were moved by a passion for imitating nature. In the North the Flemings mastered appearances by meticulous observation of external detail. In Italy the Florentines employed a profounder science to discover the laws of perspective, of foreshortening, anatomy, movement and relief.

In the early twentieth century the dominant interest was almost exactly opposite. The pictorial conquest of the external visual world had been completed and refined many times and in different ways during the previous half millennium. The more adventurous and original artists had grown bored with painting facts. By a common and powerful impulse they were driven to abandon the imitation of natural appearance.

'Abstract'

'Abstract' is the term most frequently used to describe the more extreme effects of this impulse away from 'nature.' It is customary to apologize for the word 'abstract,' but words to describe art movements or works of art are often inexact: we no longer apologize for applying the ethnological word 'Gothic' to French thirteenth-century art and the Portuguese word for an irregular pearl, 'Baroque,' to European art of the seventeenth century. Substitutes for 'abstract' such as 'non-objective' and 'non-figurative' have been advocated as superior. But the image of a square is as much an 'object' or a 'figure' as the image of a face or a landscape; in fact 'figure' is the very prefix used by geometers in naming A or B the abstractions with which they deal.

This is not to deny that the adjective 'abstract' is confusing or even paradoxical. For an 'abstract' painting is really a most positively concrete painting since it confines the attention to its immediate, sensuous, physical surface far more than does the canvas of a sunset or a portrait. The adjective is confusing, too, because it has the implications of both a verb and a noun. The verb *to abstract* means *to draw out of* or *away from*. But the noun *abstraction* is something already drawn out of or away from—so much so that like a geometrical figure or an amorphous silhouette it may have no apparent relation to concrete reality. 'Abstract' is therefore an adjective which may be applied to works of art with a certain latitude, and, since no better or more generally used word presents itself, it shall be used from now on in this essay without quotation marks.

[. . .]

Two Main Traditions of Abstract Art

At the risk of grave oversimplification the impulse towards abstract art during the past fifty years may be divided historically into two main currents, both of which emerged from Impressionism. The first and more important current finds its sources in the art and theories of Cézanne and Seurat, passes through the widening stream of Cubism and finds its delta in the various geometrical and Constructivist movements which developed in Russia and Holland during the War [WWI] and have since spread throughout the World. This current may be described as intellectual, structural, architectonic, geometrical, rectilinear and classical in its austerity and dependence upon logic and calculation. The second – and, until recently, secondary – current has its principal source in the art and theories of Gauguin and his circle, flows through the *Fauvisme* of Matisse to the Abstract Expressionism of the pre-War paintings of Kandinsky. After running underground for a few years it reappears vigorously among the masters of abstract art associated with Surrealism. This tradition, by contrast with the first, is intuitional and emotional rather than intellectual; organic or biomorphic rather than geometrical in its forms; curvilinear rather than rectilinear, decorative rather than structural, and romantic rather than classical in its exaltation of the mystical, the spontaneous and the irrational. Apollo, Pythagoras and Descartes watch over the Cézanne-Cubist-geometrical tradition; Dionysus (an Asiatic god), Plotinus and Rousseau over the Gauguin-Expressionist-non-geometrical line.

Source: From Alfred H. Barr, Jr., *Cubism and Abstract Art,* New York: Museum of Modern Art, 1936, pp. 11–12, 19.

Document 13   WALTER BENJAMIN, 'THE WORK OF ART IN THE AGE OF MECHANICAL REPRODUCTION'

Walter Benjamin (1892–1940) was one of the influential critical theorists to emerge from the Frankfurt School of intellectuals that included Leo Löwenthal, Max Horkheimer and Theodor Adorno. A visionary intellectual with far ranging interests that included aesthetic and literary theory, German idealism, Western Marxism, and Jewish mysticism, Benjamin's great unachieved **Passagenwerk** *('The Arcades Project') was dedicated to the rise of modernity and modernist sensibilities in the nineteenth and early twentieth centuries. In 'The Work of Art in the Age of Mechanical Reproduction' (1935), Benjamin reflects upon the loss of the 'aura' of authenticity in art reproduced by technical and commercial means, while contemplating the revolutionary potential of such art as a means for political liberation.*

Even the most perfect reproduction of a work of art is lacking in one element: its presence in time and space, its unique existence at the place where it happens to be. This unique existence of the work of art determined the history to which it was subject throughout the time of its existence. This includes the changes which it may have suffered in physical condition over the years as well as the various changes in its ownership. The traces of the first can be revealed only by chemical or physical analyses which it is impossible to perform on a reproduction; changes of ownership are subject to a tradition which must be traced from the situation of the original.

The presence of the original is the prerequisite to the concept of authenticity. Chemical analyses of the patina of a bronze can help to establish this, as does the proof that a given manuscript of the Middle Ages stems from an archive of the fifteenth century. The whole sphere of authenticity is outside technical

– and, of course, not only technical – reproducibility. Confronted with its manual reproduction, which was usually branded as a forgery, the original preserved all its authority; not so *vis-à-vis* technical reproduction. The reason is twofold. First, process reproduction is more independent of the original than manual reproduction. For example, in photography, process reproduction can bring out those aspects of the original that are unattainable to the naked eye yet accessible to the lens, which is adjustable and chooses its angle at will. And photographic reproduction, with the aid of certain processes, such as enlargement or slow motion, can capture images which escape natural vision. Secondly, technical reproduction can put the copy of the original into situations which would be out of reach for the original itself. Above all, it enables the original to meet the beholder halfway, be it in the form of a photograph or a phonograph record. The cathedral leaves its locale to be received in the studio of a lover of art; the choral production, performed in an auditorium or in the open air, resounds in the drawing room.

The situations into which the product of mechanical reproduction can be brought may not touch the actual work of art, yet the quality of its presence is always depreciated. This holds not only for the art work but also, for instance, for the landscape which passes in review before the spectator in a movie. In the case of the art object, a most sensitive nucleus – namely, its authenticity – is interfered with whereas no natural object is vulnerable on that score. The authenticity of a thing is the essence of all that is transmissible from its beginning, ranging from its substantive duration to its testimony to the history which it has experienced. Since the historical testimony rests on the authenticity, the former, too, is jeopardized by reproduction when substantive duration ceases to matter. And what is really jeopardized when the historical testimony is affected is the authority of the object.

One might subsume the eliminated element in the term 'aura' and go on to say: that which withers in the age of mechanical reproduction is the aura of the work of art. . . .

[. . .]

The uniqueness of a work of art is inseparable from its being imbedded in the fabric of tradition. [. . .] We know that the earliest art works originated in the service of a ritual – first the magical, then the religious kind. It is significant that the existence of the work of art with reference to its aura is never entirely separated from its ritual function. In other words, the unique value of the 'authentic' work of art has its basis in ritual, the locale of its original use value. This ritualistic basis, however remote, is still recognizable as secularized ritual even in the most profane forms of the cult of beauty. The secular cult of beauty, developed during the Renaissance and prevailing for three centuries, clearly showed that ritualistic basis in its decline and the first deep crisis which befell it. With the advent of the first truly revolutionary means of production, photography, simultaneously with the rise of socialism, art senses the approaching crisis which has become evident a century later. At the time, art reacted with the doctrine of *l'art pour l'art*, that is, with a theology of art. This gave rise to what might be called a negative theology in the form of the idea of 'pure' art, which not only denied any social function of art but also any categorizing by subject matter. (In poetry, Mallarmé was the first to take this position.)

An analysis of art in the age of mechanical reproduction must do justice to these relationships, for they lead us to an all-important insight: for the first time in world history, mechanical reproduction emancipates the work of art from its parasitical dependence on ritual. To an ever greater degree the work of art reproduced becomes the work of art designed for reproducibility. From a photographic negative, for example, one can make any number of prints; to ask for the 'authentic' print makes no sense. But the instant the criterion of authenticity ceases to be applicable to artistic production, the total function of art is reversed. Instead of being based on ritual, it begins to be based on another practice – politics.

Source: From Walter Benjamin, 'The Work of Art in the Age of Mechanical Reproduction' in Hannah Arendt (ed. and intro.) *Illuminations* (trans. Harry Zohn), Pimlico, 1999. Originally published by Schocken Books, new York, 1969, pp. 217–251. Reprinted in the UK and Commonwealth (excluding Canada) courtesy of The Random House Group Limited.

Document 14   RICHARD HAMILTON, 'FOR THE FINEST ART TRY – POP'

A member of the Independent Group at the Institute of Contemporary Arts in London, Richard Hamilton (1922–2011) was a leading figure in the Pop Art movement of the 1950s and 1960s. Drawing upon mass media and consumer products, he specialised in collage and painting. In sharp contrast to Clement Greenberg's advocacy of abstract modernism to assume a 'high culture' role, in 'For the Finest Art try – POP' (1961) Hamilton appeals to contemporary artists to seize upon the 'low culture' realm of mass consumer culture for source materials.

In much the way that the invention of photography cut away for itself a chunk of art's prerogative – the pictorial recording of visual facts – trimming the scope of messages which Fine Art felt to lie within its true competence, so has popular culture abstracted from Fine Art its role of mythmaker. The restriction of his area of relevance has been confirmed by the artist with smug enthusiasm so that decoration, one of art's few remaining functions, has assumed a ridiculously inflated importance.

Isn't it surprising, therefore, to find that some painters are not agog at the ability of the mass entertainment machine to project, perhaps more pervasively than has ever before been possible, the classic themes of artistic vision and to express them in a poetic language which marks them with a precise cultural date-stamp.

It is the *Playboy* 'Playmate of the month' pull-out pin-up which provides us with the closest contemporary equivalent of the odalisque in painting. Automobile body stylists have absorbed the symbolism of the space age more successfully than any artist. Social comment is left to TV and comic strip. Epic has become synonymous with a certain kind of film and the heroic archetype is now buried deep in movie lore. If the artist is not to lose much of his ancient purpose he may have to plunder the popular arts to recover the imagery which is his rightful inheritance.

Two art movements of the early part of this century insisted on their commitment to manifest the image of a society in flux: Dada, which denied the then current social attitudes and pressed its own negative proposition, and Futurism with its positive assertion of involvement. Both were fiercely, aggressively propagandistic. Both were rebellious, or at least radical, movements. Dada anarchically seditious and Futurism admitting to a core of authoritarian dogma – each was vigorous and historically apposite.

A new generation of Dadaists has emerged today, as violent and ingenious as their forebears, but Son of Dada is accepted, lionized by public and dealers, certified by state museums – the act of mythmaking has been transferred from the subject-matter of the work to the artist himself as the content of his art.

Futurism has ebbed and has no successor, yet to me the philosophy of affirmation seems susceptible to fruition. The long tradition of bohemianism which the Futurists made their bid to defeat is anachronic in the atmosphere of conspicuous consumption generated by the art rackets.

Affirmation propounded as an avant-garde aesthetic is rare. The history of art is that of a long series of attacks upon social and aesthetic values held to be dead and moribund, although the avant-garde position is frequently nostalgic and absolute. The Pop-Fine-Art is a profession of approbation of mass culture, therefore also antiartistic. It is positive Dada, creative where Dada was destructive. Perhaps it is Mama – a cross-fertilization of Futurism and Dada which upholds a respect for the culture of the masses and a conviction that the artist in twentieth century urban life is inevitably a consumer of mass culture and potentially a contributor to it.

Source: From Richard Hamilton, *Collected Works, 1953–1982,* London and New York: Thames & Hudson, 1982, pp. 42–43. Reprinted with permission of Hansjorg Mayer, on behalf of Rita McDonough.

Document 15   PETER BÜRGER, 'THE NEGATION OF THE AUTONOMY OF ART BY THE
AVANT-GARDE'

*In the wake of the mixed results from student and political uprisings of May
1968, German literary critic Peter Bürger (1936–) re-evaluated the aesthetic,
intellectual, and political goals of artistic and literary avant-gardes. Strongly
influenced by Theodor Adorno's imperative for critical autonomy in art,
Bürger examined the role of the avant-garde within the contexts of the culture
industry of mass consumption and the official institutionalisation of modernism in art museums. In this excerpt from* The Theory of the Avant-Garde
*(1974), Bürger argues that, unlike the historical avant-garde of the 1920s
and 1930s, which directly attacked bourgeois society and advocated political
revolution, the critical function of the contemporary avant-garde under late
twentieth century capitalism lies in its ability to produce new art that critiques
and surpasses previous works of modernism.*

The European avant-garde movements can be defined as an attack on the
status of art in bourgeois society. What is negated is not an early form of art
(a style) but art as an institution that is unassociated with the life praxis of
men. When the avant-gardistes demand that art has become practical once
again, they do not mean that the contents of works of art should be socially
significant. The demand is not raised to the level of the contents of individual
works. Rather, it directs itself to the way art functions in society, a process
that does as much to determine the effect that works have as does the particular content.

     The avant-gardistes view its dissociation from the praxis of life as the
dominant characteristic of art in bourgeois society. One of the reasons this
dissociation was possible was that Aestheticism had made the element that
defines art as an institution the essential content of works. Institution and
work contents had to coincide to make it logically possible for the avant-
garde to call art into question. The avant-gardistes proposed the sublation of
art – sublation in the Hegelian sense of the term: art was not to be simply
destroyed, but transferred to the praxis of life where it would be preserved,
albeit in a changed form. The avant-gardistes thus adopted an essential
element of Aestheticism. Aestheticism had made the distance from the praxis
of life the content of works. The praxis of life to which Aestheticism refers
and which it negates is the means-ends rationality of the bourgeois everyday.
Now, it is not the aim of the avant-gardistes to integrate art into *this* praxis.
On the contrary, they assent to the aestheticists' rejection of the world and
its means-end rationality. What distinguishes them from the latter is the
attempt to organize a new life praxis from a basis in art. In this respect
also, Aestheticism turns out to have been the necessary precondition of the

avant-gardiste intent. Only an art the contents of whose individual works is wholly distinct from the (bad) praxis of the existing society can be the center that can be the starting point for the organization of a new life praxis.

With the help of Herbert Marcuse's theoretical formulation concerning the twofold character of art in bourgeois society . . . the avant-gardiste intent can be understood with particular clarity. All those needs that cannot be satisfied in everyday life, because the principle of competition pervades all spheres, can find a home in art, because art is removed from the praxis of life. Values such as humanity, joy, truth, solidarity are extruded from life as it were, and preserved in art. In bourgeois society, art has a contradictory role: it projects the image of a better order and to that extent protests against the bad order that prevails. But by realizing the image of a better order in fiction, which is semblance (*Schein*) only, it relieves the existing society of the pressure of those forces that make for change. They are assigned to confinement in an ideal sphere. Where art accomplishes this, it is 'affirmative' in Marcuse's sense of the term. If the twofold character of art in bourgeois society consists in the fact that the distance from the social production and reproduction process contains an element of freedom and an element of the noncommittal and an absence of any consequences, it can be seen that the avant-gardistes' attempt to reintegrate art into the life process is itself a profoundly contradictory endeavor. For the (relative) freedom of art vis-à-vis the praxis of life is at the same time the condition that must be fulfilled if there is to be a critical cognition of reality. An art no longer distinct from the praxis of life but wholly absorbed in it will lose the ability to criticize it, along with its distance. During the time of the historical avant-garde movements, the attempt to do away with the distance between art and life still had all the pathos of historical progressiveness on its side. But in the meantime, the culture industry has brought about the false elimination of the distance between art and life, and this also allows one to recognize the contradictoriness of the avant-gardiste undertaking.

[. . .]

In summary, we note that the historical avant-garde movements negate those determinations that are essential in autonomous art: the disjunction of art and the praxis of life, individual production, and individual reception as distinct from the former. The avant-garde intends the abolition of autonomous art by which it means that art is to be integrated into the praxis of life. This has not occurred, and presumably cannot occur, in bourgeois society unless it be a false sublation of autonomous art. Pulp fiction and commodity aesthetics prove that such a false sublation exists. A literature whose primary aim it is to impose a particular kind of consumer behavior on the reader is in fact practical, though not in the sense the avant-gardistes intended. Here, literature ceases to be an instrument of emancipation and becomes one of subjection. Similar comments could be made about commodity aesthetics that treat form as mere enticement, designed to prompt purchasers to buy what they do not need. Here also, art becomes practical but it is an art that enthrals. This brief allusion will show that the theory of the avant-garde can also serve to make us understand popular literature and commodity aesthetics as forms of a false sublation of art as institution. In late capitalist society, intentions of the historical avant-garde are being realized but the result has been a disvalue. Given the experience of the false sublation of autonomy, one will need to ask whether a sublation of the autonomy status can be desirable at all, whether the distance between art and the practice of life is not requisite for that free space within which alternatives to what exists become conceivable.

Source: From Peter Bürger, *Theory of the Avant-Garde* (trans. Michael Shaw), series 'Theory and History of Literature' vol. 4, Minneapolis: University of Minnesota Press, 1984, pp. 49–50, 54.

Document 16   JEAN BAUDRILLARD, *SIMULATIONS*

Jean Baudrillard (1929–2007) was a French sociologist, philosopher and cultural theorist of post-structuralism. Baudrillard belonged to a generation of French intellectuals that included Roland Barthes, Michel Foucault, Jacques Derrida, and François Lyotard, who adopted Ferdinand de Saussure's linguistic semiotics of difference as a theoretical corrective to the Marxist and Existentialist intellectual trends characteristic of the post-war era. In Simulations *(1981), Baudrillard pushed the implications of post-structuralism to extremes by arguing that the predominance of imagistic and abstractly hyperreal culture had cut off access to all references in the actual world and had emptied language of meaning altogether.*

> The simulacrum is never that which conceals the truth – it is the truth which conceals that there is none. The simulacrum is true.
>
> —*Ecclesiastes*

If we were able to take as the finest allegory of simulation the Borges tale where the cartographers of the Empire draw up a map so detailed that it ends up exactly covering the territory (but where the decline of the Empire sees this map become frayed and finally ruined, a few shreds still discernible in the deserts – the metaphysical beauty of this ruined abstraction, bearing witness to an Imperial pride and rotting like a carcass, returning to the substance of the soil, rather as an aging double ends up being confused with the real thing) – then this fable has come full circle for us, and now has nothing but the discrete charm of second-order simulacra.

Abstraction today is no longer that of the map, the double, the mirror or the concept. Simulation is no longer that of a territory, a referential being or a substance. It is the generation by models of a real without origin or reality: a hyperreal. The territory no longer precedes the map, nor survives it. Henceforth, it is the map that precedes the territory – PRECESSION OF SIMULACRA – it is the map that engenders the territory and if we were to revive the fable today, it would be the territory whose shreds are slowly rotting across the map. It is the real, not the map, whose vestiges subsist here and there, in the deserts which are no longer those of the Empire, but our own. *The desert of the real itself.*

In fact, even inverted, the fable is useless. Perhaps only the allegory of the Empire remains. For it is with the same Imperialism that present-day simulators try to make the real, all the real, coincide with their simulation models. But it is no longer a question of either maps or territory. Something has disappeared: the sovereign difference between them that was the abstraction's charm. For it is the difference which forms the poetry of the map and the charm of the territory, the magic of the concept and the charm of the real. This representational imaginary, which both culminates in and is engulfed by the cartographer's mad project of an ideal coextensivity between the map and the territory disappears with simulation – whose operation is nuclear and genetic, and no longer specular and discursive. With it goes all of metaphysics. No more mirror of being and appearances, of the real and its concept. No more imaginary coextensivity: rather, genetic miniaturisation is the dimension of simulation. The real is produced from the miniaturised units, from matrices, memory banks and command models – and with these it can be reproduced an indefinite number of times. It no longer has to be rational, since it is no longer measured against some ideal or negative instance. It is nothing more than operational. In fact, since it is no longer enveloped by an imaginary, it is no longer real at all. It is hyperreal, the product of an irradiating synthesis of combinatory models in a hyperspace without atmosphere.

[. . .]

So it is with simulation, insofar as it is opposed to representation. The latter starts from the principle that the sign and the real are equivalent (even if this equivalence is utopian, it is a fundamental axiom). Conversely, simulation starts from the *utopia* of this principle of equivalence, *from the radical negation of the sign as value*, from the sign as reversion and death sentence of every reference. Whereas representation tries to absorb simulation by interpreting it as false representation, simulation envelops the whole edifice of representation as itself a simulacrum.

This would be the successive phases of the image:

— it is the reflection of a basic reality.
— it masks and perverts a basic reality.
— it masks the *absence* of a basic reality.
— it bears no relation to any reality whatever: it is its own pure simulacrum.

[. . .]

When the real is no longer what it used to be, nostalgia assumes its full meaning. There is a proliferation of myths of origin and signs of reality; of second-hand truth, objectivity and authenticity. There is an escalation of the true, of the lived experience; a resurrection of the figurative where the object and substance have disappeared. And there is a panic-stricken production of the real and the referential, above and parallel to the panic of material production: this is how the simulation appears in the phase that concerns us – a strategy of the real, neo-real and hyperreal whose universal double is a strategy of deterrence.

Source: From Jean Baudrillard, *Simulations* (trans. Paul Foss, Paul Patton and Philip Beitchman), New York: Semiotext(e), 1983, pp. 1–13.

Document 17 FREDRIC JAMESON, 'POSTMODERNISM, OR THE CULTURAL LOGIC OF LATE CAPITALISM'

Fredric Jameson (1934–) is a contemporary American literary critic and cultural theorist. From intellectual origins in Existentialism and Marxist literary theory, Jameson participated in the 'linguistic turn' of the 1980s that was sceptical of totalising 'metanarratives' and emphasised the dissolution of the individual subject. In 'Postmodernism, or The Cultural Logic of Late Capitalism' (1984), an essay later developed into a full-length work, postmodernism becomes the metanarrative of high modernism, constituting neither a radical avant-garde nor its parody, but a pastiche of all previous modernist styles that serve the commercial purposes of corporate capitalism.

The last few years have been marked by an inverted millenarianism, in which premonitions of the future, catastrophic or redemptive, have been replaced by senses of the end of this or that (the end of ideology, art, or social class; the 'crisis' of Leninism, social democracy, or the welfare state, etc., etc.): taken together, all of these perhaps constitute what is increasingly called postmodernism. The case for its existence depends on the hypothesis of some radical break or *coupure*, generally traced back to the end of the 1950s or the early 1960s. As the word itself suggests, this break is most often related to notions of the waning or extinction of the hundred-year-old modern movement (or to its ideological or aesthetic repudiation). Thus, abstract expressionism in painting, existentialism in philosophy, the final forms of representation in the novel, the films of the great *auteurs*, or the modernist school of poetry (as institutionalized and canonized in the works of Wallace Stevens): all these are now seen as the final, extraordinary flowering of a high modernist impulse which is spent and exhausted with them. The enumeration of what follows then at once becomes empirical, chaotic, and heterogeneous: Andy Warhol and pop art, but also photorealism, and beyond it, the 'new expressionism'; the moment, in music, of John Cage, but also the synthesis of classical and 'popular' styles found in composers like Phil Glass and Terry Riley, and also punk and new wave rock (the Beatles and the Stones now standing as the high-modernist moment of that more recent and rapidly evolving tradition); in film, Godard, post-Godard and experimental cinema and video, but also a whole new type of commercial film (about which more below); Burroughs, Pynchon, or Ishmael Reed, on the one hand, and the French *nouveau roman* and its succession on the other, along with alarming new kinds of literary criticism, based on some new aesthetic of textuality or *écriture* . . . The list might be extended indefinitely; but does it imply any more fundamental change or break than the periodic style- and fashion-changes determined by an older high-modernist imperative of stylistic innovation?

[. . .]

Pastiche Eclipses Parody

The disappearance of the individual subject, along with its formal consequence, the increasing unavailability of the personal style, engender the well-nigh universal practice today of what may be called pastiche. This concept, which we owe to Thomas Mann (in *Doktor Faustus*), who owed it in turn to Adorno's great work on the two paths of advanced musical experimentation (Schoenberg's innovative planification, Stravinsky's irrational eclecticism), is to be sharply distinguished from the more readily received idea of parody.

This last found, to be sure, a fertile area in the idiosyncrasies of the moderns and their 'inimitable' styles: the Faulknerian long sentence with its breathless gerundives, Lawrentian nature imagery punctuated by testy colloquialism, Wallace Stevens' inveterate hypostasis of non-substantive parts of speech ('the intricate evasions of as'), the fateful, but finally predictable, swoops in Mahler from high orchestral pathos into village accordion sentiment, Heidegger's meditative-solemn practice of the false etymology as a mode of 'proof' . . . All these strike one as somehow 'characteristic', insofar as they ostentatiously deviate from a norm which then reasserts itself, in a not necessarily unfriendly way, by a systematic mimicry of their deliberate eccentricities.

Yet, in the dialectical leap from quantity to quality, the explosion of modern literature into a host of distinct private styles and mannerisms has been followed by a linguistic fragmentation of social life itself to the point where the norm itself is eclipsed. . . . If the ideas of a ruling class were once the dominant (or hegemonic) ideology of bourgeois society, the advanced capitalist countries today are now a field of stylistic and discursive heterogeneity without a norm. Faceless masters continue to inflect the economic strategies which constrain our existences, but no longer need to impose their speech (or are henceforth unable to); and the postliteracy of the late capitalist world reflects, not only the absence of any great collective project, but also the unavailability of the older national language itself.

In this situation, parody finds itself without a vocation; it has lived, and that strange new thing pastiche slowly comes to take its place. Pastiche is, like parody, the imitation of a peculiar mask, speech in a dead language: but it is a neutral practice of such mimicry, without any of parody's ulterior motives, amputated of the satiric impulse, devoid of laughter and of any conviction that alongside the abnormal tongue you have momentarily borrowed, some healthy linguistic normality still exists. Pastiche is thus blank parody, a statue with blind eyeballs. . . .

It would therefore begin to seem that Adorno's prophetic diagnosis has been realized, albeit in a negative way: not Schoenberg (the sterility of whose achieved system he already glimpsed) but Stravinsky is the true precursor of the postmodern cultural production. For with the collapse of the high-modernist ideology of style – what is as unique and unmistakable as your own fingerprints, as incomparable as your own body (the very source, for an early Roland Barthes, of stylistic invention and innovation) – the producers of culture have nowhere to turn but to the past: the imitation of dead styles, speech through all the masks and voices stored up in the imaginary museum of a now global culture.

Source: From Fredric Jameson, 'Postmodernism, or the cultural logic of late capitalism', *New Left Review* 142 (1984): 53–65.

Document 18   LUCY R. LIPPARD, 'TROJAN HORSES: ACTIVIST ART AND POWER'

Lucy R. Lippard (1936–) is a politically engaged writer and activist in America who has written extensively on contemporary and feminist art. A co-founder of Political Art Documentation/Distribution (PADD), Heresies

Collective publications and the art bookstore Printed Matter, during the 1980s Lippard was coordinator of Artists Call Against U.S. Intervention in Central America. In 'Trojan Horses: Activist Art and Power' (1984), Lippard argues forcefully against purely stylistic and deracinated art, and calls for engaged artists to form community linkages to address continuing issues of racism, sexism, and classism in the contemporary political landscape.

The power of art is subversive rather than authoritarian, lying in its connection of the ability to make with the ability to see – and then in its power to make others see that they too can make something of what they see . . . and so on. Potentially powerful art is almost by definition oppositional – that work which worms its way out of the prescribed channels and is seen in a fresh light.

Despite art's public image of haughty powerlessness and humiliating manipulatability, a growing number of activists in and out of the cultural sphere are beginning to confront its potential power. However, the culture that is potentially powerful is not necessarily the culture that those in cultural power think will or should be powerful. Power is generally interpreted as control – control over one's own and others' actions. The myth of culture's powerlessness stems from a misunderstanding of the basis of art's authority and authenticity. Art is suggestive. The motions it inspires are usually *e*-motions. In the art world, a powerful artist is one whose name can be used. Name, not art. ('I bought a Starr,' like 'I bought a piece of Starr,' dangerously close to 'I bought Starr.')

Or perhaps it's more accurate to say the power of the artist is separated from the power of the object. Once art objects had literal power – magical, political power – and the artist shared in this because s/he was needed by the community. (Who needs artists today? What for? Who decided the art object was to have such a limited function?)

If the first ingredient of art's power is its ability to communicate what is seen – from the light on an apple to the underlying causes of world hunger – the second is control over the social and intellectual contexts in which it is distributed and interpreted. The real power of culture is to join individual and communal visions, to provide 'examples' and 'object lessons' as well as the pleasures of sensuous recognition. Ironically, those artists who try to convey their meanings directly are often accused of being propagandists, and their accessibility is thus limited to those not afraid of taking a stand. The ability to produce visions is impotent unless it's connected to a means of communication and distribution.

Political realism is usually labeled propaganda. Yet racism, sexism, and classism are not invisible in this society. The question of why they should be generally invisible in visual art is still a potato too hot to pick up. Because it is so embedded in context, activist art often eludes art critics who are neither the intended audience nor as knowledgeable about the issues and places as the artists themselves have become. The multiple, drawn-out forms can also be confusing because innovation in the international art world is understood as brand-name, stylistic, and short-term, geared to the market's brief attention span. Conventionally, artists are not supposed to go so far beneath the surface as to provoke changed attitudes; they are merely supposed to embellish, observe, and reflect the sites, sights, and systems of the status quo.

[. . .]

The degree to which an activist art is integrated with the artist's beliefs is crucial to its effectiveness. Much well-meaning progressive and activist art does not truly reflect the artist's lived experience, and often the artist's lived experience bears little resemblance to that of most other people. Work with tenants' organizations, feminist, radical, or solidarity groups, labor unions, or in the cultural task forces of the many small left parties, or with environmental, pacifist, and anti-nuclear groups offers ways to connect with those who are interested. Another option is to see the changing self as a symbol of social change, using personal histories (not necessarily one's own) to illuminate world events and larger visions. In this process local, ethnic, gender, and class identifications can augment individual obsessions. The extraordinary Afro-Brazilian film *Jom* shows the *griot* (storyteller, historian, shaman, artist) as the backbone of daily political consciousness in the community, the source of continuity through which power is maintained or lost.

I like to keep reminding myself that the root of the word 'radical' is the word 'root.' Grassroots then means not only propagation – spreading the word – but is based on the fact that each blade of grass has its own roots. Power means 'to be able' – the ability to act vigorously with 'strength, authority, might, control, spirit, divinity.' And the word 'craft' comes from Middle English and means strength *and* power, which later became 'skill.' Neither the word 'art' nor the word 'culture' bear these belligerent connotations. Art originally meant 'to join or fit together,' and 'culture' comes from cultivation and growth. An artist can function like a lazy gardener who cuts off the weeds as a temporary holding action. Or s/he can go under the surface to the causes. Social change can happen when you tear things up by the roots, or – to collage metaphors – when you go back to the roots and distinguish the weeds from the blossoms and vegetables . . . the Trojan horses from the four horses of the Apocalypse.

Source: In Brian Wallis (ed.), *Art After Modernism: Rethinking Representation*, New York: The New Museum of Contemporary Art, 1984, pp. 345–358.

RAYMOND WILLIAMS, 'WHEN WAS MODERNISM?'   **Document 19**

Raymond Williams (1921–1988) was a renowned New Left intellectual and journalist in the United Kingdom, as well as a foundational figure in the development of cultural studies. Considering himself a 'humanist Marxist,' Williams ran against the theoretical grain of post-structuralism to insist upon a 'cultural materialism' that remains enmeshed in concrete social and political relations. In 'When Was Modernism?' (1987), Williams views modernism in historical terms, from the revolutionary bohemianism of the 1840s to the present, and considers the state of contemporary art less 'postmodern' than the 'next challenge' in a continuing task to realise a more human modern culture.

'Modernism' as a title for a whole cultural movement and moment has . . . been retrospective as a general term since the 1950s, thereby stranding the dominant version of 'modern' or even 'absolute modern' between, say, 1890 and 1940. We still habitually use 'modern' of a world between a century and half a century old. When we note that in English at least (French usage still retaining the meaning for which the term was coined) 'avant-garde' may be indifferently used to refer to Dadaism seventy years after the event or to recent fringe theatre, the confusion both willed and involuntary which leaves our own deadly separate era in anonymity becomes less an intellectual problem and more an ideological perspective. By its point of view, all that is left to us is to become post-moderns.

   [. . .]

   But this version of Modernism cannot be seen and grasped in a unified way, whatever the likenesses of its imagery. Modernism thus defined *divides* politically and simply – and not just between specific movements but even *within* them. In remaining anti-bourgeois, its representatives either choose the formerly aristocratic valuation of art as a sacred realm above money and commerce, or the revolutionary doctrines, promulgated since 1848, of art as the liberating vanguard of popular consciousness. Mayakovsky, Picasso, Silone, Brecht are only some examples of those who moved into direct support of Communism, and D'Annunzio, Marinetti, Wyndham Lewis, Ezra Pound of those who moved toward Fascism, leaving Eliot and Yeats in Britain and Ireland to make their muffled, nuanced treaty with Anglo-Catholicism and the Celtic twilight.

   After Modernism is canonized, however, by the post-war settlement and its accompanying, complicit academic endorsements, there is then the presumption that since Modernism is *here* in this specific phase or period, there is nothing beyond it. The marginal or rejected artists become classics of organized teaching and of travelling exhibitions in the great galleries of the metropolitan cities. 'Modernism' is confined to this highly selective field and denied to everything else in a pure act of ideology, whose first, unconscious irony is that, absurdly, it stops history dead. Modernism being the terminus, everything afterwards is counted out of development. It is *after*, stuck in the past.

The ideological victory of this selection is no doubt to be explained by the relations of production of the artists themselves in the centres of metropolitan dominance, living the experience of rapidly mobile émigrés in the migrant quarters of their cities. They were exiles one of another, at a time when this was still not the more general experience of other artists, located as we would expect them to be, at home, but without the organization and promotion of group and city – simultaneously located *and* divided. The life of the émigré was dominant among the key groups, and they could and did deal with each other. Their self-referentiality, their propinquity and mutual isolation all served to represent the artist as necessarily estranged, and to ratify as canonical the works of radical estrangement. So, to *want* to leave your settlement and settle nowhere like Lawrence or Hemingway, becomes presented, in another ideological move, as a normal condition.

What has quite rapidly happened is that Modernism quickly lost its anti-bourgeois stance, and achieved comfortable integration into the new international capitalism. Its attempt at a universal market, transfrontier and transclass, turned out to be spurious. Its forms lent themselves to cultural competition and the commercial interplay of obsolescence, with its shifts of schools, styles and fashion so essential to the market. The painfully acquired techniques of significant *dis*connection are relocated, with the help of the special insensitivity of the trained and assured technicists, as the merely technical modes of advertising and the commercial cinema. The isolated, estranged images of alienation and loss, the narrative discontinuities, have become the easy iconography of the commercials, and the lonely, bitter, sardonic and skeptical hero takes his ready-made place as the star of the thriller.

These heartless formulae sharply remind us that the innovations of what is called Modernism have become the new but fixed forms of our present moment. If we are to break out of the non-historical fixity of *post*-modernism, then we must search out and counterpoise an alternate tradition taken from the neglected works left in the wide margin of the century, a tradition which may address itself not to this by now exploitable because quite inhuman rewriting of the past but, for all our sakes, to a modern *future* in which community may be imagined again.

Source: From Raymond Williams, 'When was Modernism?' in *The Politics of Modernism: Against the New Conformists,* London: Verso, 2007, 32–35.

References

Barr, Jr., Alfred H., *Cubist and Abstract Art* (rpnt edn), New York: Arno Press, 1996.

Baudelaire, Charles, *The Painter of Modern Life and Other Essays* (trans. Jonathan Mayne) London: Phaidon Press, 1995.

Baudrillard, Jean, *Simulations* (trans. Paul Foss, Paul Patton and Philip Beitchman), New York: Semiotexte, 1983.

Bayer, Herbert, Walter Gropius and Ise Gropius, *Bauhaus 1919–1928*, New York: The Museum of Modern Art,1938.

Benjamin, Walter, *Illuminations* (trans. Harry Zohn), Pimlico, 1999.

Berman, Marshall, *All That Is Solid Melts Into Air: The Experience of Modernity*, New York: Penguin, 1988.

Blake, Jody, *Le Tumulte noir: Modernist Art and Popular Entertainment in Jazz-Age Paris, 1900–1930*, University Park, PA: The Pennsylvania State University Press, 1999.

Bradbury, Malcolm and James McFarlane (eds), *Modernism: A Guide to European Literature 1890–1930* (new Preface), New York: Penguin, 1991.

Breton, André, *The Manifestoes of Surrealism* (trans. Richard Seaver and Helen R. Lane), Ann Arbor: University of Michigan Press, 1972.

Brown, Betty Ann, *Gradiva's Mirror: Reflections on Women, Surrealism and Art History*, New York: Midmarch Arts Press, 2002.

Bürger, Peter, *Theory of the Avant-Garde* (trans. Michael Shaw; Foreword Jochen Schulte-Sasse), Minneapolis: University of Minnesota Press, 1984.

Butler, Christopher, *Early Modernism: Literature, Music and Painting in Europe 1900–1916,* Oxford: Oxford University Press, 1994.

Calinescu, Matei, *Five Faces of Modernity: Modernism, Avant-Garde, Decadence, Kitsch, Postmodernism*, Durham: Duke University Press, 1987.

Caws, Marianne, Rudoph Kuenzli and Gwen Raab (eds), *Surrealism and Women*, Cambridge, MA.: MIT Press, 1991.

Childs, Peter, *Modernism* (Series 'The New Critical Idiom'), London and New York: Routledge, 2000.

Eksteins, Modris, *Rites of Spring: The Great War and the Birth of the Modern Age*, New York: Mariner Books, 2000.

Eysteinsson, Astradur, *The Concept of Modernism*, Ithaca: Cornell University Press, 1990.

Fineberg, Jonathan, *Art since 1940: Strategies of Being*, New York: Harry N. Abrams, 1995.

Flamm, Jack, *Matisse on Art* (revd edn), Berkeley: University of California Press, 1995.

Flaubert, Gustave, *The Letters of Gustave Flaubert, 1857–1880* (ed. and trans. Francis Steegmuller), Cambridge, MA.: The Belknap Press of Harvard University Press, 1982.

Foster, Hal, Rosalind Krauss, Yve-Alain Bois and Benjamin H.D. Buchloh, *Art since 1900: Modernism, Antimodernism, Postmodernism*, New York: Thames and Hudson, 2004.

Freud, Sigmund, *The Interpretation of Dreams* (ed. and trans. James Strachey), New York: Basic Books, 1955.

Gaiger, Jason (ed.), *Frameworks for Modern Art*, New Haven and London: Yale University Press/The Open University Press, 2003.

Gates, Jr., Henry Louis and Karen C.C. Dalton, *Josephine Baker and La Revue Nègre: Paul Colin's Lithographs of Le Tumulte noir in Paris, 1927*, New York: Harry N. Abrams, 1998.

Genova, Pamela A., *Symbolist Journals: A Culture of Correspondence*, Aldershot, Hampshire: Ashgate Publishing, 2002.

Ghirardo, Diane, *Building New Communities: New Deal America and Fascist Italy*, Princeton: Princeton University Press, 1989.

Gleason, Abbot, Peter Kenez and Richard Stites (eds), *Bolshevik Culture: Experiment and Order in the Russian Revolution*, Bloomington: Indiana University Press, 1985.

Gluck, Mary, *Popular Bohemia: Modernism and Urban Culture in Nineteenth-Century Paris*, Cambridge, MA: Harvard University Press, 2005.

Gorsky, Susan Rubinow, *Virginia Woolf* (revd edn) 'Twayne's English Authors Series', Boston: Twayne, 1989.

Greeley, Robin Adèle, *Surrealism and the Spanish Civil War*, New Haven: Yale University Press, 2006.

Green, Christopher (ed.), *Picasso's Les Demoiselles d'Avignon*, Cambridge: Cambridge University Press, 2001.

Greenberg, Clement, *Art and Culture: Critical Essays*, Boston: Beacon Press, 1989.

Hamilton, Richard, *Collected Words, 1953–1982*, London and New York: Thames Hudson, 1982.

Harrison, Charles and Paul Wood (eds), *Art in Theory 1900–2000: An Anthology of Changing Ideas* (new edn), Oxford: Blackwell, 2003.

Harrison, Charles, Francis Frascina and Gill Perry, *Primitivism, Cubism, Abstraction: The Early Twentieth Century* (series: 'Modern Art: Practices and Debates'), New Haven and London: Yale University Press/The Open University, 1993.

Harvey, David, *The Condition of Postmodernity*, Oxford: Blackwell, 1990.

Harvey, David, *Paris, Capital of Modernity*, New York: Routledge, 2006.

Healey, Kimberly J., *The Modernist Traveler: French Detours, 1900–1930*, Lincoln: University of Nebraska Press, 2003.

Herbert, Robert L. (ed. and trans.), *Modern Artists on Art* (2nd edn), Mineola, NY: Dover, 2000.

Hopkins, David, *After Modern Art, 1945–2000*, Oxford: Oxford University Press, 2000.

Huelsenbeck, Richard (ed.), *The Dada Almanac* (English edn, Malcolm Green, trans.), Malcolm Green et al. (eds.), Lodon: Atlas Press, 1993.

Hughes, H. Stuart, *Consciousness and Society: The Reorientation of European Social Thought 1890–1930*, New York: Alfred A. Knopf, 1958.

Hughes, H. Stuart, *Between Commitment and Disillusion*, Middletown, CT: Wesleyan University Press, 1986.

Huyssen, Andreas, *After the Great Divide: Modernism, Mass Culture, Postmodernism*, Bloomington: Indiana University Press, 1986.

Jameson, Fredric, 'Postmodernism, or The Cultural Logic of Late Capitalism', *New Left Review* 142 (1984), 53–65.

Jervis, John, *Exploring the Modern*, Oxford: Blackwell, 1998.

Kandinsky, Wassily, *Concerning the Spiritual in Art* (trans. M.T.H. Sadler), New York: Dover Publications, 1977.

Kaplan, Alice Yeager, *Reproductions of Banality: Fascism, Literature, and French Intellectual Life*, Minneapolis: University of Minnesota Press, 1986.

Kern, Stephen, *The Culture of Time and Space 1880–1918*, Cambridge, MA: Harvard University Press, 1983.

Knabb, Ken (ed.), *Situationist International Anthology* (revd edn), Berkeley: Bureau of Public Secrets, 2006.

Levenson, Michael (ed.), *The Cambridge Companion to Modernism*, Cambridge: Cambridge University Press, 1999.

Lottman, Herbert R., *The Left Bank: Writers, Artists, and Politics from the Popular Front to the Cold War*, New York: Houghton Mifflin, 1982.

Lowe, Donald M., *History of Bourgeois Perception*, Chicago: University of Chicago Press, 1982.

Lunn, Eugene, *Marxism and Modernism: An Historical Study of Lukács, Brecht, Benjamin, and Adorno*, Berkeley: University of California Press, 1984.

Marx, Karl, *The Communist Manifesto* (ed. and intro. David McLellan), Oxford: Oxford University Press, 1992.

Mondrian, Piet, *The New Art—The New Life: Collected Writings* (trans. and ed. Harry Holtzman and Martin S. James), New York: Da Capo Press, 1993.

Morton, Patricia A., *Hybrid Modernities: Architecture and Representation at the 1931 Colonial Exposition, Paris*, Cambridge, MA: MIT Press, 2000.

Motherwell, Robert (ed.), *The Dada Painters and Poets: An Anthology* (2nd edn, trans. Ralph Manheim), Cambridge, MA: Belknap Press of Harvard University Press, 1988.

Nadeau, Maurice, *The History of Surrealism* (trans. Richard Howard), Cambridge, MA: The Belknap Press of Harvard University Press, 1989.

Poggioli, Renato, *The Theory of the Avant-Garde* (trans. Gerald Fitzgerald), New York: Harper and Row, 1968.

Proust, Marcel, *The Way by Swann's* (trans. Lydia Davis), *In Search of Lost Time*, Vol. 1 (gen. ed. Christopher Prendergast), London: Penguin, 2002.

Rainey, Lawrence (ed.), *Modernism: An Anthology*, Oxford: Blackwell, 2005.

Ross, Alex, *The Rest is Noise: Listening to the Twentieth Century*, New York: Picador, 2007.

Rubin, William (ed.), *'Primitivism' in 20th Century Art: Affinity of the Tribal and the Modern,* 2 vols, New York: The Museum of Modern Art, 1984.

Rubin, William, Hélène Seckel and Judith Cousins, *Les Desmoiselles d'Avignon*, New York: The Museum of Modern Art, 1994.

Saler, Michael T., *The Avant-Garde in Interwar England: Medieval Modernism and the London Underground*, Oxford: Oxford University Press, 1999.

Schorske, Carl E., *Fin-de-Siècle Vienna: Politics and Culture*, New York: Vintage Books, 1981.

Schwartz, Vanessa, *Spectacular Realities: Early Mass Culture in Fin-de-Siècle France*, Berkeley: University of California Press, 1998.

Siegel, Jerrold, *Bohemian Paris: Culture, Politics, and the Boundaries of Bourgeois Life*, New York: Penguin Books, 1986.

Stovall, Tyler, *Paris Noir: African Americans in the City of Light*, New York: Houghton Mifflin, 1996.

Varnedoe, Kirk and Adam Gopnik, *High & Low: Modern Art, Popular Culture*, New York: The Museum of Modern Art, 1991.

Wallis, Brian (ed.), *Art After Modernism: Rethinking Representation* New York: The New Museum of Contemporary Art, 1984.

Walz, Robin, *Modernism* (Series: 'Short Histories of Big Ideas'), Harlow: Pearson/Longman, 2007.

Walz, Robin, *Pulp Surrealism: Insolent Popular Culture in Early Twentieth-Century Paris*, Berkeley: University of California Press, 2000.

Weiss, Jeffrey, *The Popular Culture of Modern Art: Picasso, Duchamp, and Avant-Gardism*, New Haven: Yale University Press, 1994.

Willet, John, *Art and Politics in the Weimar Period: The New Sobriety 1917–1933*, New York: Pantheon Books, 1978.

Williams, Raymond, *The Politics of Modernism: Against the New Conformists*, London: Verso, 1989.

Wood, Paul (ed.), *Varieties of Modernism* (Series: 'Art of the 20th Century'), New Haven and London: Yale University Press/The Open University, 2004.

Wood, Paul et al., *Modernism in Dispute: Art since the Forties* (Series: 'Modern Art: Practices and Debates'), New Haven and London: Yale University Press/The Open University, 1993.

Woolf, Virginia, *Collected Essays*, Vol. I, New York: Harcourt, Brace & World, 1967.

Index

'abstract': defined 135

abstract art: in America 86; Barr on xxvii, 134–6; Cabaret Voltaire and 56; development of xxvii, 43–4, 47, 84–5; Supremacist movement 59; two main traditions of 135–6

Abstract-Creationism 83

Abstract Expressionism 8, 63, 72, 83, 85, 86, 87–8, 89, 92–3, 97; defined xxii

abstraction: Baudrillard on 143; experiments in 11, 71; use in contemporary culture 107

Académie des Beaux-Arts 20

ACT-UP (AIDS Coalition to Unleash Power) 109

action painting 87–8

Adorno, Theodor 96, 140, 145, 146

advertising: images used in collage and montage 47, 58, 88, 98–9, 103; modernist techniques used in 11, 100, 150; Pop art and 98; posters 22, 60, 70

Aestheticism 140–1

African-Americans 75–6, 84

African culture 23, 48, 58, 74, 75

AIDS 109

Akhmatova, Anna 27

AKhRR (Association of Artists of Revolutionary Russia) 71

Aldington, Richard 45

Alembert, Jean le Rond d' 7

Althusser, Louis 95

American Abstract Artists group 86

Americanism 96

ancient cultures, influence of 7, 26, 118, 122

Anderson, Sherwood 84

anthropometrics 90–1

apaches 75

Apollinaire, Guillaume xiv, 3, 41, 46, 48, 49; calligrammes 46, 76; 'La colombe poignardée et le jet d'eau' Plate 2, 46

Aragon, Louis xiv, 60, 77, 78, 86

Arbeiter-Illustrierte-Zeitung (A.-I.-Z.) 72–3

architecture: Bauhaus 63, 64, 69; Constructivist 60; De Stijl 47, 83; exhibition buildings 66–7, 74–5; housing 64, 69–70; International Style 69; London Underground 70; Mondrian on 121; neo-classical 66, 68; postmodern 103–4; Purist 62–3, 129–32; Rationalist 69–70; Socialist Realism 66–7, 68

Arensberg, Walter and Louise 84

Argentina: Neo-Concretists 92

Arman 91

Armory Show, New York 84

Arp, Hans (also Jean) 43, 56, 58, 83

art: activist 146–8; American 84–8, 89–90; ascending triangle in 44, 119; and authenticity 136–7, 138; brothel painting 3; defined 148; early avant–garde 43–4, 46–51; heroic 68, 71, 73, 139; minimalist 102; neo-avant-garde 89–93; ritualistic basis 137–8; Stalinist 71; symphonic paintings 44; women artists 108–9; see also abstract art; and specific movements

art brut 90

Art Deco 62

Art Nouveau: Austrian Secession 26; defined xxii; Jugendstil 43; Symbolists and 22

Art of this Century gallery, New York 83–4, 86, 87

art pour l'art, l' (art for art's sake) 19, 99, 138; defined xxii; rejection of 59

Art Students' League 97, 98

arts and crafts movement 70

atomic physics 32–3

atonality 10, 44–5

authenticity 136–7, 138
automatism 61, 86, 87, 128
avant-garde: Bürger on 104, 140–2; defined xxii; and dehumanisation 10–11; early 41–53; effect of institutionalisation on 99; and entertainment 49–50; gay and lesbian 109; gender and 108–9; goal of transforming Western civilisation 49, 50, 51; Hamilton on 139; looseness of term 149; and mass culture 77, 85, 96–7; Nazis and 73; and 1930s politics 68; poetry 36–7, 45–6; in post-1918 France 60; radical 5, 54–65; and 'shock of the new' 42; 21st century 108; see also modernism; neo-avant-garde; and specific movements

Baader, Johannes 54, 58
Bacon, Francis xiv, 89, 90
Baker, Josephine xiv, 76
Ball, Hugo xiv, 56; 'Karawane' 57
Balla, Giacomo 50
Ballets Russes 41–2
Balzac, Honoré de 17, 20, 36
Barbusse, Henri 77
Barnes, Djuna 84, 108
Barr, Jr., Alfred H. xiv; as director of MoMA 84; flowchart by xxvii, 84–5; Cubism and Abstract Art xxvii, 134–6
Barthes, Roland 146; Mythologies 100–1
Baudelaire, Charles xiv, 15–16, 20, 27; Les fleurs du mal 15; 'The Painter of Modern Life' 15, 19, 112–13
Baudrillard, Jean: Simulations 101, 142–4
Bauhaus 63–5, 69; defined xxii; Gropius on 132–4
Beardsley, Aubrey 23
Bechet, Sidney 75
Beckmann, Max 72
Belle Époque 23, 26
Benda, Julian: The Treason of the Intellectuals 77
Benjamin, Walter xiv, 96, 98; 'The work of art in the age of mechanical reproduction' 136–8
Bennett, Arnold 114
Benton, Thomas Hart 87
Berg, Alban 45
Bergson, Henri 34
Berlin: Dada 57–8; Dada Fair (1920) 54–5, 58, 73; Expressionism 51; modernist housing 69; Spartacist uprising (1919) 55, 58; theatre 26–7; wrapping of Reichstag (as artwork) 91
Bernard, Émile 48
Beuys, Joseph 92
Biely (Bugayev), Andrei 27

billboards 98
binary code 101
black culture: in Paris 75–6; see also African-Americans; African culture
Blaue Reiter (Blue Riders) 43–4; defined xxii
Blok, Alexandr 27
Bloomsbury Group 70
Blum, Léon 66, 78
Boccioni, Umberto 50
bohemianism 18–19
Bohr, Neils 33
Bolsheviks 55, 58, 59, 66, 70
Bonnard, Pierre 21, 86, 89
Borlin, Jean 76
bourgeois society 7, 18, 58, 72, 140–1, 146
Boyle, Kay 84
Brânşusi, Constantin 83
Braque, Georges xiv, 43, 46, 83, 86, 89
Brazil: Brazilia architecture 63; Jom (film) 148; Neo-Concretists 92
Brecht, Bertolt xv, 59, 77, 149
Breton, André xv, 4, 60, 61, 78, 86, 95; Manifesto of Surrealism 61, 127–9
Brittany 24, 25
Brodsky, Isaak 71
brothel painting 3
Brouwer, L. E. J. 33
Brücke group 49, 122
Bugayev, Andrei see Biely, Andrei
Burchard, Otto 54
Bürger, Peter: The Theory of the Avant-Garde 99, 104, 140–2

Cabaret Voltaire 56
Cage, John xv, 89, 109, 145
Cahun, Claude 108
Calder, Alexander xv, 83, 86
calligrammes 46, 76
Cambridge Heretics Society 28
capitalism: critiques of 29–30, 58–9; Jameson on 146; postmodernism and 104; Weber on 31; Williams on 150
Carli, Mario 50
Carrà, Carlo 50
Carrington, Leonora 108
Casa del Fascio, Como 69
Casebere, James 103
Catalonia 67, 78
cenacles 22
Cendrars, Blaise xv; La prose du Transsibérien et de la Petite Jehanne de France 36–7

Centre Georges Pompidou, Paris 95
Cézanne, Paul xv, 21, 43, 44, 48, 84, 86, 116, 135
Chagall, Marc 86
Charlesworth, Sarah 103
Chicago, Judy: *The Dinner Party* 108
Chirico, Giorgio de 83, 86
Christo and Jeanne-Claude xv, 91
CIAM *see* International Congress of International
    Architecture
cinema and film: Constructivist 60; epic 139;
    Futurist 51; *Jom* 148; *Kino-glaz* techniques 71;
    modernist techniques commonly used in 107,
    150; montage 60, 107; music 103; *Neue
    Sachlichkeit* 72; 1920s 55–6; postmodern 145;
    reproduction of 96; Warhol and 98
cities, European 16–17, 26–7, 49; *see also specific
    cities*
civilisation *see* Western civilisation
Cixous, Hélène 108
Club Dada, Berlin 57–8
Cocteau, Jean xv, 41, 83
Colin, Paul: *Le Tumulte noir* 76–7
collage 10, 47, 87, 88, 96, 97; feminist 108–9
colonialism 16, 23, 24, 25, 29; Surrealist critique of
    74–5; *see also* imperialism
colour: Expressionism and 48, 49; Impressionism
    and 21; Kandinsky's theory of 44; Lichtenstein
    and 97–8; Matisse on 116–17; Miró and 67;
    Mondrian and 47
comics 97–8
commercialism 17, 68–9, 96–100, 107
communications technologies 16–17, 28, 55–6
communism 30, 55, 58–9, 61, 149; in 1930s 78;
    Soviet 66, 71, 78
composition: Matisse on 43, 116
'compositions' 44, 47
computer processing 101
Comte, Auguste 29
'concrete': defined xxii
concrete performance art 88, 91, 92, 97
concrete poetry 45, 46, 57
Conrad, Joseph 26
consciousness: effect of dissonance on 44–5;
    expansion of 74; Mondrian on 120;
    refashioning 8; study of 34–5
Constructivism 4, 47, 96, 99, 135; Bauhaus and 63,
    64; defined xxii; international 60; Russian 45,
    59–60, 63, 64, 71, 75
Constructivist Manifesto 59
consumption, mass 17, 95–100, 107, 141–2
Cora, Bruno 50

corporate branding 104
Counter-Colonial Exposition (Paris, 1931) 75, 77
crafts 63, 122, 132–3; origin of word 148
'crisis of the referent' 100–3, 107–8
criticism: and activist art 148; American 85, 92; by
    Apollinaire 46; of Pollock 88; postmodern 145;
    queer theory and 109; Symbolist 22; Tzara on
    126
Crowley, Malcolm 77
Cubism 4, 46–7, 48, 50, 51, 52, 62, 63, 70, 72, 84,
    96, 99, 135; in America 86; defined xxiii;
    parody of 76; Picasso's *Guernica* 67–8
'Cubism and Abstract Art' exhibition, MoMA 84–5
Cubo-Futurism 51, 60
cultural materialism 149
Cunard, Nancy 108
Cunningham, Merce 89, 109

Dada 6, 47, 51, 54–5, 56–8, 64, 84, 96, 99;
    defined xxiii; Hamilton on 139; meeting with
    Constructivists (1922) 60; origin of word 56;
    Paris 61; Zurich 56, 57, 64
Dada Advertising Company 58
Dada Almanach 57, 58
Dada Fair 54–5, 58, 73
Dada Manifesto 1918 (Tzara) 57, 125–7
Dakar-Djibouti ethnographic mission 74
Dalí, Gala 108
Dalí, Salvador xv, 61, 83
Darwin, Charles 10, 30, 31
Daumier, Honoré 17, 20
Davis, Stuart 84, 87
de Beauvoir, Simone: *The Second Sex* 108
Debussy, Claude xv, 25; *Prélude à 'L'Après-midi d'un
    faune'* 25, 41
Decadent movement 22, 23, 31
Degas, Edgar 21
de Gaulle, Charles 94, 95
degeneration 31; *Entartete Kunst* 73
dehumanisation 10–11
Deineka, Alexander 71
de Kooning, Willem xv, 83, 85, 86, 88
Delacroix, Eugène 23; *Liberty Leading the People* 17
Delaunay, Robert 46, 51
Delaunay, Sonia 37
Demuth, Charles 84
Depression, Great 72, 84
Dérain, André 3, 43, 49
Design and Industries Association (DIA), UK 70
desire 94, 95
Desnos, Robert 86

Dessau: Bauhaus 64, 69
De Stijl 47, 62, 83; defined xxiii
Destruction in Art Symposium (London, 1963) 92
Diaghilev, Sergei 41, 42
Diderot, Denis 7, 29
digression 36
Dine, Jim 88
dissonance: in art 47; in music 44–5
Dix, Otto xv, 72, 54, 58
Doesburg, Theo van 63
Doolittle, Hilda *see* H. D.
Dos Passos, John 77, 84
Doucet, Jacques 4
Dove, Arthur 84
dreams 10, 34, 61
Drieu la Rochelle, Pierre xv, 61–2
Dubuffet, Jean xvi, 89–90
Duchamp, Marcel xvi, 49–50, 61, 83, 84, 86, 89, 91
Durkheim, Émile 23–4, 31

écriture féminine, l' 108
Ehrenberg, Ilya 78
Einstein, Albert 32, 33
Eisenstein, Sergei 60, 72
Eliot, T. S. xvi, 26, 45, 49, 149
Éluard, Paul 60–1, 86
émigrés 150
Encyclopédie (*eds.* Diderot and Alembert) 7, 29
Enlightenment 7, 29, 30
Entartete Kunst ('Degenerate Art') 73
episteme 101
Epstein, Jacob 70
Ernst, Max 61, 83, 86
Esprit Nouveau, L' (review) 62
ethnography 23, 24, 58, 74
Europe: neo-avant-garde 89–91; 19th century 16–17; *see also* cities, European
evolution 30–1, 130–1
Existentialism 87, 89, 90; defined xxiii
exotic other 22–5, 75–6
exots 25, 58
experimentation 9
Exposition Universelle (Paris, 1889) 18
Expressionism 4, 24, 43–4, 48, 49, 56, 63, 84; criticism of 59; defined xxiii; Futurism and 51; Matisse on 116–17; 'new' 145; see also Abstract Expressionism
'exquisite corpse' games 61
Eysteinsson, Ástráođur 42

fairs, world 17, 18, 23, 24, 25, 66–7, 74–5, 77
fascism 55, 61–2, 149; Futurism and 51, 61, 62, 64, 68; Italian 61, 62, 66, 68, 69–70, 77; Popular Front and writers against 66–7, 68, 77–8
Fauves 43, 49, 50, 70, 84, 116; defined xxiii
Feiniger, Lyonel 63
feminism 107–9
film *see* cinema and film
First All Union Congress of Writers (1934) 71
First World War 51, 52, 56, 84; art depicting 54; traumatic effects of 55, 58, 60–2
Fitzgerald, F. Scott 84
flâneurs 19, 20
Flanner, Janet 84
Flaubert, Gustave xvi, 20; *Salammbô* 23
Fluxus 92; defined xxiii
folk art 44, 48
Formalism 33; Russian 100
Forster, E. M. 26, 77
Foster, Hal 104
Foucault, Michel 95, 101
France: colonialism 74–5; entertainers 75–6; fascism 61–2; feminism 108; Popular Front government 66–7, 78; post-1918 60–2; primitivism 74–7; student protests and general strike (1968) 94–5; Surrealism 61, 64, 74; Vichy/Nazi-occupied 62, 83, 85–6; *see also* Paris
Franco, Francisco 66, 67, 78
Frankfurt School 95, 96, 136
Freud, Sigmund xvi, 10, 26, 31–2, 61, 74, 128; *The Interpretation of Dreams* 10, 34
Fry, Roger 70
Futurism 4, 50–2; defined xxiii; and fascism 51, 61, 62, 64, 68; Hamilton on 139; international influence 51; Italian 45, 50, 51, 61, 64; Marinetti's 'Manifesto of' 50, 123–5
Futurismo (journal) 61

Gallimard (publisher) 62
Gauguin, Paul xvi, 21, 24–5, 48, 84, 135
Gautier, Théophile xvi, 19
Gehry, Frank xvi, 103–4
geometric designs 62–3, 86
Gerasimov, Alexander 71
Germany: Bauhaus 63–5, 69, 132–4; effects of First World War 55; Expressionism 43, 51; modernist housing 69; Nazis 58, 66, 68, 72–3, 78, 85; Weimar Republic 54–5, 58, 64, 69, 72–3; *see also* Berlin
Gesamtkunstwerk 25
Giacometti, Alberto xvi, 83, 89, 90

Giacometti, Augusto 56, 90
Gide, André 77
Ginna, Arnaldo 50
Glass, Philip xvi, 102–3, 145; *Einstein on the Beach* (with Robert Wilson) 102–3
Gluck, Mary 20
Gober, Robert 109
Goering, Hermann 73
Golding, John 46
Gonzalez-Torres, Felix 109
Gorky, Arshile xvi, 86, 87
Gorky, Maxim 72, 77
Gorsky, Susan Rubinow 35
Goudeau, Émile 22
Gourmont, Remy de xvi, 22
graffiti 94–5
Gramsci, Antonio: *Prison Notebooks* 77
graphics 107
Graves, Michael 103
'Great Work' (cultural fusion) 25
Greeks, ancient: art 26, 118, 122
Greenberg, Clement xvi, 85, 88; *Modernist Painting* 92
Gris, Juan 46, 51
Gropius, Walter xvi, 63–4, 69; 'Art and Technology: A New Unity' 63; 'The Theory and Organisation of the Bauhaus' 132–4
Gross, Valentine *see* Hugo, Valentine
Großen Deutschen Kunstausstellung, Munich 73
Grosz, George xvii, 54, 57, 58–9, 72
Guernica massacre 67
Guggenheim, Peggy xvii, 83–4, 86, 87
Gutai 91–2
Guys, Constantin ('Monsieur C.G.') 15, 19, 112–13

H. D. (Hilda Doolittle) xvii, 26, 45, 108
Hamilton, Richard xvii; 'For the Finest Art try – POP' 138–9; *Just What Is It That Makes Today's Homes So Different, So Appealing?* 97
Haring, Keith 109
Harlem Renaissance 75, 84
Hartley, Marsden 84
Hausmann, Raoul xvii, 54–5, 58
Haussmann, Georges-Eugène 18, 21
Heartfield, John xvii, 54, 57, 58, 72–3
Heckel, Erich 49
Hegel, Georg Wilhelm Friedrich 29, 30, 140
Heisenberg, Werner 33
Hemingway, Ernest 84, 150
Henderson, Nigel 97
Hennings, Emmy 56

heroic art 68, 71, 73, 139
Herzfeld, Helmut *see* Heartfield, John
Herzfelde, Wieland 57
Higgins, Dick 92
Hilbert, David 33
Hill, Eric 70
Hiroshige, Ando 23
history: as evolutionary process 29, 30–1
Hitler, Adolf 68, 72, 73
Höch, Hannah xvii, 54, 73, 108; *Aus einem ethnographischen Museum* 58
Hofmann, Hans 85, 86
Hokusai, Katsushika 23, 25
Holden, Charles 70
Horkheimer, Max 96
housing, modernist 64, 69–70
Huelsenbeck, Richard 56, 57, 58
Hughes, Langston 77, 84
Hugo, Valentine (*née* Gross) 41–2, 108
Hugo, Victor 19; *Les Misérables* 17
Hulme, T. E. xvii, 45
Hurston, Nora Neale 84
Husserl, Edmund 34
Huxley, Aldous 77
Huysmans, Joris Karl 22, 25
Hydropathe group 22
hyper-masculinity 50, 51

Ibsen, Henrik 26, 27
ICA *see* Institute of Contemporary Arts
Idealism 29
ideynost, principle of 71
imagination: Breton on 128; the *flâneur* and 19; Symbolism and 22
Imagism 8, 45; defined xxiii
imperialism 16, 27, 30, 143; *see also* colonialism
Impressionism 5, 18, 20–3, 43; defined xxiv; Neo- 43, 50; and music 25; Post- 21, 48, 70, 84
Independent Group 97
industrial design: Bauhaus and 63–4, 132–4; Constructivists and 59
industrial production: Futurists and 50, 51–2, 123–5; of mass culture 96, 97–8; scientific management (Taylorism) 62
Industrial Revolution 16–17
Ingres, Jean-Auguste-Dominique 23
innovation 4, 9, 11
installations 91, 108
Institute of Contemporary Arts, London 97
institutionalisation 95, 99, 107, 149–50

International Colonial Exposition (Paris, 1931) 74–5, 77

International Congress of Modern Architecture (Congrès International d'Architecture Moderne, CIAM) 69

International Exhibition, Paris 1937 (Exposition Internationale des Arts et Techniques dans la Vie Moderne) 66–7

International Exposition of Decorative Arts (Paris, 1925) 62–3

International Style 69

International Writers Association for the Defence of Culture 78

International Writers Congress for the Defence of Culture (Paris, 1935) 66, 77–8

intuitionism 33

Iofan, Boris 66–7

Irigaray, Luce 108

Italia Futurista, L' (review) 50

Italy: fascism 61, 62, 66, 68, 69–70, 77; Futurism 45, 50, 51, 61; 'New Towns' project 69–70

James, Henry 26

James, William xvii, 34

Jameson, Frederic: 'Postmodernism, or The Cultural Logic of Late Capitalism' 104, 144–6

Janco, Marcel 56

Japan: neo-avant-garde 91–2

japonisme 23, 25; defined xxiv

jazz 60, 75–6

Johns, Jasper 88, 109

Jom (film) 148

journals: arts 59, 74; fascist 61; literary 50, 62; Surrealist 74; Symbolist 22; Wagnerian 25; see also magazines

Joyce, James xvii, 26, 49; Ulysses 36

Judith (Jewish heroine) 23, 26

Jugendstil 43

junk, neo-avant-garde use of 91

Kahlo, Frida 108

Kandinsky, Wassily xvii, 43–4, 63, 73, 83, 86; Concerning the Spiritual in Art 44, 118–19

Kant, Immanuel 7, 129

Kern, Stephen 28, 52

Kiesler, Frederick 83

kinaesthesia 51

Kino-glaz techniques 71

Kirchner, Ernst Ludwig 49

Kitsch 73, 85; defined xxiv

klassovost, principle of 71

Klee, Paul xvii, 43–4, 73, 83

Klein, Yves xvii, 90–1

Klimt, Gustave xvii, 23, 26

knowledge: participation of the investigator 32; pluralities of 33; transformation of 29–30

Krasner, Lee 84, 86, 87, 108

Kristeva, Julia 108

Kruger, Barbara xviii, 108–9; Untitled (your body is a battleground) Plate 4, 109

Kunstblatt, Das (journal) 59

language: in Imagist poetry 45; invented (Dada) 57; of music 44; semiotics 100–1

Lautgedicht (sound poem) 57

Lawrence, D. H. 26, 45, 145, 150

Le Corbusier (Charles-Édouard Jeanneret) xviii, 62–3, 64, 69; on Purism 129–32

LEF (Left Front of the Arts) 71

LEF (review) 59–60

Le Fauconnier, Henri 46

Lefebvre, Henri 95

Léger, Fernand xviii, 46, 51, 62, 83, 86, 89

Leiris, Michel 74

Lenin, Vladimir Ilyich 60, 71

Leonard, Zoe 109

Levine, Sherrie: Untitled, After Edward Weston 103

Lévy-Bruhl, Lucien xviii, 24, 74

Lewis, Wyndham xviii, 51, 62, 149

Lichtenstein, Roy xviii, 97–8

Lingeri, Pietro 69

Lipchitz, Jacques 86

Lippard, Lucy R.: 'Trojan Horses: Activist Art and Power' 146–8

Lissitzky, El 63, 72

literature: African-American 84; early 20th century 34–7; French 19th century 17, 18–19, 20, 23; Futurist 51–2; and mass culture 77; Orientalism 22–3, 25; postmodern 145–6; roman feuilleton 19; stream of consciousness 10, 34, 35, 113–14; Surrealist 61; Symbolist 26; time and space in 34–6; 'uselessness of' 19; women writers 108; Woolf on 28, 113–15; see also poetry

Littoria, Italy: housing 69

logic 33, 127–8; 'of the unconscious' 44–5

London: Destruction in Art Symposium (1963) 92; galleries 83, 97; 19th century 16, 17, 26; 20th century (early) 26; Underground art and architecture 70

'Lost Generation' 84

Loti, Pierre 23, 24

Lowe, Donald M. 28

Lunacharsky, Anatoly 59
Lunn, Eugene 9–11
Lyotard, François: *The Postmodern Condition* 101

McFarlane, James 9
McHale, John 97
McKay, Claude 84
Mackensen, Fritz 48
McKnight Kauffer, Edward 70
McTaggart Ellis, John 28
Maeterlinck, Maurice 25
magazines: in montages 58; 19th century 17, 18, 23;
        satirical 72; *see also* journals
magical thinking 24
Magritte, René 61
Mallarmé, Stéphane xviii, 21, 25, 26, 138
Malraux, André 77, 86
Mandelstam, Osip 27, 72
Manet, Édouard xviii, 20–1, 23
Mann, Thomas xviii, 145; *Buddenbrooks: The Decline
        of a Family* 35
Mapplethorpe, Robert 109
Marc, Franz 43
Marcuse, Herbert 95, 141
Marin, John 84
Marinetti, Filippo Tommaso xviii, 50–2, 61, 149;
        'The Founding and the Manifesto of Futurism'
        50, 123–5
Marquesas Islands 25
Martin, Agnes 109; *Leaf* 102
Marx, Karl 8, 29–30
Marxism 74, 95, 149
mass culture: Hamilton on 138–9; 19th century 17,
        18, 19, 23, 27; Pop art and 97–100;
        postmodern photography and 103;
        structuralism on 100–1; tensions between
        avant-garde and 77, 85, 96–7
mass media 55–6, 58, 72, 101
masses, reaching the 50, 52, 55–6, 59; London
        Underground art 70; in Soviet Union 71
Masson, André 61, 86
materialism: cultural 149; Kandinsky on 118–19
mathematics 33, 130, 131
Matisse, Henri xviii, 3, 23, 43, 49, 86, 89;
        'Notes of a Painter' 43, 116–17
Mauss, Marcel 23–4
Mayakovsky, Vladimir xviii, 51, 60, 71, 72, 149
meaning: uncertainty of 10, 25
mechanical reproduction 96, 98, 136–8
mechanical selection 131
mechanized work: Gropius on 132

medieval era 7, 24
Mehring, Walter 58
melodrama 19
Mendès, Catulle 22
Mexican muralists 84, 87
Meyer, Adolf 69
Mies van der Rohe, Ludwig xviii, 69
Miller, Lee 108
Millet, Jean-François 48
minimalism 101–2; defined xxiv
Minotaure (review) 74
Miró, Joan xix, 67, 68, 83, 86, 87; *Aidez L'Espagne*
        (poster) *Plate 3*, 67
'modern': defined 5, 6–7, 149
modernisation 6, 7–8; 19th century 29; as source of
        discontent 31
modernism: American 86–9; contemporary
        acceptance of 4; defined 4, 6–11; diversity 8–9;
        early 41–53; effects of First World War 55;
        experimentation 9; and gender 107–8; high
        3–4, 5, 39–79; historical origins 5, 13–38;
        influence on contemporary culture 11;
        institutionalisation of 95, 99, 107, 149–50;
        literary (perceptual revolution) 34–7; Lunn's
        four dimensions of 9–11; late 1920s and 1930s
        66–79; networks and geographic displacement
        49; reaching the masses 50, 52, 55–6, 59, 70,
        71; relationship with consumerism 96;
        relationship with modernity 8, 9; shift from
        linearity to multi-perspectivity 28–9; Williams
        on 149–50; *see also* avant-garde; postmodernism
modernity 3, 6, 8, 9; Baudelaire on 15–16, 113;
        defined xxiv; early 20th century 28; 19th
        century and 17, 20–1; perceptual revolution
        and 32
Modersohn, Otto 48
Modersohn-Becker, Paula xix, 48
Moffet, Donald 109
Moholy-Nagy, László 63
MoMA *see* Museum of Modern Art
Mondrian, Piet xix, 47, 49, 83, 86; 'Neo-plasticism:
        the general principle of plastic equivalence'
        120–1
Monet, Claude 21, 23
montage 10, 11, 58, 71, 98–9, 103, 107; in film 60,
        107; *see also* photomontage
Moore, Charles Willard 103
Moore, Henry 70
Moore, Marianne 45, 108
Moréas, Jean 22
Moreau, Gustave xix, 21–2, 23

Morisot, Berthe xix, 21
Morris, Robert 92
Morris, William 70
Motherwell, Robert xix, 83, 86–7
Mukhina, Vera 66
multimedia 47
Mulvey, Laura: 'Visual Pleasure and Narrative Cinema' 108
Munich: Expressionists 43; Nazi exhibitions 73
Murakami, Saburo 92
murals 84, 87
Murger, Henry: *Scenes from Bohemian Life* 18
Museum of Modern Art (MoMA), New York 84–5, 91, 134
museums: Marinetti on 125; modernist art in 95, 99, 107; Nolde on 122; postmodern architecture 104
music: atonal 10, 44–5; 'brutist' 56; Dada 57; early avant-garde 44–5; Impressionist 25; jazz 60, 75–6; minimalist 102–3; multitonality 10; neo-avant-garde 89; popular 145; Wagnerian 25
Musil, Robert 77
Mussolini, Benito 61, 62, 69
mythology 49

naïve art 48
narodnost, principle of 71
Nash, Paul 70
nation-states 29
National Union of Students, France 94
nationalism 51, 55
natural selection 30–1, 130–1
nature 10, 48
Nazis 58, 66, 68, 72–3, 78, 85–6
neo-avant-garde 6, 88–93, 96–7, 99; defined xxiv; European 89–91; Japanese 91–2; music 89; student protests as 94–5;
neo-classical style 60, 66, 73; defined xxiv
Neo-Concretists 92
Neo-Impressionism 43, 50
Neo-Plasticism 8, 47, 63; defined xxv; Mondrian on 120–1
Neue Sachlichkeit (New Objectivity) 58–9, 64, 72; defined xxv
New Artists' Association (*Neue Künstlervereinigung*; NKV) 43
New Towns project 69–70
New York 78, 83–90; ACT-UP 109; Armory Show 84; art criticism 85; Art of this Century gallery 83–4, 86, 87; Eight Spruce Street skyscraper 104; Fluxus performances 92; Harlem

Renaissance 75, 84; modernity and cosmopolitanism 85–6; MoMA 84–5, 91, 134; museums and galleries 88
New York School 87–8
Newman, Barnett 87
'new sobriety' 5, 68–9, 72
newspapers: 19th century 17; in montages 58
Newtonian physics 32–3
Nietzsche, Friedrich 10, 26, 31, 49
nihilism 31
Nijinsky, Vaslav 41–2
Nizan, Paul: *The Watchdogs* 77
NKV *see* New Artists' Association
Nolde, Emil xix, 44, 49, 73; 'On Primitive Art' 122–3
Nouveau Réalisme (New Realism) 90–1; defined xxv
Nouvelle Revue Française (*NRF*) 62
novels *see* literature
nudes 20–1, 23, 26, 46, 48, 49, 73

odalisque 23, 139
Ogden, Charles Kay 28
O'Keeffe, Georgia 84
Oldenburg, Claes 88
Olson, Charles 89
Ono, Yoko 92
opera 18, 25, 102–3
Oppenheim, Meret 108
order: Purism and 131; return to 62
Orientalism 22–5
Orozco, José Clemente 84
Ortega y Gasset, José 42; *The Revolt of the Masses* 77
Orwell, George: *Homage to Catalonia* 78
other: exotic 22–5, 75–6; woman as 108
Ozenfant, Amédée xix, 62, 63, 86; on Purism 129–32

Pabst, G. W. 72
pacifists 56
Paik, Nam June 92
Paolozzi, Edoardo 97
Paris: black culture in 75–7; bohemianism 18–19; Centre Georges Pompidou 95; cosmopolitanism 49; Dada 61; *flâneurs* 19, 21; Futurism 51; Guggenheim in 83; Haussmann's renovation of 18, 21; Impressionism 21; international events 62–3, 66–8, 74–5, 77–8; Jardin des Plantes 48; negative response to modernism 49–50; 19th century 17–19; *Nouveau Réalisme* 90–1; premier of *The Rite of Spring* 41–2; student protests (1968) 94–5; Surrealism 61, 90

parody 100, 146
participation, audience 10
partiynost, principle of 71
Parysis, Marcelle 76
Pasternak, Boris 72, 77
pastiche 58, 88, 96–7, 100, 103, 104, 146
pastoral theme 49
peasantry, portraying 48
perceptual revolution 28–38
Péret, Benjamin 61
performance art 90–2
phenomenology 34, 44
philosophy 29–30, 31, 34, 87; postmodern 101
photography 51, 59–60, 96, 137, 138;
     postmodern 103
photomontage 54, 58, 72–3, 96
physics 32–3
Picabia, Francis 58, 61
Picasso, Pablo xix, 44, 49, 73, 83, 86, 87, 149; and
     Cubism 46, 67–8; return to Neo-Classical style
     60; *Les Demoiselles d'Avignon Plate 1*, 3–4, 46,
     48; *Guernica* 67–8
Pick, Frank 70
Pierson, Jack 109
Piscator, Edwin 59
Pissarro, Camille 18, 21
Pivot, Bernard 95
plastic art: Le Corbusier and Ozenfant on 130;
     see also Neo-Plasticism
poem-object 46
poetry: Acmeist 27; avant-garde 36–7, 45–6;
     concrete 45, 46, 57; Dadaist 57; Futurist 123,
     124; Symbolist 21, 22, 27
political engagement 59, 61, 68–9, 72, 77
political struggles 29–30; *see also* revolution
Pollock, Jackson xix, 8, 83, 85, 87–8, 91
Polynesia 24–5
Pop art 6, 47, 97–100, 109, 145; defined xxv;
     Hamilton on 138–9
Popular Front 66–7, 68, 78, 85
portraits: Nazi 73; *Neue Sachlichkeit* 72; Pop art 98;
     Soviet 71
positivism 29, 30, 32; revolt against 10, 31
posters 22, 58, 60, 67, 76; London Underground 70;
     Miró's *Aidez L'Espagne Plate 3*, 67
Post-Impressionism 21, 48, 70, 84
postmodernism 6, 47, 99–104, 107–8, 109–10, 150;
     defined xxv; Jameson on 144–6
post-structuralism 100, 142–4, 149; defined xxv
Pound, Ezra xix, 8, 26, 45, 49, 51, 149; and fascism
     62

power: art and 146–8; defined 148
Prague: Futurism 51; Structuralism 100
Prendergast, Christopher 36
Prendergast, Maurice: *The Promenade* 84
primary forms 131
primitive, the: fascination with 22–5, 44, 46, 74–7;
     Matisse on 118; Nolde on 122
Primitivism 48–9; Dada and 56, 57, 58; defined xxv;
     French and 74–7; Surrealists and 74–5
Prince, Richard 103
printmaking techniques 98
progress, notion of 29, 30–2
Prolekult 59; defined xxv
propaganda 60, 73, 147
Proust, Marcel xix: *À la recherche du temps perdu*
     (*In Seach of Lost Time*) 35–6
psychic field 10
psychoanalysis 31–2, 34
psychology 34, 51, 75
Puccini, Giacomo: *La Bohème* 18
Pudovkin, Vsevolod 60
Purism 62–3; defined 5; Le Corbusier and Ozenfant
     on 129–32

quantum mechanics 33
queer theory 107–8, 109

Rachilde 22
'radical': origin of word 148
radical avant-garde 5, 54–65
radio 55, 96
Rationalism 69–70
Rauschenberg, Robert 88, 89, 109
Ray, Man 70, 83
Realism 5, 20, 48, 85; defined xxv; *see also Nouveau
     Réalisme*; Socialist Realism
reality: material 20, 30; pluralities of 33
record covers 98
recording technology 55, 96, 100
referent *see* 'crisis of the referent'
Reich, Steve xx, 102
Reinhardt, Ad: *Abstract Painting, No.5* 102
Renaissance 7, 44
Renoir, Pierre-Auguste 21, 23
revolution: Marinetti on 124; political 51, 52, 58, 62,
     74, 94–6
Rhys, Jean 108
Ribemont-Dessaignes, Georges 58
Richards, M. C. 89
Riefenstahl, Leni 73
Riley, Terry xix, 145; *In C* 102

Rimbaud, Arthur 21
Rivera, Diego 84
Rivers, Larry 88, 109
Rodchenko, Alexander xx, 60, 71, 72
roman feuilleton 19
Romanticism 8, 19; defined xxv
Rosenberg, Harold 6, 88
Rosenquist, James xx, 97, 98–9; *F-111* 99
Rothko, Mark xx, 83, 87
Rousseau, Henri xx, 48
Ruskin, John 70
Russell, Bertrand and Whitehead, Alfred North:
    Principia Mathematica 33
Russia: Bolshevik Revolution 55, 58, 59, 70, 78;
    Cubo-Futurism 51; *see also* Soviet Union
Rutherford, Ernest 32
Ryman, Robert: *VIII* 102

Saint Petersburg 27
Sainte-Beuve, Charles Augustin 20
Salomé 23
Salon des refusés, Paris 21
satire 72–3
Saussure, Ferdinand de xx, 100, 142
Schoenberg, Arnold xx, 44–5, 89, 145, 146
Schopenauer, Arthur 26, 31
Schwitters, Kurt xx; *Sonate in Urlauten* 57
science 7, 28, 29, 30, 31, 32–3
scientific management 62
scientific racism 30
scientism *see* positivism
sculpture 54, 70, 83, 90, 118, 120
Secession 26
Second World War 62, 78, 83, 85–6
Segalen, Victor xx, 25
self-reflexivity 9
semiotics 100–2, 142
Serge, Victor 78
Settimelli, Emilio 50
Seurat, Georges 21, 135
Shahn, Ben 84
Shaw, George Bernard 26
Sherman, Cindy: *Untitled Film Still* 103
Shiraga, Kazuo 92
'shock of the new' 42
signs *see* semiotics
Simmel, Georg 31
Simplicissimus 72
simulation 142–4
simultaneity 9–10
Siqueiros, David Alfaro 84

Sissle, Noble 75
Situationist International 91
Smith, Ada Louise 'Bricktop' 75
Smith, David 87
social sciences 31
Socialist Realism 68, 71–2, 78; defined xxvi
Soupault, Philippe 56, 58, 61
Soviet Union: AKhRR 71; Constructivism 45, 59–60,
    63, 64, 71, 75; Formalism 100; Greenberg on
    85; New Economic Policy (NEP) 59, 70–1, 72;
    Prolekult 59; and Socialist Realism 68, 71–2,
    78; and Spanish Civil War 66, 78; Stalinist
    66–7, 68, 70–2, 78; *see also* Russia
Spanish Civil War 66, 67, 78
Spanish Republic, Second 66, 67–8, 78
Speer, Albert 66, 73
Stalin, Joseph 68, 70–2, 78
standardisation 62
stations: architecture 70
Stein, Gertrude xx, 3, 41, 49, 108
Stella, Joseph 84
Stevens, Wallace 45, 145
Stieglitz, Alfred 84
Still, Clyfford 83
Stravinsky, Igor xx, 145, 146; *Le Sacre du printemps
    (The Rite of Spring)* 41–2
stream of consciousness 10, 34, 35, 113–14
Strindberg, Arthur 27
structuralism 100; defined xxvi
Sue, Eugène: *Les Mystères de Paris* 17–18
suicide rates 31
Supremacist movement 59
Surrealism 47, 51, 61–2, 67, 70, 83, 90, 95, 99,
    136; in America 86, 87; anti-colonialism and
    primitivism 74–6; Breton's manifesto of 61,
    127–9; defined 5; and politics 61–2; rift with
    communists 78; women artists 108
Surréalisme au service de la révolution, Le (journal)
    74
Sutherland, Graham 70
Symbolism 5, 21–3, 25, 26, 27, 31, 50, 95;
    defined 6; Imagists' view of 45
synesthesia 51

Tahiti 24–5
Tanaka, Atsuko 92
Tanguy, Yves 61, 83, 86
Tatlin, Vladimir 60
Taylorism 62
technology *see* industrial design; industrial production;
    mechanical reproduction; recording technology

television 96, 101, 107
Terragni, Giuseppe 69
theatre: *Neue Sachlichkeit* 59
time and space 28–9, 32–3; experience of 34, 35–7
Tinguely, Jean xx, 81
tipichnost, principle of 71
Toulouse-Lautrec, Henri de 23
transportation 16, 18, 28
triangle, ascending 44, 119
trouvaille, la 61
Tudor, David 89
Turnbull, William 97
typography, use of 46, 57
Tzara, Tristan xx, 56, 58, 61, 86; 'Dada Manifesto 1918' 57, 125–7
tzigane 75

uncertainty of meaning 10, 25
uncertainty principle 33
unconsciousness, the 26, 31–2, 34, 44, 47, 61, 74, 86, 120
Union of Soviet Writers 71
United States of America: modernists displaced from 49; Pop art 97–9; *see also* New York
universal, the: Gropius on 132; Mondrian on 120–1
urbanisation 16–17

Valéry, Paul 95
Van Gogh, Vincent 21, 23, 48, 84
Varo, Remedios 108
Vautier, Ben 92
Venturi, Robert 103
Verlaine, Paul 22
Vertov, Dziga xxi, 60, 71
Vidocq, Eugène-François 18
Vienna: Ringstrasse architecture and art 26; composers 45
Villiers de l'Isle-Adam, Auguste, Comte de 22
virtual reality 100
Vlaminck, Maurice de 49
violence, glorification of 51–2
Vorticism 45, 51, 62; defined xxvi
Vostell, Wolf 92

Wadsworth, Edward 70
Wagner, Richard 25
warfare 51, 52, 124
Warhol, Andy xxi, 97, 98, 145
Weber, Max 31
Webern, Anton 45
Weimar: Bauhaus 63; Dada-Constructivist meeting (1922) 60
Weimar Republic 54–5, 58, 64, 69, 72–3
Welling, James 103
West, Rebecca 108
Western civilisation: goal of changing 49, 50, 51, 107; rejection of 56–7
Wharton, Edith 108
Whitechapel Art Gallery, London: 'This is Tomorrow' exhibition 97
Whitehead, Alfred North 33
Wilde, Oscar 23, 26
Willett, John 68
Williams, Raymond 109–10; 'When Was Modernism' 149–50
Williams, William Carlos 45
Wilson, Robert 102–3
Wittig, Monique 108
Wojnarowicz, David 109
women: feminism 107–9; Futurist contempt for 50, 51, 124; as idealised peasantry 48; nudes 20–1, 23, 26, 46, 48, 49, 73
Women's Liberation Movement 108
woodcut block-print methods 49
Woolf, Virginia xxi, 108; and stream of consciousness 35, 113–14; 'Mr. Bennett and Mrs. Brown' 28, 35, 113–15
working class: portrayal of 71, 71–2
Works Progress Administration (WPA): Federal Arts Project 84, 85
Worpswede painters 48
wrapping installations 91

Yeats, William Butler 26, 45, 149

Zhdanov, Andrei 71
Zola, Émile 17, 36
Zurich Dada 56, 57, 64